You: For Sale

You: For Sale
Protecting Your Personal Data and Privacy Online

Stuart Sumner

Mike Rispoli, Technical Editor

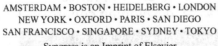

AMSTERDAM • BOSTON • HEIDELBERG • LONDON
NEW YORK • OXFORD • PARIS • SAN DIEGO
SAN FRANCISCO • SINGAPORE • SYDNEY • TOKYO
Syngress is an Imprint of Elsevier

Acquiring Editor: Chris Katsaropoulos
Editorial Project Manager: Benjamin Rearick
Project Manager: Punithavathy Govindaradjane
Designer: Matthew Limbert

Syngress is an imprint of Elsevier
225 Wyman Street, Waltham, MA 02451, USA

ISBN: 978-0-12-803405-7

British Library Cataloguing-in-Publication Data
A catalogue record for this book is available from the British Library

Library of Congress Cataloging-in-Publication Data
A catalog record for this book is available from the Library of Congress

For information on all Syngress publications
visit our website at store.elsevier.com/Syngress

www.elsevier.com • www.bookaid.org

Contents

Foreword

Everywhere, privacy is under attack. Even those who actively try to protect their own privacy, a dying breed, are no longer safe from intrusion. The ability of companies and governments to extract information, regardless of our protections and liberties, is growing at a fearsome rate.

So even with the powerful tools now available to us, such as encryption, online anonymity is fast becoming a myth.

One of the most worrying aspects of this is the development of ground-breaking pattern recognition technologies, allowing marketing technology firms to identify people regardless of how they identify themselves online. That is to say, even if people try to maintain their anonymity, these programmes can recognise your activities from other data that is held.

Complex programmes now match partial data about people from different sources to create a complete picture. They can do this due to the multitude of data available on everyone, for example from electoral and government records to online surveys.

Even your medical records are now considered fair game by the Government. The UK Government's temporarily delayed 'care.data' scheme would have opened up patients' records, supposedly anonymised, to a multitude of private bodies, including insurers and research organisations, before objectors forced the Government to rethink its plans. With the advances in pattern recognition, there is no way that the majority of medical records could have been kept anonymous.

Once you know someone's name, date of birth and postcode, data we all readily give up on request, then it is only a small step to identify further data belonging to that person. For example, I have had my nose broken five times. Once you know that, I'm probably in a group of 100 people in England. Then you figure out when I had my diphtheria jab, usually done shortly after birth. With this two pieces of information it is a simple task to identify me from my medical records. You wouldn't even need to rely on the high-tech pattern recognition software in development.

Because metadata can mathematically manipulated, it is susceptible to very sophisticated analysis, and that sophistication increases exponentially every year. Google are already extraordinarily adept at this; several years ago they managed, using their recognition algorithms, to predict the H1N1 outbreak about two weeks ahead of official sources.

And if companies can do it, states certainly can. Although governments across the world are tight-lipped about their intelligence gathering, a number of leaks in recent years have shone a light on some of their clandestine workings. The most obvious of these was the data publicised by Edward Snowden.

The enormity of Snowden's revelations are often underrated. The sheer scale of surveillance by governments of their civilian populations, and of foreign communications, came as a surprise even to those who were supposedly informed of such matters – including the Parliamentary oversight committee.

Snowden revealed previously unknown, and even largely unsuspected, details of global surveillance apparatus run by the United States' NSA, together with three of the so-called 'Five Eyes' intelligence partners, Australia, the United Kingdom and Canada.

Between the exposure of PRISM, TEMPORA, XKEYSCORE and stellarwind, Snowden showed the world the tip of an iceberg – a global surveillance network designed to catch the personal communications and information not just of terrorists and criminals, but of everyone.

What was so shocking about the revelations was not that such widespread surveillance was being done, but that it was completely legal, and fully sanctioned. Until Snowden, no-one was aware of the shocking extent to which they were under surveillance.

As Sir John Sawers, the ex-head of MI6 recently said, "Snowden threw a massive rock in the pool," and the ripples have not yet stopped. We must hope that by the time the waters have stilled, Governments, the intelligence agencies and the public debate have all caught up with our ever-changing technological capabilities, and started to understand and respect our digital rights.

But the danger that mass collection of private data poses does not just come from overwhelming the intelligence services with largely useless data. It comes from the power that this data grants over the lives of ordinary citizens. A power that states are unwilling to give up, and too ill-disciplined to resist using. It is not that we are actually watched at all times, but that we could all potentially be watched at any time.

This level of intrusion goes totally against public opinion. Survey after survey show that the vast majority of people are not happy that their communications are monitored by governments, or that their data is hoovered up by companies.

As more and more is known about mass data collection, four things have become clear. Firstly, that people do not like it. Secondly, that the data collected is frequently excessive and is not always used in the interests of the public. Thirdly, the risks inherent in the collection of this data are often very large. Finally, the data collection is often done in a covert or sneaky way. Sometimes this is in the interests of the public, and sometimes it very much is not.

This book is being published at a time when the issues that it addresses are central to the current public debate. Under intense pressure from journalists, from the courts and especially from the public, Britain is having to rewrite the rules on state snooping. All of the organisations involved will have to face up to this shift in public opinion and cope with the inevitable changes.

There is no doubt that big data can be a force for good; it allows markets to run more efficiently, helps for the better provision of services, and plays a large role in our security. But governments will only be able to deliver on this if they accept the need to change their approach to people's rights and liberties.

This excellent book highlights these points, and brilliantly exemplifies them in an eminently digestible manner. The author's recommendations are smart and practical: I recommend them to policymakers everywhere.

—David Davis MP

About the Author

Stuart Sumner is a journalist, writer and broadcaster. He has written for and edited a number of both business and consumer titles, and specialises in technology, security, privacy and the law.

He has a bachelor's degree in law, but escaped a legal career for the glamour of sitting alone in a darkened room, typing.

Stuart is an experienced speaker and events chairman, and has presented hundreds of live and recorded television broadcasts. He is also a regular technology pundit on BBC News.

He is married, with two children who wake him up at 6am without fail every day. He is not a morning person.

Twitter: @stuartsumner

About the Technical Editor

Mike Rispoli is the Press Freedom Director at the U.S.-based media reform organization Free Press, where he oversees campaigns to protect reporters' rights, promote free speech, and fight government and corporate surveillance. He previously worked at Privacy International, an international advocacy and research organization that fights for the right to privacy, and Access, an international organization that defends and extends the digital rights of users at risk around the world. He lives in New Jersey with his family, and not in a cave in the mountains, despite being aware of all the ways governments and companies can spy on you.

Acknowledgments

There are a number of people who were an enormous help in not just writing this book, but in gestating the ideas, and connecting me to the right interviewees and resources. My memory being what it is, I'm unlikely to give proper credit to all the necessary parties, so apologies in advance to anyone I've missed.

The first person I need to thank is Mike Rispoli, who was kind enough to be technical editor on the book. His many insights, and his vast knowledge in the subject area were an incalculable help.

Secondly I'd like to thank Ben Rearick, my editor at Elsevier, and Chris Katsaropolous, also of Elsevier, who put me in touch with Ben. Thanks also go to everyone else at Elsevier who made the whole process so clear and simple throughout.

I'd also like to express a special thank you to David Davis MP, who was kind enough to write the forward. David is a staunch privacy advocate and more figures like him are needed in government.

It would be remiss of me not to thank my interviewees, every one of whom improved the book hugely with their insight. Privacy International were extremely forthcoming with spokespeople and information whenever asked, and special mention too must go to Acxiom, who were happy to speak to me despite the tricky nature of the book's subject and its relation to their business model.

Finally I'd like to thank Raj Samani for suggesting I write the book in the first place, and my wife for putting up with my need to spend weekends keeping up with my writing schedule instead of chasing after our screaming, unruly children.

Author's Note

As a journalist I'm lucky enough to be able to spend time with some very well-informed and interesting people. I recently had lunch with a group of senior technology leaders from various well-known brands across several industries, and soon enough the conversation turned to privacy.

The prevailing view in the group seemed to be one of irritation at what some of them clearly saw as a meddlesome community of privacy advocates, who, in their opinion, were always on the lookout for things to be offended by. 'So what if someone takes your data, no one really cares,' was one comment, with which some in the group seemed to agree.

This is concerning, and is one of the reasons I decided to write this book. I can see the perspective of some of those technologists and business people. On the face of it, there is little harm in our data being harvested, even without our knowledge or consent. No one dies or gets ill. You don't come out in an ugly rash when Facebook logs every action you've ever taken on its site. Your hair doesn't fall out, nor suddenly sprout from unseemly places when Google scans your emails looking for advertising and profiling opportunities.

But what is worrying is the rate and extent of the many erosions of our privacy in the digital age. This rapid wearing down of one of our fundamental human rights might not seem important now, but it does affect lives, and those effects are growing year on year. It influences your credit rating, insurance premiums, medical options, and it feeds a clandestine corporate bonanza seeking to surreptitiously change your behaviour for its own advantage, not yours. And it's not just private organizations, but governments if anything have their hands even deeper in the data trough.

At the same time much of the existing internet economy revolves around the basic human desire to get something for (at least seemingly) nothing. Web search, and many types of internet services and apps are free to use, and the firms behind them need to recoup their investment somehow. This book doesn't argue that firms like Google and Facebook should shut down, nor completely change their business models, but rather that most of their revenue generating activities could be altered to better respect their users' privacy with little loss of income.

This book aims to present a balanced view of the arguments for and against the current state of digital privacy, and to show the direction of travel. The reader is invited to decide for his or herself how they feel about where we're going to end up if we stay on this course.

If nothing else, I hope the reader emerges having read this book able to debate the views of some of the technologists I had lunch with that day. Privacy does matter.

Stuart Sumner
Summer 2015

CHAPTER 1

Introduction

WHY ALL THIS FUSS ABOUT PRIVACY?

Does privacy really matter? In fact, do we all agree on what it actually is? As Paul Sieghart said in his 1975 book 'Privacy and Computers', privacy is neither simple nor well defined. "A full analysis of all its implications needs the skills of the psychologist, the anthropologist, the sociologist, the lawyer, the political scientist and ultimately the philosopher," wrote Sieghart.

For our purposes we'll dispense with the committee necessary for this full analysis, and start with a summary of the definition which came out of the International Commission of Jurists in Stockholm in May 1967:

'The right to privacy is the right to be let alone to live one's own life with the minimum degree of interference.'

That statement may be around 50 years old, but it still hits the right note. Then there's the Universal Declaration of Human Rights, signed by the UN a few years earlier in 1948:

"No one shall be subjected to arbitrary interference with his privacy, family, home, or correspondence."

Privacy is also enshrined in national laws. Under US Constitutional law it's considered to be the right to make personal decisions regarding intimate matters (defined as issues around faith, moral values, political affiliation, marriage, procreation, or death).

Under US Common Law (which is the law to come out of the courtroom – where legal precedents are routinely set and followed), privacy is defined as the right of people to lead their lives in a manner that is reasonably secluded from public scrutiny, whether that scrutiny comes from a neighbor, an investigator, or a news photographer's for instance.

Finally, under US statutory law, privacy is the right to be free from unwarranted drug testing and electronic surveillance.

CONTENTS

In the UK the legal protection of privacy comes from the 'Privacy and the Human Rights Act 1998', which basically corresponds to the rights conferred under the 1948 UN declaration. But the law is changing, and we'll explore how in chapter 7.

As we shall see, literally every aspect of these definitions of privacy is under attack from both public and private organizations today. Individuals' privacy is being eroded at an alarming rate. In fact, some commentators are even beginning to ask if there can be such a thing as privacy in a world of cookies, government surveillance, big data and smart cities (to name just a handful of recent technology trends in part culpable for the situation).

And it's not just commentators and experts who are fretting about the privacy-free world we appear to be unwittingly signing up to. The results of the Pew Research Internet Project of 2014 reveal that 91 per cent of Americans believe that consumers have lost control of their personal information. They trust the government only slightly more; 80 per cent agreed that Americans should be concerned about the government's monitoring of their communications, which we'll explore in the next chapter.

A White House Big Data Survey from May 2014 shows that 55 per cent of respondents in the EU and 53 per cent in the US see the collection of big data (which can be used to identify individuals from supposedly anonymized data) as a negative.

Privacy is an aspect of our freedom. It's about being free to think and act with autonomy, and where desired, without those thoughts and actions being broadcast to others.

This book aims to explain how and why privacy is under threat, and give some basic recommendations for individuals, corporations and governments to follow in order to arrest this slide towards a world that is less free.

HERE'S MY COW, NOW WHERE'S MY CHANGE?

What's better than a great product at a reasonable price? What about a great product for free? It sounds too good to be true, and it is, and yet that's the lie that's repeatedly sold to all of us who use the internet or download apps to our tablets and smartphones. It's such an obvious duplicity that you'd think more of us would see through it. That we don't is a result of the way our brains are wired, but before we come to that, let's have a brief look at the path humanity has taken in its history to bring us to this point.

Next time you pass a dairy farm, you could surprise and delight your friends by remarking that it's an early form of bank (neither surprise nor delight guaranteed).

That's because the earliest form of currency is thought to be cattle. If you don't possess the ability to mint coins or at least make something that's easy and cheap to reproduce accurately yet hard to copy, a cow is a pretty good substitute. As something which produces milk and can be slaughtered for meat, leather and various other products, it has its own value. Despite small variances in size, one cow is pretty much as valuable as another. You can even get change from a cow – in many early economic systems it was considered to be worth two goats.

This worked well enough for many societies from about 9,000BC to 1,200BC, until they were replaced by Cowrie shells. After all, it's great having a form of currency you can eat when times get tough, but it's less good when your entire life savings gets wiped out by disease or is devoured by a pack of wolves or even hungry neighbors.

Cowrie shells – egg-shaped shells belonging to a species of sea snail common to the coastal waters of the Indian and Pacific Oceans - were popular because they were almost impossible to forge, portable, and neither too rare to stymie trading, nor so common that even an egg was worth several wheelbarrowloads (and if that was the exchange rate, how would anyone have transported enough shells to afford the wheelbarrow?). The classical Chinese character for money (貝) originated as a stylized drawing of a cowrie shell, and they are still used today in Nepal in a popular gambling game.

Things became more recognizable to us in modern societies in 1,000BC when China first began to manufacture bronze and copper coins, originally designed to resemble Cowrie shells to help people grasp what they were for. Five hundred years later came electrum (an alloy of gold and silver) coins in Sardis, the capital city of ancient Lydia (an area which roughly corresponds to Turkey today).

Paper money first appeared in China in 806 AD, during the Tang dynasty. It's interesting to wonder what those financial pioneers would have made of the fact that their idea endures over 1,400 years later.

You might think your credit card is a relatively recent invention, but plastic money has been used in various forms since the late 19th century when celluloid 'charge coins' were used by some hotels and department stores to enable transactions to be charged to their clients' accounts.

Credit cards as we know them now however were first used in September 1958 when Bank of America launched the somewhat unimaginatively named 'BankAmericard' in Fresno, California. This eventually became the first successful recognizably modern credit card and nineteen years later changed its name to Visa.

That's the past, but what of the future of money? Some believe it to be digital currency, the most recognizable example of which today is Bitcoin, an open-source, online software payment system unaffiliated to any central authority or bank. Anyone can download the software and use their computer to help verify and record payments into a public ledger, sometimes being rewarded with bitcoins themselves for their efforts.

Others see potential in the smartphone as a wallet, with its near-field communication capabilities enabling transactions at the push of a button or simple wave in the air. If you've ever suffered the inconvenience of losing your smartphone, or worse having it stolen, then the prospect if it also being your wallet might leave you with a knotted feeling in your stomach and an empty feeling in your bank account, in which case you might prefer the idea of a chip embedded under your skin, or even a barcode branded onto your arm.

There are apps which claim to offer simpler ways of transacting money, and many mainstream services are now diversifying into cash transfers: Facebook, Twitter and Snapchat to name a few.

These would be free services, because nothing is precisely the amount modern online consumers expect to pay for anything. So how would these offerings make money? One way is serving advertising, and another is to sell the data they collect on their customers. Information like what size of transaction you tend to make, when you tend to make them, and what you tend to buy. Snapchat in particular has a sketchy recent history as a guardian of personal data. The popular app (and 'popular' hardly does it justice, with over 700 million photos and videos shared each day) allows users to send data in the form of pictures, videos and written messages to one another. So far so pedestrian, but the supposed unique selling point is that the pictures are permanently deleted after a few seconds. Neither the receiver of the image, nor Snapchat itself can retrieve the picture once it has been deleted. Or at least, that's the idea. In practise it's the work of moment for a savvy user to make a permanent record whatever appears on their screen – for example by activating the phone's screenshot mode, or by using a third party app specifically designed for the task (an example of which is SnapBox, an app designed to allow users to keep Snapchat images without the sender's knowledge). And worse, in October 2014 a hacker published 12.6 gigabytes of images stolen from Snapchat's users, none of which were ever supposed to have been recorded in the first place.

However in this instance Snapchat itself isn't to blame. The breach itself occurred when now defunct third party site Snapsaved.com - which contained archived photos and videos from some Snapchat users - was attacked. However, Snapchat itself is guilty of a failure to act when in August 2013 Australian security firm Gibson Security alerted it to a vulnerability. In December that same year Snapchat finally put what it called mitigating features in place to plug the hole, but a few days later a hacking group bypassed the security measures calling them "minor obstacles", and then released 4.6 million Snapchat usernames and passwords in via a website called SnapchatDB.info. Snapchat apologized a week later.

But whichever economic system wins out, and the likelihood is that it will be some combination of all of the above, the one certainty seems to be that the illusion of a free lunch will continue.

HEY I THOUGHT THIS LUNCH WAS FREE!

Have you ever downloaded Angry Birds to a mobile device? How carefully did you read the user agreement that flashed up before you started catapulting creatures across the screen? If you didn't so much as glance at it, then you're with the vast majority of people, but in this case there is scant safety in numbers, the entire herd is being preyed upon, and most are totally oblivious.

We're picking on Angry Birds here as it's a common example, but most of this applies to many of the most common and well-known apps and other online services popular today, and no doubt to tomorrow's apps currently in development.

By the beginning of 2014 Angry Birds had been downloaded over 1.7 billion times. That's an incredible figure. According to the population clock at www. worldofmeters.info, there are over 7.2 billion people in the world at the time of writing. So that's almost a quarter of the entire population of the planet, potentially playing the game. Of course the real figure attacking green pigs with multi-coloured birds is actually less than that, as many people will download the app several times to different devices, but the essential point is that an incredible number of people have downloaded that particular game, and the proportion who read the user agreement is probably significantly fewer than one in a million.

What you'd know if you read it, is that the app makes its money by taking your personal information and selling it on to advertisers. And given that your smartphone is so, well, smart, there's a real wealth of information for Angry Birds and apps like it to mine.

Your phone knows your location. It knows your routine, where you live, which coffee shop you stop at on the way to work, and of course where you work. It knows the route you take on your commute. It's got the contact details for just about everyone you know, and if you use it for email, it's got everything you write to them, and everything they send back to you. It contains your photos, videos, and browsing habits.

Rovio, the developers behind Angry Birds, admits that the data it collects may include but is not limited to your email, device ID, IP address and location. It then sells this data on to advertisers who hope to be better able target you, and sometimes where those third parties have a presence within the app itself, perhaps via an in-app advert, then they can siphon data directly from your phone.

Many apps behave the same way, most gather up way more data than they need, and the vast majority employ very poor or non-existent security. In fact, it's such a treasure trove of personal information that the security agencies have got in on the act. One of the secrets uncovered by the revelations of former CIA contractor Edward Snowden is the fact that the National Security Agency (NSA) in the US and the Government Communications Headquarters (GCHQ) in the UK have developed capabilities to take advantage of leaky apps like Angry Birds to help them compile their dossiers on their citizens (and those of other countries).

The chances are that you use more than one app on your phone, and between them, the combination of apps and websites we all use gather just about everything we do.

Google is one of the worst offenders. Via its free webmail service 'Gmail', Google happily scours what you thought were your private emails looking for keywords, again in order to target ads at you. And it doesn't stop there, but makes full use of the potential of its wide array of products and services. Google is also able to track you across multiple devices. For example if you use Google Maps on your smartphone whilst out and about, that data will be stored and used to help target you with ads the next time you log into Google at home.

In 2013 a group of users had had enough of Google's data gathering activities, banded together and sued the company. Their argument was that Google combs its customers' emails in order to extract a broad meaning – or "thought data" – from them.

"Google creates and uses this 'thought data' and attaches it to the messages so Google can better exploit the communication's 'meaning' for commercial gain," they said in response to legal counter-action from Google designed to dismiss their case from the courts.

"Google collects and stores the 'thought data' separately from the email message and uses the 'thought data' to: (1) spy on its users (and others); and, (2) amass vast amounts of 'thought data' on millions of people (secret user profiles)."

Google argued that federal and state wiretap laws exempt email providers from liability, as it's a basic tenet of their business. So there was no attempt to deny the claims, just a shrug of the shoulders and a 'Yeah, so what?'

"These protections reflect the reality that [electronic communication service] providers like Google must scan the emails sent to and from their systems as part of providing their services," Google said in its motion.

But the plaintiffs added a further point, and a crucial one. Google does not disclose its "thought data" mining activities to anyone. It's one thing to take someone's data in exchange for a valuable service, it's quite another to do it without permission.

"Google's undisclosed processes run contrary to its expressed agreements. Google even intercepts and appropriates the content of minors' emails despite the minors' legal incapacity to consent to such interception and use. Thus, these undisclosed practices are not within the ordinary course of business and cannot form the basis of informed consent," the plaintiffs said.

In March 2014, the plaintiffs lost their case. Lucy Koh, a federal judge in California, ruled in favor of Google, at the same time handing a potent defense to every company which takes its users data without their express consent.

There was a similar case in the UK in 2013. A group of internet users sued Google through law firm Olswang, complaining that the search giant had installed cookies (small files designed to track when someone visits a website, and what they do there) on their desktops and mobile devices despite their expressed preference to avoid precisely that activity. The individuals had used a feature in Apple's Safari browser to block third party cookies.

In this case Google had gone way beyond simply obfuscating its intentions – it had effectively hacked its own users! For a firm whose motto is 'don't be evil', it doesn't appear to be trying very hard to be good.

Google uses the data contained in these cookies about users' browsing habits to enable its partners to buy ads targeted at well-defined sections of society, for instance 'high-earners', 'gadget-buyers', or 'home owners'. It also sells some of this data on directly to advertisers, once it has been anonymized. However, as we'll come to later in the book, in the age of big data it's fairly trivial to identify individuals even from supposedly anonymized information.

There are legitimate reasons why you might not want advertisers to know what you've been using the internet for. A teenage girl might search for contraceptive advice, then be embarrassed when related ads come up when her parents are helping her with her homework. A more serious impact to the girl (or boy for that matter) than embarrassment could be a disinclination to search for information on contraception for precisely this reason. Or you might search for a wedding ring, or some other surprise gift for your partner. Do you want similar products then appearing when they sit down to do their own browsing? The situation wouldn't be so bad if you could opt out, but when the firm in question doesn't even deign to tell you it's happening, then there's a problem.

The Olswang case was brought by 12 Apple users, all of whom had been using Apple's Safari browser. Google was fined $22.5m (£14.2m) by the Federal Trade Commission (FTC) in the US in late 2012 for exactly the same issue - putting cookies onto Safari users' devices - when a case was brought about by a different group.

Nick Pickles, director of civil liberties campaign group Big Brother Watch at the time, told UK-based newspaper The Telegraph: "This episode was no accident. Google tracked people when they had explicitly said they did not want to be tracked, so it's no surprise to see consumers who believe their privacy had been steamrollered by corporate greed seeking redress through the courts.

"This case could set a hugely important legal precedent and help consumers defend their privacy against profit-led decisions to ignore people's rights."

In August 2013 the Independent, another UK-based newspaper, reported that Google described the case as "not serious… the browsing habits of internet users are not protected as personal information, even when they potentially concern their physical health or sexuality."

Google had refused to acknowledge the case in the UK, saying it would only recognize it in the US.

The Independent went on to quote Judith Vidal-Hall, a privacy campaigner and one of the claimants, who said: "Google's position on the law is the same as its position on tax: they will only play or pay on their home turf. What are they suggesting; that they will force Apple users whose privacy was violated to pay to travel to California to take action when they offer a service in this country on a .co.uk site? This matches their attitude to consumer privacy. They don't respect it and they don't consider themselves to be answerable to our laws on it."

It also quoted another claimant named Marc Bradshaw, who argued: "It seems to us absurd to suggest that consumers can't bring a claim against a company which is operating in the UK and is even constructing a $1 billion headquarters in London.

"If consumers can't bring a civil claim against a company in a country where it operates, the only way of ensuring it behaves is by having a robust regulator. But the UK regulator, the Information Commissioner's Office, has said to me that all it can do is fine Google if it breaks the law, but Google clearly doesn't think that it is bound by that law."

"Fines would be useless – even if Google agreed to pay them - because Google earns more than the maximum fine in less than two hours. With no restraint Google is free to continue to invade our privacy whether we like it or not."

We'll return to Google in chapter 4.

WHY SHOULD WE CARE ABOUT PRIVACY?

But does any of this really matter? The short answer is that it's up to each individual to decide how much he or she values their privacy – or how accepting they are with faceless corporations trading their most intimate secrets for fractions of a cent.

It's useful to put this into context by comparing it with our privacy out in the 'real', physical world. The following is true story from late 2014. The names have been changed to protect the parties involved.

Ashley, a technology journalist, was waiting in a publisher's office. He was there to help produce a piece of content encompassing mobility, big data, and other technology trends for one of the publisher's media brands. To kill time, he was messing around with a few apps on his smartphone, just as many of us do with a few minutes spare.

But what Ashley had that most of us don't, was access to a brand new service from a UK-based startup. This product enables its customers to rig up a cheap home CCTV system using a few old smartphones, and then allows them to watch the live stream over the internet. Being a technology journalist, Ashley was trialing the service, and had set it up in his home office to test it out. He idly flicked over to the feed. There, caught unknowingly by one of the seemingly dead and redundant phones lying around the room, was Emma, a friend of Ashley's wife who had been staying with the family. She was rummaging through Ashley's papers – and not just papers lying around for anyone to see, she was actively rooting through his filing cabinet.

Since smartphone cameras, even ones from a few years ago, boast decent resolution, Ashley was able to clearly make out which drawers she was going through, and even which section of which drawer – all happening live before his disbelieving eyes.

Emma was searching through Ashley's financial details – bank statements, invoices and salary slips. Ashley watched silently as she pulled out bundles of paper and carefully arranged them on the floor, before sitting cross-legged among them, seemingly ready for a good, long read.

At this point Ashley's contacts at the publisher turned up, and that was the end of his viewing for now. He was rattled, but as a professional was forced to put it to one side of his mind for the moment to get on with his job.

A natural break in his morning's work arose some hour and a half later. Checking the feed again, he found Emma still sat in the same place, still going through his private details. What could be so fascinating? What was she looking for that she hadn't managed to find yet?

These questions and more went through Ashley's mind as he watched the feed. Should he call the house and confront her? That might stop her going through his papers, but then what would she do, alone in his house with basically nothing to lose, now that her favor with Ashley's household was basically zero, and her welcome expired?

He called his wife and asked her to ring the house. Not to confront Emma, but just to get her out of his office. He went back to the feed, and soon enough

Emma heard the phone and left the room. Not having installed cameras anywhere else in the house, Ashley watched an empty room for a few minutes. Maybe once out of the room and her concentration broken, Emma would find something else to occupy her, or better still, leave the house.

But no. Moments later, she was back. She resumed her position amongst his personal papers, and carried on reading.

We can imagine how Ashley felt during this ordeal. Violated, betrayed, shaken and angry. He had no business or other financial relationship with Emma, there was absolutely no reason for her to read his financial information. He had by no means given her permission to go into his office, and certainly not to go through his filing cabinet. And yet she had done both, and waited for both he and his wife to be out in order to do so. Clearly she knew it was wrong, and also knew that if she had asked for permission to go through Ashley's details, it would have been denied.

This is a similar situation to the one in which the various groups to have brought claims against Google in recent years found themselves. A common situation with internet services today is that users don't give permission for their private information (as browsing habits are defined) to be accessed and sold on to the extent that it is. Sometimes people give permission for some of these activities, but they very really understand the full extent to which their data will be mined, traded, and stored. In the Google cases mentioned in this chapter, the complainants had actively denied permission for their data to be used in this way. In either case, whether users actively deny consent, or simply aren't sufficiently well informed (if at all) of the full range of activities they're consenting to, their data is taken and used to generate profit without their knowledge. They are effectively out of the house when Google rifles through their filing cabinets.

Emma's stay with Ashley's family ended that night. Not because of her actions, she was always planning to go home that evening. Ashley and his wife decided not to confront her that night because they didn't want to risk a scene with their children in the house. Instead, Ashley's wife called Emma the next day.

"Hi Emma. Ash wants to know if you found what you were looking for," she said, before explaining that her husband had seen everything, and that Emma was no longer welcome to stay with them.

We're not used to caring as much about digital information as that stored on paper, even when it reveals the same facts about us. Having a stranger break into your house is inevitably more violating than having one hack into your email. Given the choice, who wouldn't prefer to find that someone had taken over their Facebook account rather than discover that person in their kitchen late at night?

But ask anyone who has had their computer infected by malware, or their email or social media taken over by a hacker, and they'll tell you it's unpleasant and disturbing.

CAUTION: HACKERS AT WORK

Another true story, this one slightly more personal as it happened to the author, so we'll break out into the first person for a moment:

In the summer of 2010 I was at work, in the midst of a lengthy magazine feature. As a displacement activity I checked my Hotmail, to find several messages from friends titled 'Re: TERRIBLE VACATION.........Stuart Sumne'.

I hadn't recently had a terrible vacation, and would hardly misspell my own name. I checked a few of the emails in bemusement, still not realizing the obvious. Had a disparate group of my friends, some of whom didn't even know one another, somehow come together to play a practical joke?

As understanding slowly dawned, my first reaction was indignation that someone had used my email account to send such a badly worded message, full of spelling and grammatical mistakes – as a journalist and editor this was hugely damaging to my personal brand! Even worse, it had begun by describing me as having 'tears in my eyes'. As if I'd admit I'd been crying to all my friends!

Here's the original email in full, sent by a hacker:

Subject: TERRIBLE VACATION.........Stuart Sumne

I'm writing this with tears in my eyes,I came down here to HIERRO MADRID SPAIN for a short vacation unfortunately i was mugged at the park of the hotel where i stayed,all cash,credit card and cell were all stolen from me but luckily for me i still have my passports with me.

i 'have been to the embassy and the Police here but they're not helping issues at all and my flight leaves in few hrs from now but I'm having problems settling the hotel bills and the hotel manager won't let me leave until i settle the bills..I am so confused right now and thank God i wasn't injured because I complied immediately.

Well all i need now is just £1,250Pounds you can have it wired to my name via Western Union I'll have to show my passport as ID to pick it up here and i promise to pay you back as soon as i get back home. Here's the info you need at western union location below

Receiver name: Stuart Sumne

Amount: £1,250Pounds

Address : Hierro 9, 28045

Country: Madrid,Spain

Kindly email me the transfer details as soon as you have it done.Please let me know if you are heading out to western union now.

Thanks

Love Stuart.

Fortunately very few of my friends were taken in by the con, and those that were sent only their sympathies. What was interesting was that I caught the hack very early on in the process, as it was just starting. I was logged into my account at the same time as the hacker, so I was able to send out simultaneous messages to friends telling them that I was fine, and definitely not to send any money no matter what subsequent messages from my address might claim.

There was even a real-time conversation that afternoon over MSN Messenger, the instant messaging service associated with Hotmail at the time, between the hacker, my cousin, and me. The hacker made his demands, my cousin sympathized, meanwhile I told her to delete me until further notice and respond to nothing until I called her.

The exchange went something like this:

Stuart:	Have you sent the money yet? (this was the hacker typing as me)
Cousin:	Are you okay?
Stuart:	I'm fine, I've been hacked, block me! (this was really me)
Stuart:	Don't block me, send the money quickly!
Cousin:	What's going on?
Stuart:	I've been hacked, block block block! I'll call you!

From my cousin's perspective I was suddenly schizophrenic. It was farcical, but worse was to come. I was soon locked out of my Facebook account, then Gmail (like many people I run several email accounts, in part to separate personal and professional lives) soon followed. I had made the rookie mistake of using one password for multiple online services, particularly embarrassing for a technology journalist who specializes in privacy and security. The hacker had no interest in these other accounts, he (it could have been a 'she', but statistically speaking it's unlikely) just wanted control of my main email address for a few hours in an attempt to extort money from as many people as possible. Barring me from other services was simply a way of preventing me from telling my friends not to pay up.

Eventually the day was over and it was time to leave work. I knew that the hacker had changed my passwords, and that once my office computer was switched off, I would be locked out of Hotmail until I could convince Microsoft that I was the account's true owner. The hacker would have it to himself for as long as that took. I needed to contact him. What I wanted to do was to rage at him for the inconvenience, embarrassment and outrage he'd caused, but that wouldn't help. Instead, I wrote a polite message to my own email address titled 'To the hacker', in which I explained that my friends weren't falling for the scam, and to please reset my password to 'Password' once he felt his work was done so I could have my digital life back.

The email appeared, unread, in my deleted items folder moments after I sent it. The hacker could have simply ignored it, but was sending me a clear message in return.

It took about two weeks to get all of my accounts back, with as it turned out, Hotmail being the hardest to retrieve. But get it all back I did, with no lasting ill effects, except a lingering feeling of violation. Just because something only exists in the digital ether, doesn't mean it doesn't matter.

Interestingly, one of the things I was able to do after I got ownership of my accounts back, was see where my Facebook account had been accessed from. It turned out that the hacker had been just outside a military base in Canada. I was sorely tempted to pay the area a visit, but the likelihood is that I would have found a proxy server operating as part of a botnet, or in layman's terms, nothing at all.

SERIOUS BUSINESS

Few groups value digital objects as highly as gamers. In March 2005, a Chinese man was stabbed to death in an argument over a sword in online game Legends of Mir 3. Shanghai-based gamer Qiu Chengwei killed his friend Zhu Caoyuan when he learnt that Caoyuan had sold his 'dragon sabre' for 7,200 yuan ($720). Chengwei had first gone to the police, but had been told that there was no crime since the weapon did not constitute 'real property'. Perhaps the outcome might have been different and Caoyuan still be alive had the police recognized the value of virtual property, although of course Chengwei's actions must be unequivocally condemned either way. He was given a suspended death sentence for his crime.

Police in the Netherlands however, seem to be more prepared to accept the value of digital obecjts. In 2007 a 17-year old man was charged with burglary and hacking after stealing $5,900 worth of virtual furniture in online game Habbo Hotel (now known simply as 'Habbo'). He managed to steal other players' passwords by creating fake Habbo sites. This is pretty standard fare for hackers. Making a website which is virtually indistinguishable from another is a simple task for anyone with a small measure of web development experience. For instance, you could register the URL 'www.Habohotel.com' (not the subtle difference from the official 'www.Habbohotel.com'), and make it look identical to the real site. Then, when a few luckless individuals who have mistyped the URL enter their usernames and passwords – hey presto, you've got their account details.

This is a classic way to get access to gamers' accounts on everything from Moshi Monsters to World of Warcraft, and many hacking groups make good profits this way. It also works perfectly well as a way to procure account details to other services too, including online banking.

Back to our 17-year old Netherlands-based entrepreneur, and he used his ill-gotten data to log into Habbo Hotel players' accounts, take their belongings and stash them in his own room in the game, and those of five accomplices. That's a shade under $6,000 for a few hours' work, most of us would be delighted with such an effort / reward ratio.

Around the same time, a woman posted an ad on online classified service Craigslist. In it, she offered her body for 5,000 gold in the aforementioned World of Warcraft. Stating that she needed the money to purchase an 'Epic Flying Mount' – a way of travelling around the game's world more quickly – she offered a variety of sexual acts for the virtual currency. Specifically, in her post she said that if someone were to send her an in-game mail with the 5,000 gold pieces attached to purchase the mount, then that person could "mount" her. She later said that her inbox was full by the next day with offers from people willing to comply.

Whatever your thoughts as to the ethics of prostitution, the fact remains that virtual property will always hold real-world value as long as people are willing to exchange real-world services and currency for it.

This is far from a new concept. In 1st century BC, Pubilius Syrus, a Syrian, was brought as a slave to Italy by the Romans. He wasn't to remain a slave for long though, as he used his wit to win the sympathies of his master, who both freed and educated him. He then found success as a writer, and a performing mime and improviser. In fact that latter pursuit was so successful that he was awarded a prize by Julius Caesar himself in 46 BC for his performance in a public contest.

Pubilius has given us several maxims that we use even today, like: 'The judge is condemned when the guilty is acquitted.' More famous, however, is: 'Something is only worth what someone is willing to pay for it'.

So the fact that something is made up purely of ones and zeroes does not preclude it from holding value. Many people might not think an item in an online game is worth anything at all in the real world, but they're entirely wrong as long as someone somewhere is willing to pay for it.

But what if this collection of ones and zeroes says something important about us, our habits, preferences, who we are, our relationships, sexual orientation, income and just about everything else besides? That makes its value more obvious, and we should be more vigilant about what happens to that information.

Frank Buytendijk, research vice president at analyst firm Gartner, explains that there are other reasons why we should care about our online privacy.

"There are a lot of companies who think they have an understanding of us," says Buytendijk. "Personas of us are flying around on the internet, and every one of them delivers a piece of us, but no one really knows exactly what's out there about you and me.

"Algorithms interpret from a partial point of view about what I do or don't do, and that might lead to embarrassing situations like pregnancy product coupons being sent to a non-pregnant teenage girl."

His point is that despite the sophistication of the monitoring and tracking that we each suffer online, there is no one overarching service collating everything. There are multiple companies all striving for the same goal – a complete picture and understanding of us all. But the likelihood is that none of them have that complete picture, meaning that not only do we suffer the injury of having our privacy infringed, but also the insult of being misunderstood!

Buytendijk's second point, intriguingly, is the opposite of his first. What if these companies don't have a partial understanding of us? What if one or more of them builds a perfect profile?

"You could have a profile so precise that it starts to influence you," he says. "So every time I respond to a recommendation because it was spot on, it further sharpens the profile. Then the profile is so sharp I become the slave of the profile. If that profile specifies that I like hamburgers, how will I ever learn to eat Mexican? It will keep me where I am," he explained, referring to the idea that if we only see special offers and advertising for things we already like, we are less likely to explore the alternatives.

Buytendijk also mentioned identity theft, something which becomes even easier once scarily accurate profiles of us are available for sale online.

"Identity theft is about to overtake normal theft in terms of economic damage. With just a little bit of combination of that fragmented data that's out there, all of a sudden you don't have a life anymore," warns Buytendijk, before concluding "I hope none of this comes true." We'll come back to this point around identity theft in Chapter five.

Everything highlighted in this chapter will be explored in more depth later. First, we'll take a close look at the governments of the US and UK, whose activities, thanks to Edward Snowden, we now know rather a lot about.

References

https://www.hostmerchantservices.com/articles/the-history-of-currency-from-bartering-to-the-credit-card-2/

http://www.forbes.com/sites/cherylsnappconner/2012/12/05/your-privacy-has-gone-to-the-angry-birds/

http://www.law360.com/articles/457089/gmail-users-rip-google-s-bid-to-sink-data-harvesting-suit

http://www.law360.com/articles/520437

http://www.telegraph.co.uk/technology/google/9831135/Apple-iPhone-users-suing-Google.html

http://www.independent.co.uk/life-style/gadgets-and-tech/news/google-claims-that-uk-law-does-not-apply-to-them-8774935.html

http://www.oddee.com/item_96657.aspx

http://www.mondaymorningmtg.com/p/blog-page_21.html#THS

CHAPTER 2

The Snowden Revelations

One of the greatest threats to our privacy comes not from cyber criminals, nor profiteering corporates, but from those we elect to govern us. When US government contractor Edward Snowden started releasing secret intelligence documents to the press in June 2013, the world was shocked and outraged at the revelations. The leaks showed that western governments, notably those of the so-called 'Five Eyes'; the US, UK, Canada, Australia and New Zealand, although others across Europe were similarly implicated, conspired to illegally mine telecommunications networks (in part by tapping undersea cables carrying around 90 per cent of the world's communications traffic), install malware onto millions of personal devices, actively attempt to undermine encryption standards, and infiltrate various internet providers, in order to spy on their own citizens and indeed anyone who makes use of digital communications.

The question on most people's lips was 'why'? Popular consensus held that this was the sort of behavior expected of totalitarian regimes, despots, and undemocratic governments of backward societies. Not our nice, socially aware, democratically elected western law-makers. But take a glance at the history books, and you'll quickly realize that the most surprising thing about the Snowden revelations was that any of us were surprised at all.

A GLANCE AT THE HISTORY BOOKS

We begin this glance almost a century ago, in early April 1917, when the US Congress declared war on Germany, signaling the nation's involvement in World War I. Communications are critical in any military activity, the difference in World War I was that there were new ways to glean crucial information from enemy broadcasts. The problem was that since the enemy was simultaneously trying to eavesdrop on your communications, each side was all too aware that its own exchanges were far from secure, and so encrypted them.

The 'Cipher Bureau and Military Intelligence Branch Section 8' was set up in Washington D.C. on April 28 1917, with the aim of cracking the coded transmissions from foreign powers. For an organization that was to eventually become the National Security Agency (NSA) and employ over 93,000 people at

CONTENTS

(Continued)

CONTENTS

its peak, it had humble origins. Originally it comprised merely of three people: cryptographer Herbert O Yardley and two clerks.

In 1919 Yardley's group set up the appropriately sinister sounding 'Black Chamber', which was located on East 37th Street in Manhattan. Its goal was to monitor communications from foreign governments and crack their codes. The Chamber made a deal with Western Union, the largest US telegram company of the day, to be allowed to monitor the supposedly private communications passing across the organization's networks. It was a sign of things to come. Western Union allowed this to go on for ten years, until 1929 when the chamber was shut down by US Secretary of State Henry L Stimson, who gave his wonderfully genteel reasoning as: "Gentlemen do not read each other's mail".

Other nations seemed less concerned by such refined codes of conduct. 'Black Chambers' were also set up by the British and French governments, with the rather less sophisticated designs of steaming open and reading written letters, before resealing them and sending them on, they hoped surreptitiously.

We'll now skip forward to World War II, specifically 1941 when an informal agreement was set up under the Atlantic Charter (which described Allied goals for the post-war era) for the UK and USA (or more accurately the organizations that were to become Government Communications Headquarters (GCHQ) and the National Security Agency (NSA)) to collaborate and share signals intelligence. Shortly after the war the other members of the Five Eyes were included.

Around the same time as the Atlantic Charter was being developed, the Signal Security Agency (SSA) was set up to gather and decipher communications between the Axis powers. After the war it was reformed into the Army Security Agency (ASA), then just months later, because there are never enough acronyms in government, it became part of the Armed Forces Security Agency (AFSA). But the AFSA's remit outstripped its abilities, and in 1951 President Harry S Truman ordered an investigation into its failings. The results of this investigation led to the formation of the NSA, although this was all utterly opaque to the US public, since the Presidential memo ordering the agency's creation was a classified document. In fact, members of the intelligence service began referring to the NSA as 'No Such Agency'.

Now let's jump forward to another war, this time Vietnam. In the 1960s the NSA was heavily involved in determining the US' involvement in the conflict, principally by gathering information on a North Vietnamese attack on the American destroyer USS Maddox during what became known as the Gulf of Tonkin Incident.

YOU SAY INCIDENT, I SAY SHAM; LET'S CALL THE WHOLE THING OFF

Confusingly, the Gulf of Tonkin Incident refers to two separate confrontations involving the USS Maddox and the North Vietnamese navy within two days of August 1964. On the 2nd August, the Maddox engaged three North Vietnamese torpedo boats from the 135th Torpedo Squadron. In the ensuing battle, the Maddox peppered the Torpedo Boats with shells, and four US Navy F-8 Crusader jet fighter bombers joined the fray, also firing on the boats. One of the jets was damaged in the fighting, as was the Maddox, whilst all three North Vietnamese Torpedo Boats took a pummeling, with four North Vietnamese sailors killed and six wounded. There were no US casualties.

Two days later came the second incident, with another tussle between the USS Maddox and North Vietnamese Torpedo Boats.

These events resulted in the US Congress passing the Gulf of Tonkin Resolution which enabled President Lyndon B Johnson to assist any Southeast Asian country whose government was potentially being "jeopardized by communist aggression". And the result of that was the Vietnam War.

It wasn't until 41-years later, in 2005, that the US public was to learn the truth about the Gulf of Tonkin Incident, when an internal NSA historical study was declassified. The document stated that although the Maddox had indeed engaged the North Vietnamese Navy in the first incident, the second battle had been entirely fictitious; there had been no North Vietnamese boats present. Furthermore, the Maddox had actually fired first in the battle of the August 2nd, a fact misreported to the Johnson administration at the time, who had been led to believe that it had been the Vietnamese to initiate the aggression. This was considered to be a crucial point determining further US involvement.

And the NSA's interest in the Vietnam War does not end there. In 1967 it launched a secret project code-named 'MINARET' in order to intercept electronic communications that contained the names of certain US citizens, then pass those communications on to other law enforcement and intelligence bodies within the US government.

Two of those US citizens were Senators Frank Church and Howard Baker. Another was civil rights activist Dr. Martin Luther King, and there were also various other well-known US journalists and athletes targeted including boxer Muhammad Ali. What they had in common was that they had all publically criticized the Vietnam War – actions supposedly protected and enshrined in the US First Amendment (which prohibits any law aiming to restrict freedom of speech).

In fact, the Sedition Act of 1918 aimed to do precisely that; restrict free speech. It prohibited the use of "disloyal, profane, scurrilous, or abusive language about the US government and its armed forces, and was repealed in 1920, only two years after its enactment, because of its incompatibility with the First Amendment.

The NSA was well aware of its own shaky legal position. An internal review at the agency found that its MINARET operation was "disreputable if not outright illegal." However, that acknowledgement – albeit one made privately – did not lead to the project's closure, but rather ensured that the cloak of secrecy under which it operated was drawn ever tighter.

Operational reports were printed on plain paper with no words or branding to link it to the NSA itself, and were hand-delivered to the White House, often directly to the President.

That we know any of this at all is due to an appeal made by the National Security Archive, an independent research institute, to the Security Classification Appeals Panel.

"Clearly the NSA didn't want to release this material but they were forced to do so by the American equivalent of the supreme court of freedom of information law," Matthew Aid, an intelligence historian specializing in the NSA, told the Guardian newspaper in September 2013.

Hints of what was to come appeared as far back as the aftermath of the Watergate Scandal at a congressional hearing in 1975 led by Senator Frank Church – one of the people marked for attention under the MINARET Project. The hearing revealed that the NSA, in collaboration with its UK-based counterpart GCHQ had intercepted communications from some outspoken anti-Vietnam war luminaries, including actress Jane Fonda.

After President Richard Nixon resigned as a consequence of the Watergate scandal, Senator Church discovered NSA wiretaps on other citizens, as well as a CIA plan, ordered by President John F. Kennedy's administration, to assassinate Fidel Castro.

The Church hearings resulted in the Foreign Intelligence Surveillance Act (FISA) of 1978, which aimed to limit the mass surveillance of US citizens by state-controlled bodies in the US. As we have since learnt, FISA has not proved entirely successful, but more on this later in his chapter.

All of this serves to beg the question, why were we all so surprised by the Snowden revelations?

REVELATIONS, OR JUST MORE OF THE SAME?

Let's take a brief look at the Snowden leaks themselves. According to an announcement from the NSA in 2013, Snowden took 1.7 million documents during his time at the agency, and had at the time released in the region of 200,000 of them to journalists. To analyze the results of even half of these documents would take several volumes of encyclopedic proportions, so we'll stick to the highlights. Specifically, we'll look at two of the larger government surveillance programs exposed by Snowden: MUSCULAR and PRISM.

MUSCULAR, operated principally by the UK's GCHQ, but with significant involvement from the NSA, is the name of a surveillance program where the two agencies gather private, unencrypted (as opposed to PRISM which is about accessing encrypted communications under the authority of FISA) public data from communications sent using software from internet giants Yahoo and Google. The use of the present tense here is deliberate, there is no evidence at the time of writing that either program has been stopped since its exposure – though it has experienced significant fetters more recently as we'll discuss later in this chapter.

According to one of the Snowden documents from Jan 9th 2013, the NSA sends millions of records every day from the private corporate networks of both Yahoo and Google, back to its own data warehouses located at Fort Meade, Maryland. To give a sense of the scale of the volume of data being gathered, the report went on to state that 181,280,466 new records had been sent back to Fort Meade in the 30 preceding days. It added that these records included data on who sent or received emails, and when they did so, on top the actual content of those communications, be they text, audio or video.

The intelligence agencies are able to do this because of two factors. Firstly, they have an overseas access point, thought to be in the UK (a slide from an NSA presentation leaked as part of the Snowden documents refers to a "Large international access located in the United Kingdom", see Figure 2.1, provided by an as yet unnamed telecommunications operator, which gives them an 'in' to the private networks of the targeted companies. Secondly, they have to be able to defeat the security on the networks they're trying to penetrate. We'll return to the security issue shortly – coming back to the access point; the fact that it is outside the US is important, as it means that it requires no tricky warrants, since it's outside FISA's remit.

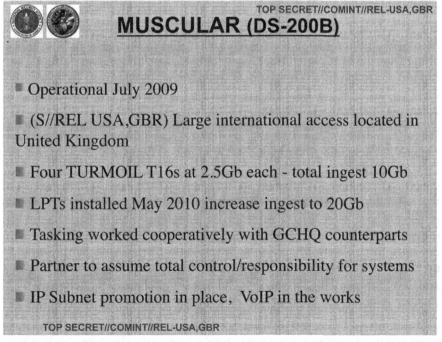

FIGURE 2.1 NSA slide on project MUSCULAR.

Executive Order 12333, signed by President Ronald Reagan on December 4th 1981, was designed to both clarify and extend the powers and responsibilities of US intelligence agencies. Just five years earlier, in 1976, the United States Senate Select Committee on Intelligence was formed with the aim of overseeing the US intelligence community. Much of its function is to review annual intelligence budgets, but another important responsibility is to conduct periodic investigations, audits, and inspections of intelligence activities and programs.

On August 16th 2013 in a press release on her own government website, Senate Intelligence Committee Chairman Dianne Feinstein admitted that Congress "…conducts little oversight of intelligence-gathering under the presidential authority of Executive Order 12333…"

She later added in the same release: "I believe… that the committee can and should do more to independently verify that NSA's operations are appropriate, and its reports of compliance incidents are accurate."

Speaking to the Washington Post in October 2013, former NSA chief analyst John Schindler said it is obvious why the agency would prefer to conduct operations overseas rather than on US soil.

"Look, NSA has platoons of lawyers, and their entire job is figuring out how to stay within the law and maximize collection by exploiting every loophole. It's fair to say the rules are less restrictive under Executive Order 12333 than they are under FISA," he said.

The NSA though, has strenuously and often denied claims of attempting to circumvent the law. In a statement reported by the Washington Post, the Office of the Director of National Intelligence denied that it was using executive authority to "get around the limitations" imposed by FISA. And at a cyber security event hosted by Bloomberg Government also in October 2013, NSA Director of the time Keith Alexander said:

"NSA has multiple authorities that it uses to accomplish its mission, which is centered on defending the nation. The Washington Post's assertion that we use Executive Order 12333 collection to get around the limitations imposed by the Foreign Intelligence Surveillance Act and FAA 702 is not true. The assertion that we collect vast quantities of US persons' data from this type of collection is also not true. NSA applies Attorney General-approved processes to protect the privacy of US persons - minimizing the likelihood of their information in our targeting, collection, processing, exploitation, retention, and dissemination. NSA is a foreign intelligence agency. And we're focused on discovering and developing intelligence about valid foreign intelligence targets only".

The point that Alexander was relying on is that the foreign access point his organization uses to take data from both Yahoo and Google allows him to assume that the data it gathers relates to foreign nationals. However, this is at best a misunderstanding, and at worst a deliberate smokescreen. The internet is a global system and huge internet firms like Yahoo and Google take a similarly worldwide view. Whilst it's true to say that these firms want to store customer data as close as physically possible to where they're accessed – which means that data belonging to Gmail customers in the US will largely reside in US-based data centers, and users in Japan will largely be accessing information in a Google data center in Asia – this is far from an absolute. Data is regularly backed up and transferred across the network to different data centers, and of course people aren't rooted to the ground, they travel and access their Gmail (and every other type of internet service) from offices, hotels and coffee shops all over the world. Also the internet is coded to send data via the most efficient route, so data could for instance pass through Japan even if neither the sender nor the recipient have ever been there. So the NSA view that data taken from overseas is from foreign nationals until proven otherwise is fundamentally flawed.

But the NSA and its related government bodies continue to deny any wrongdoing. Speaking at an American Bar Association conference in Washington on October 31st 2013, Robert S. Litt, general counsel for the Director of National Intelligence, said:

"Everything that has been exposed [by the media] so far has been done within the law. We get court orders when we are required to, we minimize information about US persons as we are required to, we collect intelligence for valid foreign intelligence purposes as we are required to."

Shortly after this speech, the NSA put out a statement backing up Litt's claims.

"Recent press articles on NSA's collection operations conducted under Executive Order 12333 have misstated facts, mischaracterized NSA's activities, and drawn erroneous inferences about those operations," it said.

Neither statement addressed the issue directly to confirm or deny the gathering of data from Google's and Yahoo's private clouds. Rather, they made the somewhat vague claims that the NSA's operations are compliant with "applicable laws, regulations, and policies." They then went on to almost beg that investigations be dropped and allegations of shady activity ceased: "…assertions to the contrary do a grave disservice to the nation, its allies and partners, and the men and women who make up the National Security Agency."

Now let's come back to the security issue – having a route into a network is well and good, but you need a way to actually understand that data, which often means decrypting it. Google and Yahoo are two of the largest firms in the world, whose customers expect a continuous, near flawless service, with the best available security.

Both firms operate multiple data centers around the world, with each one protected by armed guards, heat-sensitive cameras, biometric verification

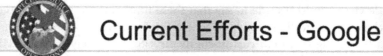

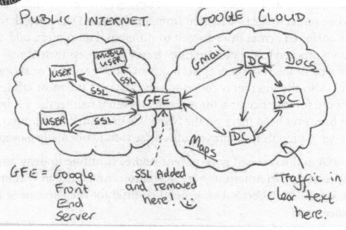

FIGURE 2.2 NSA explanation of how they cracked Google's network.

technologies, and other tools and techniques which wouldn't seem out of place protecting the villain's lair in a James Bond movie. However, a post-it note which formed part of an internal NSA presentation released as with the Snowden documents reveals a sketch showing where the "Public Internet" meets the internal "Google Cloud". At this junction, the author wrote: "Encryption is added and removed here!" See Figure 2.2.

There is even a rough sketch of a smiley face to express delight at the security agency's victory over Google's security measures.

The problem for Google was that at the time it relied on its perimeter security to keep intruders out, and away from its data. A fair analogy would be: if people can't climb over your fence, there's no need to lock your back door. So, data was unencrypted inside Google's private cloud, with the servers responsible for interfacing with the public internet stripping away Secure Socket Layer (an encryption protocol commonly used in internet communication) before it entered Google's cloud, and then adding it back as the traffic went the other way.

The Washington Post reported: "Two engineers with close ties to Google exploded in profanity when they saw the drawing."

Google later told the Post that it was "troubled by allegations of the government intercepting traffic between our data centers, and we are not aware of this activity. We have long been concerned about the possibility of this kind of snooping, which is why we continue to extend encryption across more and more Google services and links."

Google later told technology news service CNET: "We are outraged at the lengths to which the government seems to have gone to intercept data from our private fiber networks, and it underscores the need for urgent reform."

Yahoo told the Post: "We have strict controls in place to protect the security of our data centers, and we have not given access to our data centers to the NSA or to any other government agency."

After the information about the MUSCULAR program was published, Google said that it was working on deploying encrypted communication between its datacenters. A few months later, in March 2014, it announced various security improvements, including HTTPS by default, meaning no one could snoop on messages sent from a computer to Google's servers, but crucially also that traffic would be encrypted within Google's private cloud.

"… every single email message you send or receive—100% of them—is encrypted while moving internally. This ensures that your messages are safe not only when they move between you and Gmail's servers, but also as they move between Google's data centers—something we made a top priority after last summer's revelations," said Google's Gmail Security Engineering Lead Nicolas Lidzborski, in a blog posting.

And as of April 2013, Yahoo, previously considered to be a laggard in cyber security circles, has been encrypting traffic as it moves between its internal data centers.

So, whilst MUSCULAR is still going on as far as we know, it is no longer providing useful data to security agencies, unless modern encryption techniques are significantly less water-tight than is currently believed.

PRISM

Whereas MUSCULAR involves snooping on traffic illegally via a backdoor, PRISM, the other major NSA and GCHQ project which the world learnt about through the Snowden revelations, was until February 2015 considered to have been carried out through entirely legal means, whatever your views as to its ethics.

However, on February 6 2015, the Investigatory Powers Tribunal (which rules on legal challenges made against UK intelligence agencies) declared that the regulations relied on by GCHQ to access emails and phone records intercepted by the NSA breached human rights law. This was the first (and at the time of writing only) time that the IPT has upheld a legal challenge against an intelligence agency in its 15 year history.

A release on the IPT's website stated that: "The regime governing the soliciting, receiving, storing and transmitting by UK authorities of private communications of individuals located in the UK, which have been obtained by US authorities... contravened Articles 8 or 10" of the European convention on human rights. These Articles provide for the right to private and family life, and freedom of expression.

The decision followed a legal challenge from various civil liberties groups including Privacy International and Liberty.

However, every silver lining has a dark cloud. Despite this landmark ruling, there is no evidence to suggest that the program has stopped, paused, or even taken a weekend off since the challenge was upheld.

So what is PRISM? The program concerns itself with the storage of internet-based communications (video calls, emails, instant messages, file transfers, photos and other data) gathered legally via Section 702 of the FISA Amendments Act 2008. This Section enables the Attorney General and the Director of National Intelligence jointly to authorize the targeted interception of internet communications from a non-US citizen located outside the US, for up to one year. Basically what this means is that firms like Microsoft, Google, Yahoo, Facebook and many others, can be forced to hand over records relating to their customers.

Another effect of the act is to grant immunity to telecommunications firms who aided government surveillance in the past, a provision which immediately put paid to a number of lawsuits designed to expose and stop various illegal government activities. It is tempting to broadly condemn any retrospective law, after all the authors of the US Constitution expressly prohibited it in their very first Article. Article 1 Section 9 forbids the federal government to pass any *ex post facto* law, and Section 10 describes the same ban on state governments. However, the US Supreme Court has ruled on various occasions that retrospective legislation is not necessarily unconstitutional – indicating that there are occasions in which it can be justified.

PRISM is "the number one source of raw intelligence used for NSA analytic reports" according to a set of the Snowden documents. Furthermore, it comprises 91 per cent of the NSA's total internet traffic volume demanded under the authority of Section 702 of the FISA Amendments Act.

A set of NSA slides forming part of another Snowden document details the process an NSA security analyst goes through to order and collect data on a new target. The first slide shows the principle methods the NSA uses to gather private data. One it calls 'Upstream', which it describes as the "Collection of communications on fiber cables and infrastructure as data flows past." This is a fairly accurate description of the MUSCULAR program (although this activity happens in the UK under the TEMPORA program, a secret UK government project worth £1bn which attached probes to transatlantic fiber-optic cables and fed information into the PRISM program). PRISM, is described as the "collection directly from the servers of these US Service Providers: Microsoft, Yahoo, Google, Facebook, PalTalk, AOL, Skype, YouTube, Apple." A large bubble points to both types of mass surveillance program with the helpful instruction: "You should use both"!

The next slide reveals that in order to get information on a new surveillance target an NSA analyst makes a request to a supervisor who reviews it before deciding whether to authorize the analyst's "reasonable belief", described as 51 per cent confidence, that the target is a foreign national who was outside US borders at the time of the data collection.

The final slide reveals the dates when the nine companies involved in PRISM joined the program. The first was Microsoft, on 11th September 2007 – there appears to be little significance to the date being the sixth anniversary of the attack on the World Trade Center in 2001, conspiracy theories aside. Yahoo joined on the 12th March 2008, then the rest are fairly evenly spread up until Apple in October 2012. It's plausible that more firms have been added since then given that Snowden's clandestine data gathering went on up until late 2013, so either PRISM's overseers were satisfied with the companies they already had, Snowden was unable to retrieve more recent files, or others have been added since he resigned his post in October 2013.

What's interesting here is that many of the firms involved in PRISM had previously denied giving any government agency direct access to their servers. Here's what Apple has to say on the matter, on its own website.

"Our commitment to customer privacy doesn't stop because of a government information request. Government information requests are a consequence of doing business in the digital age. We believe in being as transparent as the law allows about what information is requested from us. In addition, Apple has never worked with any government agency from any country to create a "back door" in any of our products or services. We have also never allowed any government access to our servers. And we never will."

On its website, Facebook tells a similar story:

"…we scrutinize every government data request that we receive – whether from state, local, federal, or foreign governments. We've also made clear that we aggressively protect our users' data when confronted with such requests: we frequently reject such requests outright, or require the government to substantially scale down its requests, or simply give the government much less data than it has requested. And we respond only as required by law."

But Snowden himself directly contradicted these assertions in an online Q&A session with Guardian readers, claiming that all US government agencies have direct, unfettered access to the nine corporations' databases.

"They can enter and get results for anything they want [such as] phone numbers, email, user ID, cell phone handset ID," he said. "The restrictions against this are policy-based, not technically based, and can change at any time" he added. "Additionally, audits are cursory, incomplete, and easily fooled by fake justifications. For GCHQ, the number of audited queries is only 5 per cent of those performed."

He continued the point a year later in October 2014, appearing at an 'Ideas Festival' organized by the UK-based Observer newspaper via Skype from his hideout in Russia.

"The UK ... [has a] system of regulation where anything goes. They collect everything that might be interesting. It's up to the government to justify why it needs this. It's not up to you to justify why it doesn't... This is where the danger is, when we think about... evidence is being gathered against us, but we don't have the opportunity to challenge that in courts. It undermines the entire system of justice," stated Snowden.

This expands on a story reported in the Guardian newspaper in 2013, in which it quotes a GCHQ legal advisor as saying "We have a light oversight regime compared with the US".

One of the results of the turmoil wrought by the revelations was the retirement in March 2014 of NSA chief Keith Alexander, who was caught so unawares by the scrutiny of his organization at Bloomberg's cyber security conference just five months earlier.

Peter Singer, a cybersecurity academic at the Brookings Institution, said Alexander's successor, Vice Admiral Michael Rogers (who specialized in computer network attacks whilst working for the Joint Chiefs of Staff during the 2003 Iraq war), faced a huge challenge in restoring the reputation of the NSA.

"We have an immense uphill battle in the post-Snowden, post-Alexander world. It's good that we're now selling a message of restraint, but it's not clear the rest of the world is going to buy it. Therein lies the challenge for the new policymakers inheriting this all," he said.

Does this change of leadership represent also a change of direction for the NSA? After all it has faced huge public criticism for its private data dragnets since they came to light. Rogers gave some hope of a change of tack in an interview with Reuters in May 2014, discussing his memory of being a teenager and learning how the CIA, FBI and NSA had illegally spied on hundreds of thousands of American citizens – revelations which surfaced through investigations in the Watergate scandal.

"I can remember being very impassioned with my father, and telling him: 'Dad, what kind of nation would we ever want to be that would allow something like this to happen?' Rogers said. Then later, speaking at the Reuters cybersecurity Summit in Washington, he added that in his opinion current intelligence data gathering activities were lawful, but individual privacy rights needed to be weighed up against security needs.

"We have been down that road in our history, and it has not always turned out well. I have no desire to be part of that," he said.

These statements emerged at a promising time for privacy advocates. A few months earlier, in January 2014, President Barack Obama called for changes to the NSA's surveillance operations, with new privacy specialists assigned to a surveillance court in order to add an extra layer of audit and oversight to new agency requests, and a transition away from the gathering of US phone records (the NSA harvests metadata on US phone calls relying on an interpretation of the Patriot Act meaning that all internal US communications can be considered to pertain to terrorism as long as a small minority can be proven to).

However, this was some way short of the changes advocated by the Review Group on Intelligence and Communications Technology, an NSA surveillance review board set up by Obama himself, which recommended that the NSA relinquish its database of US telephone records.

"In our view, the current storage by the government of bulk meta-data creates potential risks to public trust, personal privacy, and civil liberty," said the report, released in December 2013.

"Excessive surveillance and unjustified secrecy can threaten civil liberties, public trust, and the core processes of democratic self-government," the report continued. "All parts of the government, including those that protect our national security, must be subject to the rule of law."

It went on to question the NSA's reasoning in keeping its phone records metadata collection program out of the public eye.

"We recommend that the decision to keep secret from the American people programs of the magnitude of the ... bulk telephony meta-data program should be made only after careful deliberation at high levels of government and only with due consideration of and respect for the strong presumption of transparency that is central to democratic governance. A program of this magnitude should be kept secret from the American people only if (a) the program serves a compelling governmental interest and (b) the efficacy of the program would be substantially impaired if our enemies were to know of its existence."

The report also recommended limitations on the ability of the US Foreign Intelligence Surveillance Court to force telecom carriers to disclose the private information of their customers to the government.

But Obama refused to go to the lengths recommended by the report, saying in a speech at the Justice Department: "Ultimately, what's at stake in this debate goes beyond a few months of headlines or passing tensions in our foreign policy. When you cut through the noise, what's really at stake is how we remain true to who we are in a world that's remaking itself at dizzying speed."

Whilst the President allowed the NSA to continue to collect metadata on millions of US citizens' phone records, he launched a directive requiring NSA analysts to get a court order to process that data. In addition he announced that the government would no longer be permitted to hold the data itself, with a third party to be created to store it. Other provisions included restrictions on spying on foreign heads of state – which the likes of Russia's Vladimir Putin no doubt took with an enormous pinch of salt – and permission for telecommunications providers to reveal information on government requests to access data.

"The reforms I'm proposing today should give the American people greater confidence that their rights are being protected," Obama said, "even as our intelligence and law enforcement agencies maintain the tools they need to keep us safe."

And it's the need to provide safety for US citizens that Obama pushed in attempting to justify his decision not to implement the full recommendations of his report, and allow the NSA to continue is wide-scale harvesting of phone metadata.

"We cannot prevent terrorist attacks or cyber-threats without some capability to penetrate digital communications," he said.

One huge area entirely unfettered by the reforms is US spying on everything outside of its borders. The proposals were all entirely focused on America spying on its own citizens. It seems that the Obama administration continued to see the rest of the world as fair game.

In any case, the reforms and their justifications did not go down well with privacy advocates.

Obama's call for a transition in the bulk phone records program raises new questions, Kevin Bankston, policy director of the New America Foundation Open Technology Institute, told technology website PCWorld.

"If the ultimate alternative to government collection is mandatory bulk data retention by the phone companies or mandatory bulk handover to a third party, the president should be prepared for a major legislative battle with key members of Congress, the technology industry, and the privacy community arrayed against him. Particularly when the president's own review group concluded that the records program is not essential to preventing terrorist attacks ... the right answer here is to stop the bulk collection completely—not to keep the same bulk data under a different roof."

In an interview with the same title, David Segal, executive director of digital rights group Demand Progress questioned the compatibility of the NSA's various spying programs with the basic tenets of democracy.

"We urge the president to recognize that the public concern is not only over whether mass spying programs are explicitly abused, within standards set by the NSA, but whether these programs should exist at all—whether they are fundamentally compatible with the notion that we live in a free society, a democracy."

Judge Richard Leon of the US District Court for the District of Columbia used the platform of his December 2013 68-page ruling in a case brought by Larry Klayman, lawyer and founder of educational foundation Judicial Watch, and three other plaintiffs, to attack the Department of Justice and the NSA on similar grounds.

"The threshold issue that I must address, then, is whether the plaintiffs have a reasonable expectation of privacy that is violated when the Government indiscriminately collects their telephone metadata along with the metadata of hundreds of millions of other citizens without any particularized suspicion of wrongdoing, retains all of that metadata for five years, and then queries, analyses, and investigates that data without prior judicial approval of the investigative targets.

"I have little doubt that the author of our Constitution, James Madison, who cautioned us to beware 'the abridgement of freedom of the people by the gradual and silent encroachments by those in power,' would be aghast."

Judge Leon has a final word too for Obama's justification that the various spying activities are necessary to prevent terrorism.

"The Government does not cite a single instance [in defending the case] in which analysis of the NSA's bulk metadata collection actually stopped an imminent attack."

As it subsequently turned out, at least part of the debate was purely academic. The USA Freedom Act which contained provisions to reform the NSA and end its control of phone metadata was defeated in Congress in November 2014 as it failed to get the 60 votes it needed to end debate and move it towards a final vote on legislation. Privacy advocates will find little comfort in the fact that the vote was very close, with 58 senators electing to end the debate, whilst 42 voted against it.

Where is 2015's Henry L Stimson? Who will stand up today and declare "Gentlemen don't read one another's mail"?

Whilst the Investigatory Power Tribunal found PRISM to have been illegal at least up until December 2014, it turned down the opportunity to rule likewise on the TEMPORA program at the same time, when it ruled that it is 'legal in principle'.

The reasoning, as ever murky in the world of intricate legal interpretations, basically boils down to a finding that since GCHQ were forced to disclose their policies during the case, the PRISM spying was subsequently in accordance with law. But they were illegal whilst the policies were secret prior to the case.

The case was brought against GCHQ by privacy campaign groups Privacy International, Amnesty International and Liberty, amongst others. The IPT was asked to rule on whether the government spying programs actually exist, and then whether they violate articles 8 and 10 of the European Convention on Human Rights. The complainants have decided to appeal, and the case is being brought to the European Court of Human Rights at the time of writing.

Eric King, deputy director of Privacy International, voiced his concern about the decision to technology news site Computing.

"With GCHQ's mass surveillance of undersea cables reported to have increased by as much as 7,000 per cent in the last five years, today's decision by the IPT that this is business as usual is a worrying sign for us all," he said.

"The idea that previously secret documents, signposting other still secret documents, can justify this scale of intrusion is just not good enough, and not what society should accept from a democracy based on the rule of law," he added.

PLUS CA CHANGE

So what have we learned so far? Throughout the 1920s the NSA's precursor was snooping on its citizens' details via a secret deal with a telecommunications firm. In the 1960s, after the agency's inception, it unlawfully spied on various US citizens. Then, from at least 2007, it started gathering, storing and analyzing data on a huge proportion of the internet's user base, and in fact, the world. It has at least been consistent in its actions, if nothing else.

Freedom fighter or terrorist, Snowden gave up much of his personal liberty to bring his revelations to the world. The question for him now is, was it worth it? What has actually changed since June 2013 when he began to release his documents?

"Nothing!" says Frank Buytendijk, research vice president, information innovation, at analyst firm Gartner.

But in explaining his theory that our society is in the second 'ethical wave of discussion' around new digital technology, Buytendijk sounds a more positive note.

"The first wave was smartphones and social media where we complained that kids just sit on their phones during dinner and don't look people in the eye. What did that [wave of discussion] achieve? Nothing.

"The second discussion now is around big data and privacy. How's that going? It's having limited success. When people complain [about a privacy issue], it gets fixed, the company withdraws its initiative or the government introduces some new regulations, but the firm [or the government] just waits and tries again."

He goes on to describe the third discussion as being around autonomous technology like self-driving cars, and the Internet of Things. We'll come back to this in Chaper 9.

Whilst Bujtendijk has good reason to suggest that nothing has changed since Snowden, he also points out that the sorts of major changes which may still result rarely come about quickly, giving the colorful example of standing in a pub and shouting offensively.

"To say nothing has changed doesn't mean people don't 'curve'. You could look at the next fifty years, and the fact that nothing happened in the last eighteen months is not meaningful. Society is a resilient structure, which means it can absorb [a certain level of change]. That should not be confused with inertia. It doesn't mean nothing will change, it just means we haven't worked out how it should change yet.

"If society changed drastically after every little scandal, society would lose its resilience."

He did however give one example of a fairly rapid recent societal change brought about by technology.

"For last 2,000 years, we've lived in the certainty that most of what we do and say in the grand scheme of things doesn't really matter. For example you could stand in pub after three beers and shout to your friends across the room that the Crown Prince is a sissy, then who really cares? But put it on Twitter and it'll never be forgotten."

But Anna Fielder, trustee and chair at privacy charity Privacy International explains that things are changing, but very much behind the scenes.

"It's true to some extent that nothing's changed," Fielder begins. "But generally people are psychologically torn about appearing to criticise mass surveillance, they're concerned that they might appear to condone terrorism."

Fielder acknowledges that the authorities recognise the need to keep a balance between freedom and security, but goes on to describe their argument that it's better to be alive and be able to worry about civil liberties, than be dead and unable to appreciate them.

Whilst that fact is hardly debatable, reality is rarely so starkly black and white. As Judge Leon said, where is the evidence of the terrorist plots foiled by mass government surveillance?

Back to the issue of change since Snowden, and Fielder points out that you have to look behind the scenes at the negotiations between the US and EU to see the great cogs of legislature slowly beginning to creak into life.

"If you look at what's going on at the European Commission level, there are conversations going on between the EU and US. The Umbrella Agreement is still being debated."

This 'Umbrella Law Enforcement Agreement' for the transatlantic transfer of data, to give it its full title, has been a topic for debate between the EU and US for over three years, but is now drawing close to some sort of consensus. Once enacted, it will confer the same legal protections to EU citizens whose personal data is harvested by US law enforcement agencies as US citizens.

At a press conference during the Justice and Home Affairs Ministerial meeting in Athens, Greece in June 2014, US Attorney General Eric Holder explained the reasoning for the agreement, admitting that both sides could do better when it comes to protecting personal information.

"In a world of globalized crime and terrorism we can protect our citizens only if we work together, including through sharing law enforcement information. At the same time we must ensure that we continue our long tradition of protecting privacy in the law enforcement context. We already have many mechanisms in place to do this and we have on both sides of the Atlantic an outstanding record to protect law enforcement information. But we can also do more and we can also do better," he said.

Shortly afterwards, European Commission vice president Viviane Reding released a statement in which she appeared to be impatient with the protracted negotiations.

"Now the announcement should be swiftly translated into legislation so that further steps can be taken in the negotiation. Words only matter if put into law. We are waiting for the legislative step," she said.

Although the issue may have largely fallen out of the media spotlight, it has evidently remained a burning issue for EU policymakers. Indeed in a European Parliamentary report from 21st February 2014, the legislators wrote on the impact of the NSA's mass surveillance programs:

"…the US authorities have denied some of the information revealed but have not contested the vast majority of it… the public debate has developed on a large scale in the US and in certain EU Member States… EU governments and parliaments too often remain silent and fail to launch adequate investigations."

The report goes further, recommending a suspension of the EU – US Safe Harbor agreement.

"[This report recommends that the EU] Suspend Safe Harbor until a full review has been conducted and current loopholes are remedied, making sure that transfers of personal data for commercial purposes from the Union to the US can only take place in compliance with highest EU standards."

If this caused friction with the US authorities, it was nothing compared to what came next. First, a statement that trust in US cloud services has been eroded.

"…trust in US cloud computing and cloud providers has been negatively affected by the [mass surveillance revelations]… therefore [we recommend] the development of European clouds and IT solutions as an essential element for growth and employment and for trust in cloud computing services and providers, as well as for ensuring a high level of personal data protection."

Then, like a quick 'one two' in a boxing ring, a recommendation to stick two metaphorical fingers up at US-based cloud services, and instead build an EU-only cloud.

After a section calling on "all public bodies in the Union not to use cloud services where non-EU laws might apply", it added a call to the European Commission and EU Member States to:

"…speed up the work of establishing a European Cloud Partnership while fully including civil society and the technical community, such as the Internet Engineering Task Force (IETF), and incorporating data protection aspects."

This idea was first mooted shortly before the report's publication by German chancellor Angela Merkel, herself alleged to have been the victim of an NSA wiretap by a section of the Snowden documents.

This 'European Cloud Partnership' proposal resulted in a swift and angry letter from members of US Congress to Martin Schulz, President of the European Parliament, accusing the lawmakers in Brussels (where the Parliament is based) of endangering trade between the two continents.

"…we have become increasingly concerned by the appearance of a trend in the European Union towards discriminating against foreign companies with respect to the digital economy. We are alarmed by proposals that seem to target US technology companies, create market access barriers, and limit innovation… Provisions calling for… localization of cloud computing services, which could go so far as to create a walled-off "EU cloud", are especially troubling. This and similar proposals to build walls rather than bridges, do not appear to give full consideration to the negative effect such policies might have on the broader US-EU trade relationship and our ability to address mutual concerns in third countries, and raise questions about the EU's commitment to open markets and the free flow of data worldwide."

One imagines, reading the final sentence quoted above, that the Congressman are not intending to refer to the 'free flow of data' into the NSA's servers, though that is one interpretation. The letter carried real weight too, being signed by some heavy hitters in Washington: Dave Camp, chairman of the House Committee on Ways and Means, Ron Wyden, chairman of the Senate Committee on Finance, Sander Levin, ranking member of the House Committee on Ways and Means and Orrin Hatch, ranking member of the Senate Committee on Finance.

The idea of keeping data relating to EU citizens within the EU is a beguiling one. If you're based in London, and you send an email to a friend in Berlin, why should it be routed through servers in New York where it will be stored and potentially analysed without your consent?

A good reason why not was expressed by Ralf Bendrath, Senior Policy Advisor to Member of the European Parliament Jan Philipp Albrecht in his analysis 'TTIP and TiSA: big pressure to trade away privacy'. He explained that it's not only technically difficult to specify geographically where internet traffic can and cannot go, it's also potentially dangerous.

"Technically it is not trivial because the Internet protocol with its IP addresses uses a logical address space that does not know from the underlying physical transport level where a given IP address is geographically located. While there are services to enable IP-level localisation, they only reach an approximation: my own IP address in the European Parliament in Brussels looks like I am located in Luxembourg, because of the three official seats of the Parliament in Brussels, Luxembourg and Strasbourg. Even if geo-routing was technically feasible, it cannot be our goal to re-shape the topology of the transnational and global Internet along national boundaries. This would quickly trigger undesirable consequences, such as calls for 'immigration controls' for data packets, which would be equivalent to Internet censorship," writes Bendrath.

Instead, he recommends end to end encryption of all internet traffic. That way, we can preserve the current method of geo-agnostic traffic routing, and not care through which jurisdictions our traffic flows.

Bendrath's analysis continues to dissect US governmental criticism of this proposed 'EU cloud', in particular the bandying about of the term 'localization'. US Trade Representative Michael Froman claimed that European "localization" rules which require data transport or data processing in Europe constitute an illegal trade barrier in his report on trade agreements for the telecommunication industry, for instance.

Bendrath argues that where data is processed is of greater importance than where it is routed.

"It is however important to keep routing and data processing clearly distinct here," he says in his report. "While rules on data packet routing may be ill-advised, it is highly relevant where data is processed – especially if it is personal data. Even on the European side of this debate, many have not yet fully understood that EU data protection rules are *fundamentally* rules for localization. Because data protection in Europe is a binding fundamental right with constitutional status in the EU Charter of Fundamental Rights, personal data may in principle be processed only within Europe. Any rules for the transfer of such data to third countries constitute exceptions from this principle and must meet certain conditions - such as an adequate level of protection in the respective third country.

"In the post-Snowden era, there is a wider debate now in Europe over stricter limits on transfers of personal data to the US and other third countries. The European Parliament has introduced a new Article 43a into its version of the upcoming General Data Protection Regulation, [24] which would prevent third countries' authorities from demanding a transfer from a European data controller without regard to a mutual legal assistance treaty. The European Court of Justice will now have to decide if data transfers to the US under the Safe Harbor decision are still legal, after a preliminary ruling from the Dublin High Court based on a challenge by Austrian activist Max Schrems and his group 'Europe vs Facebook'."

There are numerous dissenting voices however, on the issue of data localization. The European Centre for International Political Economy (ECIPE), which describes itself as an independent and non-profit policy research think tank dedicated to trade policy and other international economic policy issues of importance to Europe, claims that keeping critical EU-related data within the EU will result in an economic shrinkage of 1.1 per cent.

In a blog titled 'The costs of data localization', published on ECIPE's website, Hosuk Lee-Makiyama, a director at the organization, says that "one of the most drastic, yet a common policy response to the problem [of mass surveillance] has been the mandatory requirement on storing critical data on servers physically located inside the country.

"What Brazil and other countries like China, the European Union, India, Indonesia, Korea and Vietnam (who all have considered similar strategies) fail – or choose to fail – to see, is that information security is not a function of where data is physically stored or processed," he continues.

"A study by ECIPE economists shows that cross-border data flow is essential for developing economies to secure access to foreign markets and participation in global supply chains. Thus, data is a major sources of growth, jobs and new investments. Manufacturing and exports are highly dependent on access to support services at competitive prices – services that depend on secure and efficient access to data. Forced data localisation affects any business that uses the internet to produce, deliver, and receive payments for their work, or to pay their salaries and taxes."

Lee-Makiyama is unrelenting in his criticism of those who advocate data localization branding it a "counterproductive strategy… with no possibilities to mitigate the negative impact in the long term. He describes it as "…the product of poor, one-sided economic analysis, often with the surreptitious objective of keeping foreign competitors out – although economic and security gains are too small to outweigh losses in terms of jobs and output in the general economy."

Global law firm Mayer Brown appears inclined to agree. In what it describes as a 'strategic analysis', published in September 2014, Alex C Lakatos, a partner at the firm, calls any decision to deliberately hinder the free flow of data between the US and EU "both naïve and dangerously short sighted."

Lakatos argues that eschewing data localization will benefit small and medium firms, and consumers.

"Under the current internet architecture, data can be stored anywhere, accessed anywhere, and it moves along the most efficient routes, avoiding legal and physical blockages alike. The model is, if you will, a 'world wide web' - and not the internet of 'you and me and I'm not so sure about you anymore,' nor the network envisioned in Chancellor Angela Merkel's proposed Europe-only communications system. The sort of balkanisation that data localization begets would make for a much less robust and diverse internet, to the detriment of consumers who use the internet to shop and pay bills. On top of that, small and local businesses might well find it economically unfeasible to compete if faced with laws requiring them to maintain separate servers, and to separately store and track information, in myriad countries, each with its own data localization requirements."

He also contends that segregating parts of the internet off into discrete chunks will enable a raft of "bad behaviour" in "authoritarian regimes – a bad government in possession of a server containing sensitive data belonging to its citizens will think nothing of mining it for all it's worth. He acknowledges that the EU Member States have a good track record on human rights which he claims makes them unlikely to try anything so shady themselves, but rather that the principle provides a precedent which weaker democracies might seek to exploit.

This is a reasonable argument but appears to have forgotten the reason this debate is happening in the first place: Snowden. Various EU Member States, principally the UK, but also Germany, the Netherlands, Sweden and France, have been proven to operate at a very shady level when it comes to their citizens' private data, rendering their previous track record on human rights irrelevant (former NSA head Keith Alexander, in testimony to the US Congress, said that European governments were being somewhat hypocritical in terms of their protests about mass surveillance: "Some of this reminds me of the classic movie Casablanca - 'My God, there's gambling going on here'.")

Secondly, authoritarian regimes need no precedent to inflict privacy abuses (and other human rights violations) on their citizens, that's one of the reasons why we call them authoritarian. However, the central tenet stands that keeping sensitive data in one country or area doesn't actually guarantee that it won't be abused.

"The EU does itself a disservice if it refuses to discourse with the US on data protection," continued Lakatos. "For one thing, if European obstinacy derails the effort to protect the free flow of data, all the world will reap the adverse economic and human rights consequences... For another thing, why not at least try to resolve these thorny issues? The fundamental EU objection seems to be that in the post-Snowden era, and in the wake of revelations about the US tapping of Chancellor Merkel's cell phone, the US has to make amends and rebuild trust. Only then will the EU open a dialogue on privacy. Certainly, the EU's anger and frustration are understandable. But are they productive? Giving the US a chance to work collaboratively on privacy issues would be a more successful path forward than giving the US the silent treatment. To reach that conclusion, it is helpful to re-examine another bit of conventional wisdom, i.e., that the US simply does not care about data protection, and moreover, if Europe brings up the subject, the EU will inevitably have to compromise its legitimate interests in data protection to reach an accord. The truth is more complex."

Lakatos addresses the somewhat 'holier than thou' attitude the EU has taken towards the US over the data localization issue by attempting to dispel the notion that the US doesn't care about privacy, or is at least loathe to protect it properly in law. The US has strong legal protection for medical and health care data under the Health Insurance Portability and Accountability Act (HIPAA). Financial data is similarly well guarded under the Graham Leach Bliley Act. Then there are the local state laws. California, the world's ninth largest economy and home to Silicon Valley, enshrines and protects privacy in its Constitution. Also, it is home to the California Online Privacy Protection Act, which enables users of commercial websites to both review and request changes to their personal data.

"Arguing that the US is simply oblivious to privacy concerns, therefore, is dubious. The argument that the US will not work constructively to reach a resolution that respects EU privacy concerns is also grounds for scepticism."

There are reasons for optimism however, as fiery as the current cross-Atlantic privacy debate is, the EU and US have managed to find some common ground recently. The Safe Harbor framework is currently being reviewed, and EC Vice President Reding has stated that the US Department of Commerce has acceded to 12 of 13 of the EC's requirements for continuing the operation of the Safe Harbor, including accepting provisions that cover transparency, redress, enforcement and access by the US authorities to data transferred under the program.

Furthermore, there is the Umbrella Agreement mentioned earlier in this chapter. Whilst it is still being debated, the view is that a consensus is not far off.

"As part of those negotiations, the EC has not hesitated to ask that an amendment enabling court access in the US for EU citizens to be added to US legislation under consideration in Congress designed to strengthen oversight of NSA surveillance activities. These are scarcely the talismans of hopelessness. Admittedly, reaching a meaningful resolution on issues of data flows and data privacy carries stakes too high to make for anything other than tough… negotiations. But for exactly the same reason, we should not settle for anything less when it comes to such a major trade initiative," concludes Lakatos.

SNOWDEN WHO?

So the issue is occupying the minds of those in power. Strange then that it so rapidly fell from the front pages of the newspapers, and hence the public consciousness (or you could argue that the cause and effect is the other way around, still the result is the same).

Privacy International's Fielder mentions that the person on the street might not care too deeply about these issues because he or she has so little power to affect them.

"Ordinary citizens perhaps don't care because there's nothing they can do! You have no choice, you can't close yourself from the internet it's no longer possible," she says.

It's easy to look at the two years or so which have elapsed since Snowden started releasing his documents to journalists and declare that nothing has improved or changed. Our data continues to be trawled by security agencies to be stored and then analysed at their leisure, with no requirement to notify us and only a few simple legal hoops to jump through to prove that any analysis is warranted. Since the initial media frenzy, the issue has largely dropped off the public radar, but that doesn't mean the political wheels aren't spinning, and it doesn't mean nothing will change. As Gartner's Buytendijk said, major societal change doesn't happen overnight. To put it another way, Rome wasn't built in a day.

"There is a lot of fall out politically on the EU level," says Fielder. "[The Snowden revelations] are providing new impetus for the European Council to start approving new data protection regulation and they've also generated a review of the safe harbor provisions."

The data protection regulation Fielder refers to was originally proposed in 2012, and is expected to come into force in 2015, after which EU member states will have two years to reform their own data protection legislation to comply. It seems that the process of reforming privacy and security laws is not for the impatient. We'll come back to these reforms in chapter 7.

The review, or indeed suspension of safe harbor was one of the issues so to anger the US Congress from the European Parliamentary report discusses earlier. The principle of safe harbor is that a certain law or regulation which defines a specific behaviour will be considered not to violate a certain other rule or law. Since that's basically as clear as mud, let's turn to an example. A safe harbor is a safe place, unsurprisingly enough. In law, that might mean that you're protected from a conviction of dangerous driving if you're travelling below 20 kilometres per hour. In the context of this chapter, it refers to the current EU Data Protection Directive (specifically Directive 95/46/EC for committed legislature fans), adopted in 1995, which required EU member states to draw up their own legislation to govern when and how personal data can be processed within the EU (an EU Directive requires nations to create their own legislation within a time frame in order to comply with their contents, whilst Regulations automatically apply without the need for new national laws). It is this directive which will be superseded by the new legislation when it comes out in 2015.

It sets comparatively strict privacy protections for EU citizens. It prohibits European firms from transferring personal data to overseas jurisdictions with weaker privacy laws, but creates exceptions where the foreign recipients have voluntarily agreed to meet EU standards.

On top of the negotiations going on between EU and US lawmakers, a coalition of Non-Governmental Organizations (NGO) has been hard at work creating new principles for data collection and mass surveillance that they hope governments will observe.

Some of them have banded together to create 'Don't Spy on US', a group of organizations who "defend privacy, free expression and digital rights in the UK and in Europe," is how it describes itself on its website.

"We've come together to fight back against the system of unfettered mass state surveillance that Edward Snowden exposed. Right now, the UK's intelligence services are conducting mass surveillance that violates the right to privacy of internet users and chills freedom of expression."

The coalition clearly believes that existing privacy law is inadequate, as it goes on to say:

"The current laws haven't stopped the intelligence services expanding their reach into our private lives. *Don't Spy On Us* is calling for an inquiry to investigate the extent to which the law has failed and suggest new legislation that will make the spooks accountable to our elected representatives, put an end to mass surveillance… and let judges not the Home Secretary decide when spying is justified."

So should privacy advocates be quietly encouraged? Governments are negotiating over increased restrictions to their surveillance powers, and issue is red hot, if not in the mind of the man or woman on the street, then at least where it counts – in the parliamentary halls of Washington and Brussels. And then there's the action taken by the firms targeted by MUSCULAR. Major corporates like Google, Yahoo and Microsoft are now encrypting their internal traffic, a step which should greatly limit what agencies like GCHQ and the NSA are able to do with our data, even if we're unable to stop them getting at it in the first place.

Interestingly, one response from the security agencies themselves appeared in the Financial Times newspaper in November 2014. In it, GCHQ chief Robert Hannigan demanded greater co-operation from technology companies to help combat the threat of terrorism.

"The Islamic State of Iraq and the Levant (Isis) is the first terrorist group whose members have grown up on the internet. They are exploiting the power of the web to create a jihadi threat with near-global reach. The challenge to governments and their intelligence agencies is huge – and it can only be met with greater co-operation from technology companies."

Hannigan went on to describe services like Twitter and Facebook as the "command and control networks of choice" for terrorists. He lamented the rise of encryption and anonymization tools which are now available, stating that today's terrorists are undoubtedly benefiting.

A few days later came a rebuttal from the Telegraph: "Rather than acknowledge the very real misgivings that the British people have in the accountability of the services charged with protecting their security, Hannigan has used his public platform as an exercise in ex-post justification, and to launch the case for expanded powers. The audacity of such an attack, even as GCHQ is under the review of the Intelligence Services Committee, the Independent Reviewer of Terrorism Legislation and the Investigatory Powers Tribunal, is astounding.

"In any event, Hannigan's argument begins from the fundamentally flawed premise that the internet is a tool of terror, rather than an instrument for public good – the greatest tool for education, expression, connection and innovation humankind has ever seen. The emancipatory power of the internet lies in its free and democratic nature."

The article concluded: "It is not terrorists who threaten that future of the internet, but our intelligence and security services."

And in October 2014 FBI director James Comey made a speech asking Congress to ban phone encryption, warning that new technology may have brought a greater degree of privacy to individuals, but that it comes at the cost of making it impossible for law enforcement agencies to find the bad guys.

This is the head of the US principle counter-terrorism and counter-intelligence agency throwing his hands up and claiming that his organization comes grinding to a standstill as soon as certain types of communication are encrypted. One hopes, for the sake of US and indeed global political stability, that Comey was exaggerating.

Neither Hannigan nor Comey appear to have allies in the author of the EU Parliamentary report of February 2014, as it welcomed the accelerated plans for encryption from the technology firms targeted by MUSCULAR.

"...the companies identified by media revelations as being involved in the large-scale mass surveillance of EU data subjects by the US NSA are companies that have self-certified their adherence to the Safe Harbor, and that the Safe Harbor is the legal instrument used for the transfer of EU personal data to the US (examples being Google, Microsoft, Yahoo, Facebook, Apple and LinkedIn); [we are concerned] that these organizations have not encrypted information and communications flowing between their data centers, thereby enabling intelligence services to intercept information; [we welcome] the subsequent statements by some US companies that they will accelerate plans to implement encryption of data flows between their global data centers."

The NSA in particular has long campaigned against publically-available encryption technologies. It has worked to control international encryption standards, used supercomputers to rip through encryption where possible, and worked secretly with technology firms to insert back-doors into some public encryption products.

The NSA surveillance review board report commissioned by President Obama recommended that the agency stop its attempts to undermine global encryption standards. "A free and open Internet is critical to both self-government and economic growth," the report said. That was just one of the recommendations not submitted for enactment.

How then to summarise global progress since Snowden? One step forward, two steps back? Even the EU Parliamentary Report mentioned several times in this chapter, and often cited as evidence of genuine desire for change within the EU, presents an equal number of reasons to change and to maintain the status quo. Here are its arguments in full, with some amendments and commentary by the author for the purposes of clarifaction:

FIVE REASONS NOT TO ACT

The 'Intelligence/National Security Argument': no EU Competence

Edward Snowden's revelations relate to US and some Member States' intelligence activities, but national security is a national concern, the EU has no competence in such matters (except on EU internal security) and therefore no action is possible at EU level.

If the EU steps back from security matters and says basically that it's none of its business, that calls into question the EU's actual purpose. Is it merely to dictate the contents of Europe's sausages, and the shape of its bananas?

The 'Terrorism Argument': Danger of The Whistleblower

Any follow up to these revelations, or their mere consideration, further weakens the security of the US as well as the EU as it does not condemn the publication of documents which may give valuable information to terrorist groups.

This argument could be used to justify anything. If a government was discovered to be perpetrating ethnic cleansing, should we ignore it because its 'mere consideration' might weaken its security?

The 'Treason Argument: no Legitimacy for The Whistleblower

As mainly put forward by some in the US and in the United Kingdom, any debate launched or action envisaged further to Snowden's revelations is intrinsically biased and irrelevant as they would be based on an initial act of treason.

This is an enduring matter for debate. Was Snowden's act one of heroism or treason? If we undermine the concept of the whistleblower by stating that it constitutes treason by definition, then that could be something we as a society come to regret when other civil liberties are eroded and no one is able to tell the story or bring the details to the public's attention.

The 'Realism Argument': General Strategic Interests

Even if some mistakes and illegal activities were to be confirmed, they should be balanced against the need to maintain the special relationship between the US and Europe to preserve shared economic, business and foreign policy interests.

This is a fair point, purely because the wording states that activities need to be 'balanced' against other interests. Clearly a policy of ethnic cleansing would be reprehensible whatever 'economic, business and foreign policy interests' it is balanced against.

The 'Good Government Argument': Trust Your Government

US and EU Governments are democratically elected. In the field of security, and even when intelligence activities are conducted in order to fight against terrorism, they comply with democratic standards as a matter of principle. This 'presumption of good and lawful governance' rests not only on the goodwill of the holders of the executive powers in these states but also on the checks and balances mechanism enshrined in their constitutional systems.

When a model from otherwise reliable brand of car proves itself to be a lemon, there is an expression which originated in the UK that it is the 'Friday afternoon car' – the last one of the week thrown together by workers anxious to go home for the weekend. This section is the Friday afternoon justification for privacy violation. You elected your government, so it must be right. The mention of relying on checks and balances has been proven not to work earlier in this chapter.

The report though goes on to call these reasons not to act as "numerous and powerful". More worryingly still, it provides these points as potential reasons why so little has changed since the Snowden revelations.

"This may explain why most EU governments, after some initial strong reactions, have preferred not to act. The main action by the Council of Ministers has been to set up a 'transatlantic group of experts on data protection' which has met 3 times and put forward a final report. A second group is supposed to have met on intelligence related issues between US authorities and Member States' ones but no information is available. The European Council has addressed the surveillance problem in a mere statement of Heads of state or government, Up until now only a few national parliaments have launched inquiries."

Now let's take a look at the reasons the report gives for creating change, again with the author's commentary.

FIVE REASONS TO ACT

The 'Mass Surveillance Argument': in Which Society do We Want to Live?

Since the very first disclosure in June 2013, consistent references have been made to George's Orwell novel '1984'. Since 9/11 attacks, a focus on security and a shift towards targeted and specific surveillance has seriously damaged and undermined the concept of privacy. The history of both Europe and the US shows us the dangers of mass surveillance and the graduation towards societies without privacy.

Not an especially strong argument. Few of us would choose to live in a society with mass surveillance, but then few of us would choose the world's current geo-political situation, or almost any situation from history given humanity's propensity for almost continuous war. This statement presents mass surveillance as existing in a vacuum, as if the options are 'mass surveillance' or 'Utopia'.

The 'Fundamental Rights Argument'

Mass and indiscriminate surveillance threaten citizens' fundamental rights including right to privacy, data protection, freedom of press, fair trial which are all enshrined in the EU Treaties, the Charter of fundamental rights and the ECHR. These rights cannot be circumvented nor be negotiated against any benefit expected in exchange unless duly provided for in legal instruments and in full compliance with the treaties.

The strongest argument yet. Mass and indiscriminate surveillance runs counter not only to the charters and bodies listed above, but also to the US constitution, albeit subject to interpretation.

The 'EU Internal Security Argument'

National competence on intelligence and national security matters does not exclude a parallel EU competence. The EU has exercised the competences conferred upon it by the EU Treaties in matters of internal security by deciding on a number of legislative instruments and international agreements aimed at fighting serious crime and terrorism, on setting-up an internal security strategy and agencies working in this field. In addition, other services have been developed reflecting the need for increased cooperation at EU level on intelligence-related matters.

This appears to be a direct counter to the first reason not to act, and is rather more compelling, explaining similar precedents for the EU to act on internal Member State security matters.

The 'Deficient Oversight Argument'

While intelligence services perform an indispensable function in protecting against internal and external threats, they have to operate within the rule of law and to do so must be subject to a stringent and thorough oversight mechanism. The democratic oversight of intelligence activities is conducted at national level but due to the international nature of security threats there is now a huge exchange of information between Member States and with third countries like the US; improvements in oversight mechanisms are needed both at national and at EU level if traditional oversight mechanisms are not to become ineffective and outdated.

This justification follows the many admissions from various bodies, notably including Senate Intelligence Committee Chairman Dianne Feinstein, that there is insufficient monitoring and auditing of security agency actions. This is true both within the EU and US.

The 'Chilling Effect on Media' and the Protection of Whistleblowers

The disclosures of Edward Snowden and the subsequent media reports have highlighted the pivotal role of the media in a democracy to ensure accountability of Governments. When supervisory mechanisms fail to prevent or rectify mass surveillance, the role of media and whistleblowers in unveiling eventual illegalities or misuses of power is extremely important. Reactions from the US and UK authorities to the media have shown the vulnerability of both the press and whistleblowers and the urgent need to do more to protect them.

A direct counter to the treason argument. When governments make mistakes or overstep their remit – whether or not we believe that to be the case with mass surveillance – and fail to admit it to their citizens, we rely on the press and whistleblowers to spark the debate.

The report concludes with an invitation to the EU to choose either to act, or not act.

"The European Union is called on to choose between a 'business as usual' policy (sufficient reasons not to act, wait and see) and a 'reality check' policy (surveillance is not new, but there is enough evidence of an unprecedented magnitude of the scope and capacities of intelligence agencies requiring the EU to act)."

As we have seen, it has chosen to act, but we should not expect sea change imminently.

References

http://www.theguardian.com/world/2013/sep/26/nsa-surveillance-anti-vietnam-muhammad-ali-mlk

http://www2.gwu.edu/~nsarchiv/NSAEBB/NSAEBB441/

"Book IV, Supplementary Detailed Staff Reports on Foreign and Military Intelligence (94th Congress, Senate report 94-755)"

http://www.pbs.org/moyers/journal/10262007/profile2.html

http://www.washingtonpost.com/world/national-security/nsa-infiltrates-links-to-yahoo-google-data-centers-worldwide-snowden-documents-say/2013/10/30/e51d661e-4166-11e3-8b74-d89d714ca4dd_story.html

http://www.archives.gov/federal-register/codification/executive-order/12333.html

http://www.feinstein.senate.gov/public/index.cfm/2013/8/feinstein-statement-on-nsa-compliance

http://opencrs.com/document/RL32525/

https://www.google.com/work/our-approach.html

http://gmailblog.blogspot.co.uk/2014/03/staying-at-forefront-of-email-security.html

Matthew M. Aid, The Secret Sentry, 2009

http://www.washingtonpost.com/blogs/the-switch/wp/2013/11/04/how-we-know-the-nsa-had-access-to-internal-google-and-yahoo-cloud-data/

http://apps.washingtonpost.com/g/page/world/the-nsas-three-types-of-cable-interception-programs/553/

http://icontherecord.tumblr.com/post/65638965144/american-bar-association-23rd-annual-review-of

http://www.wsj.com/news/articles/SB121443403835305037?mod=googlenews_wsj&mg=reno64-wsj&url=http%3A%2F%2Fonline.wsj.com%2Farticle%2FSB121443403835305037.html%3Fmod%3Dgooglenews_wsj

What Is Wrong With Retrospective Law?, A. D. Woozley, *The Philosophical Quarterly*

http://www.washingtonpost.com/wp-srv/special/politics/prism-collection-documents/

http://www.ibtimes.co.uk/nsa-whistleblower-edward-snowden-479709

http://www.businessinsider.com/r-post-snowden-the-nsas-future-rests-on-admiral-rogers-shoulders-2014-19?IR=T

https://www.nsa.gov/public_info/_files/speeches_testimonies/ADM.ROGERS.Hill.20.Nov.pdf

http://www.whitehouse.gov/sites/default/files/docs/2013-12-12_rg_final_report.pdf

http://www.docstoc.com/docs/165628488/D.C.%20District%20Court%20NSA%20Opinion

http://www.pcworld.com/article/2089180/obama-proposes-changes-to-nsa-surveillance.html

http://ec.europa.eu/justice/data-protection/files/factsheets/umbrella_factsheet_en.pdf

http://europa.eu/rapid/press-release_STATEMENT-14-208_en.htm?locale=en

http://ec.europa.eu/justice/data-protection/

http://www.europarl.europa.eu/sides/getDoc.do?type=REPORT&mode=XML&reference=A7-2014-0139&language=EN

https://placelux.files.wordpress.com/2014/11/lettre-du-congres-americain-a-martin-schulz.pdf

https://www.congress.gov/bill/113th-congress/senate-bill/2685

http://www.ecipe.org/blog/the-costs-of-data-localization/

http://www.mayerbrown.com/files/Publication/d776facf-7d47-4043-aede-3880cf094f1f/Presentation/PublicationAttachment/34e865ff-a744-491c-8852-3c0267316202/Striking-transatlantic-data-deal.pdf

http://www.telegraph.co.uk/technology/internet-security/11213510/Destroying-online-freedom-in-the-name-of-counter-terrorism-will-make-the-world-a-more-dangerous-place.html

CHAPTER 3

Supermarkets and Data Brokers

The Snowden revelations sparked a fierce global debate, with world leaders like President Barack Obama and Germany's Angela Merkel weighing in, and lawmakers on both sides of the Atlantic frantically arguing over new regulations to govern the privacy violations they described.

But what many people have failed to grasp is that many of the forms of snooping the various implicated governments have been accused of has been happening right under our noses, with countless private sector bodies mass harvesting public data with little to no attempt to obfuscate their activities. Indeed, most of society has been positively welcoming the opportunity to hand over its data crown jewels.

This is alarming by itself, but especially in light of everything explored in the previous chapter. This overcollection of data by private organizations is a big help to mass surveillance by States. Individuals are practically forced to share huge amounts of data in order to participate in the modern world, and industry gathers, stores and sells it. This makes industry act as little brothers to Big Brother.

It all starts with the supermarkets.

CONTENTS

SIGN UP HERE FOR PRIVACY VIOLATION

We're all familiar with retail loyalty cards. You sign up once, then every time you make a purchase from that brand, you swipe your card and earn points, receive a discount, or get some other sort of benefit. In many instances customers receive a financial reward for making purchases they were intending to make anyway. Why not sign up to a scheme at your local store if it means you get money back for your weekly shop, when the alternative is simply doing the weekly shop at the same place anyway, but without the incentive? It's a compelling argument, and is one posed by many of the largest retail chains around the world. In the US some of the biggest chains to offer such programs include Smith's, Kroger and Safeway, and in the UK two of the oldest and largest schemes are run by Sainsbury's and Tesco. Whilst the supermarkets pioneered the concept at scale, it has now spread to many other retail verticals, including pharmaceuticals, books, hardware, fashion, hotel chains and airline carriers, to name a few.

At first glance, it's not just harmless, but actively beneficial, and the public has rushed in its droves to sign up.

These schemes are complex beasts, requiring sophisticated technology and significant investment to implement and run. UK-based pharmaceutical chain Boots has spent upwards of £30 million ($46 million) on its loyalty card program since its inception nearly 20 years ago. Since modern corporations are not prone to wasting cash, at least not firms who intend to survive, these schemes must generate significant value for the organizations who run them. In the case of Boots, its program has presumably generated considerably more than £30 million worth of value, otherwise it would be considered a failure. So what's in it for the supermarkets, and should it trouble the ordinary consumer?

The answers, as we're about to see, are 'a lot', and 'yes'.

For every penny / cent / loyalty point or coupon that supermarkets hand out to their customers, they harvest a wealth of data around consumers' purchasing habits. There's a Latin phrase often invoked when consumers complain, having inadequately understood the terms of their purchase: *caveat emptor*. It translates as 'let the buyer beware'. Basically, don't buy a chocolate telephone then complain that your ear is sticky.

You could argue the same point with loyalty schemes. You don't have to read the small print to guess that retailers are monitoring your shopping habits when you sign up. But what if you don't sign up, effectively opting out of the entire deal? That's also fine, right? You don't get the discounts, and they don't track you.

Wrong. Here's where it gets shady. Supermarkets also track their customers via their credit and debit cards – almost always without the consumers' knowledge.

This works in exactly the same way as the loyalty system. Every purchase made with a certain card is tracked and stored, with a profile of that individual's shopping habits slowly built up over time, and used to assess the effectiveness of things like in-store promotions, placement of certain brands of produce, and customer loyalty. The difference is that the retailer is unable to send material directly to the customers in this case because it doesn't know their home address. Although widely believed to be common practise, this form of non-consensual tracking has been expressly admitted by UK supermarket chains Morrisons, Waitrose and Asda, whilst Sainsbury's and Tesco have made statements denying that it goes on at their organizations.

And for those chains that do employ this form of customer analysis – or at least are open about it – it doesn't stop there. Not only do they track payment cards used in their stores, they pay data analytics firms, or sometimes data aggregators, to find out how certain customers spend their cash outside their stores. Waitrose, for one, has admitted to paying data analytics firm Beyond Analysis for anonymized information on customer spending patterns at rival chains.

How many members of the public are aware that detailed information on what they purchase with their credit and debit cards is available to anyone who wants to pay for it? Where is the opt-out button?

The answer of course is that there simply isn't one, how could there be when most people are totally unaware that this is going on? Or at least there isn't an opt out button that anyone concerned over retail data snooping is likely to find. Some credit card companies do offer an opt out from this sort of activity, if you're prepared to look hard enough. Mastercard offers a 'Data Analytics Opt-Out' under the global privacy notice on its website.

It also explains, in typically dense legalese, with whom it may deign to share your personal information.

"We may share the personal information we collect with our affiliates, financial institutions that issue payment cards or process electronic payment transactions, entities that assist with payment card fraud prevention, and merchants."

That final word is the key: 'merchants'. That means anyone capable of taking payment via a credit card. It's a deep pool.

It continues, in a presumably unintentionally comic moment, to suggest that the best way to stop the firm harvesting your data, is not to use its card:

"You can choose not to provide personal information to MasterCard by refraining from conducting electronic payment card transactions."

Presumably MasterCard believes that its customers take out its card purely for the pleasure of filling in forms and receiving endless junk mail.

The supermarkets of course would prefer not to have to pay to find out how you spend your money when you're not in the store, which is why the major (and plenty of not so major) brands offer even more loyalty points and discounts once you agree to take out one of their own credit cards.

But does any of this actually matter? If someone somewhere is having a blast counting how many kumquats you bought last week, isn't the best thing to do just to walk away shaking your head?

The problem is that the data tracking doesn't stop at the vegetable aisle. Think about the breadth of products sold by the modern supermarket. It includes ranges like hygiene products, pharmaceuticals, and alcohol. Most people might very reasonably find it hard to work up much of a sweat over the implications of their regular turnip consumption being tracked, but do you want your supermarket to hold what essentially amounts to your secondary medical record? To track and potentially sell on details of how much you're drinking? And retailers haven't proven themselves to be safe custodians of our data either. One of the most dramatic data breaches in recent years was when US retail chain Target was hacked in December 2013, with over 110 million customer details – including credit card data, names, email address and phone numbers – stolen. We'll discuss the security angle in more depth in chapter 6.

If you're still not feeling in some way violated, imagine a stranger coming into your home and rooting through your fridge. Then moving on to your kitchen cupboards, bathroom and wardrobes, all the while making notes on every purchase you've made. Once they've finished, they then approach you and show you a host of adverts based on what you've previously bought. Maybe they're trying to get you to switch brands, maybe they're trying to reinforce your loyalty to a particular product line. Whatever the strategy, ultimately they want your cash.

So your data is tracked, analysed, potentially sold on, and potentially lost in a hack whether or not you sign up to the loyalty scheme. But what if you give them what they're ultimately looking for and just pay with cash? Surely then you're safe?

In a sense you are (although your face could be captured by till-side cameras, as we'll come to in chapter 10), but your purchases are still being analysed and logged. Most large supermarkets use a system at the till which builds up a profile of you literally as you're standing there waiting to pay. They pinpoint your demographic, and target you with coupons and offers – either in-store or often in an attempt to entice you to their online presence where they can really grab your data. One of the most commonly used till-side systems in both the UK and the US is Catalina. As it declares on its website: "…Catalina knows the evolving purchase history and individual needs of more than three-quarters of American shoppers. We use that insight to create personalized, measurable campaigns that motivate high-value consumers to try new products, increase consumption, and stay loyal to CPG Brands and Retailers."

So even paying cash, you still can't escape the relentless attempts to convince you to spend more and stay loyal, although at least your name, address and credit card details won't be attached in any way to your profile.

Another way the supermarkets profit is by allowing brands to target loyal customers of its rivals with special offers for its own products. So ShinyWhite toothpaste might pay a supermarket chain for access to regular purchasers of its big rival NoPlaque, in an effort to tempt them to swap brands. According to industry insiders, this form of targeted advertising causes coupon redemption rates to soar from the one per cent at which many languish, to as much as fifty.

You might think you're making your own decisions as you wheel your trolley around the aisles, or your mouse around the site, but the supermarkets, brands and even payment firms are doing their damnedest to make your mind up for you.

Faced with the dizzying array of produce today's supermarkets offer, some may like the idea of having decisions made for them. But Gartner's Frank Buytendijk points out that it can be restrictive to customers.

"This sort of profiling keeps you where you are. If I'm down on a database as liking Chinese food, I'll keep seeing offers for that. So how will I find out if I like Mexican?"

Target, a chain you could either view as lax in its security efforts or simply unlucky, is one of the worst offenders when it comes to what it does with its customers' data. A good example to back this up happened in 2012, when a father found out that his teenage child – a schoolgirl - was pregnant. For many fathers that's already bad enough news for one day, but what made it worse was the way he found out. His supermarket told him.

DATA MINING ALL THE WAY TO THE WOMB

The day someone becomes a parent isn't just a big day for them and their families, it's also a red-letter day for their local supermarket. Parents of new-borns immediately start buying a host of extra products, often weeks or months before the baby arrives. On top of the extra food there are disinfectants, wipes, toys, clothes, diapers, lotions, balms, dietary supplements for the mother, and more. And parents, who tend to move home less frequently than non-parents, are often very loyal customers. Grab them while they're pregnant, and you've probably got them for years to come. Naturally supermarkets compete to become the store of choice for new parents, and they do this by first identifying them, then targeting them with advertising.

With decades of detailed data on customer spending patterns, supermarkets know what new and expectant mothers are likely to buy, and when. Target goes a step further with its baby registry, a service offering, amongst other things, help with planning a baby shower. It noticed that mothers who had signed up to the registry bought large quantities of unscented lotion about a third of the way in to their pregnancies. About half way through, they tended to start sweeping armfuls of vitamin and mineral supplements into their shopping trolleys. Then there are other triggers, like hand sanitizers and extra washcloths. In all, they found around 25 products whose purchase seemed to indicate a potential pregnancy. Taken individually none of these items tells much of a story, but analysed together they allow the supermarket to build an incredibly accurate picture of an individual customer's circumstances. In this case, it assigns them a 'pregnancy score', a percentage chance that they are pregnant based on their recent purchase history, and an extremely accurate window of their estimated due date.

This is alchemy for the modern age. Turning data into gold.

Target used this magic formula on every regular female shopper in its database, and ended up with a list tens of thousands strong of women who were highly likely to be pregnant.

And whilst this information was set to make the brand a lot of money, it knew that knowledge of how it was manipulating its customers' data was likely to upset and worry consumers.

Andrew Pole, a statistician and data analyst working at Target said as much to the New York Times in 2012.

"If we send someone a catalog and say, 'Congratulations on your first child!' and they've never told us they're pregnant, that's going to make some people uncomfortable. We are very conservative about compliance with all privacy laws. But even if you're following the law, you can do things where people get queasy," he admitted.

And not just queasy, but also livid. The New York Times article continues to tell the story of an irate customer who turned up one day at a Target store outside Minneapolis demanding to speak to the manager about a bunch of baby-related coupons which had been sent to his daughter.

"My daughter got this in the mail!" he's quoted as saying. "She's still in high school, and you're sending her coupons for baby clothes and cribs? Are you trying to encourage her to get pregnant?"

The manager checked up and verified that the man's daughter was indeed earmarked as potentially pregnant on Target's database. He apologized to the father, then a few days later called to apologize once again. But this time, the father's attitude had changed.

"I had a talk with my daughter," the NYT reports he said. "It turns out there's been some activities in my house I haven't been completely aware of. She's due in August. I owe you an apology."

Target broke off all relations with the NYT reporter shortly after this interview with Pole. It recognized that people might not react well to hearing the extent to which it, and no doubt its competitors, profiles its customers.

So, how to resolve the problem of wanting to compel pregnant women to buy goods they don't even know they want yet, without creeping them out with the realisation that their supermarket was, in a very real sense, stalking them? That was the quite literally million dollar question.

Target's solution was obfuscation. After some tests, it concluded that women would happily use their baby-related vouchers if they believed they were random, rather than targeted. If they could be convinced that the sudden appearance of diaper vouchers and disinfectant discounts through their mailboxes was nothing more than coincidence, then Target would get the jump on its rivals for these highly desirable customers. So, when it sent out its coupon brochures to these women, it interspersed the vouchers for relevant products with items it knew the women wouldn't want.

"...we started mixing in all these ads for things we knew pregnant women would never buy, so the baby ads looked random," a Target executive told the NYT. "We'd put an ad for a lawn mower next to diapers. We'd put a coupon for wineglasses next to infant clothes. That way, it looked like all the products were chosen by chance.

"And we found out that as long as a pregnant woman thinks she hasn't been spied on, she'll use the coupons. She just assumes that everyone else on her block got the same mailer for diapers and cribs. As long as we don't spook her, it works."

This programme was, financially, if not in terms of public relations, a huge success for Target. The brand's Mom and Baby sales rocketed shortly after the breakthrough was made, and between 2002 and 2010, when Pole was working on various iterations of the coupon system, the firm's revenues grew from $44 billion to $67 billion. During this period, in 2005, Target's then president, Gregg Steinhafel (he was forced to resign the post in May 2014 as a result of the massive data breach mentioned earlier in this chapter), bragged to a group of investors about the firm's "heightened focus on items and categories that appeal to specific guest segments such as mom and baby."

BROKEN PRIVACY

Many people may find some of these practices to be unattractive and undesirable, but there is an entire shady industry operating at a level below the public consciousness which makes what we have seen so far in this chapter appear relatively above board.

When supermarkets, and other organizations, feel that they have insufficient data to truly know, or more accurately, target, their customers, they turn to the data brokers. These are firms who exist to know just about everything about just about everyone. This will commonly include not just shopping habits, but home and work addresses, occupation, marital status, salary, amount of savings and pensions held, hobbies, type of house and car owned, preferred holiday destinations, regular locations visited, criminal record, credit score, credit card details and sometimes medical history. And thanks to their vast databases, what they don't know they can predict by comparing you to hundreds of thousands if not millions of people similar to you. The information will have been taken from marketing research, online surveys, government data, payment card firms and a wealth of other sources too varied to list. If you've ever wondered why you're asked to fill in your name, address and other details when you're simply trying to buy a television, or get a refund at a shop, or access various services online, this is often the reason. Your data is a valuable resource, and no one knows this better than the data brokers.

One of the largest data brokers in the world is marketing technology firm Acxiom. Based in Arkansas, and with annual revenues well in excess of $1 billion, it has been described by American columnist and documentary-maker Douglas Rushkoff as "one of the biggest companies you've never heard of."

Jed Mole, European Marketing Director at Acxiom, is at pains to point out how seriously the firm takes its privacy obligations.

"We're a stick of rock [similar to a candy cane, but famous for having words written through its middle, like 'Brighton', a coastal town in the UK]," says Mole. "Privacy, compliance and ethical use of data are written throughout."

He continues by stating that his firm is "obsessed by personal recognition". "We help the marketers do their jobs by helping them to recognise an individual regardless of how they present themselves online."

So if you thought your cunning use of online pseudonyms, or even your refusal to register and log in to a site, was fooling the digital marketers, think again.

Mole explains that before the techniques developed by Acxiom and other modern data brokers, businesses who wanted to monitor and track individuals relied on fairly unsophisticated name and address matching. From someone's interaction with your website, or a partially filled in marketing questionnaire you might get a name and a partial address. But computers are inherently bad at comparing approximations, or fractional data.

"Computers love ones and zeroes, black and white. If it's grey, binary systems hate that sort of fuzzy matching," says Mole.

To improve the ability to match individuals more accurately, Acxiom introduced what Mole describes as 'knowledge-based matching'.

He explains that traditional matching techniques would fail to match and combine separate partial records which pertain to the same person. But knowledge-based matching brings in other data "ethically brought together", as Mole is keen to emphasize, which allows Acxiom to say that regardless of the fact that two record sets may even look very little like one another, they actually relate to the same person.

"We try to build a sophisticated approach to using the best indicators we can get to recognize people. So when an individual presents him or herself [at a website for instance], we do the best job of helping brands provide a personal experience."

Not only does this system, which Acxiom calls 'Abilitec', help firms to identify customers, it does so on a massive scale, and on the fly. Ian Fremaux, Senior Consultant at Acxiom, explains that it's used by businesses who process over 100 million records in a prospect list – a record of potential new customers. And Fremaux has an extremely high level of confidence in the solution.

"We take the approach that once we've got the tool right, we either return a result as a 100 per cent match, or we don't declare it as a match at all. Once we've identified the individual, we know it's the right person. If we're not 100 per cent, we don't return a positive result at all."

The system can process millions of records per hour, all operating 'in-memory' – in other words running rapidly in a computer's RAM instead of needing to be written to disc, which takes longer – across large networks of machines. This is a vastly more efficient way of trawling through data looking for potential matches than was used in the past.

"Around the year 2,000 a lot of clients spent big money on large UNIX servers [for this sort of activity]. Acxiom invested effort to build our grid-based infrastructure. We now have around 6,000 computers linked together in separate data centres around the world."

The workload is spread across multiple machines, trying to achieve the best results in the shortest possible time. The goal? To identify us, even when we attempt to remain anonymous.

Mole continues, explaining that Acxiom holds data on around 50 million adults in the UK. What's interesting about this number is that there are in total, around 50 million adults in the UK. So Acxiom has collected data on practically all of them.

"We cover the whole population, every household," adds Fremaux. "Give us any name and address in the country and we'll return something."

So where does Acxiom get all of this data from?

"Until recently we were the last company in the market to run large-scale offline questionnaires, like household surveys," says Mole. "But the propensity for people to return a paper survey has declined; they're more interested in online surveys now. So we've moved with the times, and that transition has improved the quality of the data. Now we're moving more towards working with partners who collect data from online and offline surveys, warranty registration cards and the like. Then there's open government data, like DVLA [the UK's vehicle registration body], and electoral open records.

"The consumer is also fragmenting into using more devices and channels, and that leaves an exhaust trail of data. As a business we're trying to build marketing insight on individuals, so we need to be more varied and sophisticated in how we source it."

And that neatly explains why we're asked to hand over everything from our name and address, to our former college room-mate's favourite soccer team, when we buy a television or a fridge. That information ends up in the hands of firms like Acxiom, and from there to any marketer who can afford their services.

The data brokerage industry, and Acxiom in particular, has been on the receiving end of more than few outpourings of anger and fear from privacy advocates and the press, only some of it justified. Mole attempts to explain why his firm's business model shouldn't be something for consumers to worry about.

"Say our client, which we'll call Brand X, has a customer who has bought a TV from them. That creates a marketing record, we know they've bought a TV. But we don't know if they have a Blu-Ray player, or a mobile phone. So Brand X can either buy in transactional data to see what that customer has bought in the past, or they might perform their own data capture on their website – they ask visitors if they like movies, and if they own a Blu-Ray player."

Mole states that most brands have a reasonable idea of the "golden set of data" they want to bring together. Some of it is around who the person is and what motivates them (because after all if you understand their behavioural triggers you can make sure they're set off at your products), but some of it is more practical.

"If you're a hardware store, you don't want to send promotional material for a lawn mower to someone living in a high-rise," he says.

Mole goes on to discuss the benefits of retargeting, a somewhat controversial advertising method popular with marketers and website owners, but less so with privacy advocates.

Retargeting is the term used to describe the ads which follow you around the web. So let's say you visit our aforementioned Brand X, an electronics company who sell televisions, Blu-Ray players and other consumer technology. Their website sports a small JavaScript tag which drops an anonymous cookie (a small file designed to track internet users) into visitors' web browsers. This cookie is used by Brand X's retargeting vendor to track that user wherever he or she goes across the internet.

And there is now a similar but far stealthier system called 'canvas fingerprinting', which is incredibly hard to detect or stop. It works by extracting information from a user's browser and building an identifiable token from it which it then places within the browser on that user's device. What it boils down to is that your browsing history can be collected by websites without even the use of cookie, and certainly without you knowing. Researchers from Belgium's Ku Leuven Univeristy together with Princeton University in the States found that 5.5 per cent of the world's 100,000 most visited sites had deployed the technology.

So why do websites feel the need to do this?

The web is largely free. If you're a typical internet user, the vast majority of sites you visit are not behind any form of paywall, or even registration wall. So you're able to consume any content you like without the pain of having to pay for it. Since content is created by people, and people generally like to be paid, there's a disconnect there. If you're a publisher of a website and you have content creators requiring regular salaries and an audience who are reluctant to break out their wallets, you turn to advertising to make it all work (see Figure 3.1, provided by Acxiom). And since it's a lot of effort to approach every firm who might want to advertise on your site to try to sell to them, and like-wise it's inefficient for a firm who wants to buy some web advertising space to contact and negotiate with dozens, hundreds or up to hundreds of thousands of individual websites, both sides use ad exchanges – middle men who sort out the deals with both parties and place ads on many sites at once.

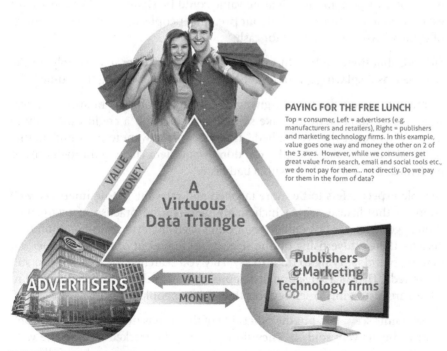

PAYING FOR THE FREE LUNCH

Top = consumer, Left = advertisers (e.g. manufacturers and retailers), Right = publishers and marketing technology firms. In this example, value goes one way and money the other on 2 of the 3 axes. However, while we consumers get great value from search, email and social tools etc., we do not pay for them... not directly. Do we pay for them in the form of data?

FIGURE 3.1 The data trade.

The other issue with web advertising is that only around two per cent of shoppers buy something the first time they visit a website. Retargeting ensures that if a potential customer has searched for 'running shoes' on your site, they'll see your ads for running shoes almost wherever they go on the web. Your retargeting vendor will have deals with various ad exchanges to make sure that if there's ad space on a site, it'll be your ad specifically trying to sell something which you know that person is interested in which they see.

Marketers get excited by this because it means their advertising spend is focused on people who are already familiar with their brand, and who are proven to have at least a passing interest in the products their trying to push.

"Retargeting converts window-shoppers into buyers." That's how AdRoll, one of the largest retargeters, describes its services on its own website.

Firms like Axciom help companies not just find out who's visiting them – even if they fail to hand over their personal details by themselves – but add further colour to the picture either way.

"In an ideal world we do a better job of helping firms to identify people," says Mole. "Then we can go into their transaction data and say they've already bought a Plasma screen TV, but they don't have a Blu-Ray player, so let's serve an ad for one of those. And in fact, let's add in a special offer because the visitor is a good prospect and the lifetime value could be significant. We can see for example that it's a household of four [wealthy] people, rather than say a bunch of students who are strapped for cash."

He adds that there's a benefit to the consumer too, rather than simply for the marketer, as displaying an irrelevant advert would be "wasting their time".

Fremaux picks up the thread, giving an example from the financial services sector. "You don't want to make someone an offer on a credit card, only to decline them once they've applied," he says. "So you want to be confident that you're picking the right people. You don't want them clicking through only to be denied, that leaves them with a bad taste."

"People expect offers to be more targeted and relevant," Mole interjects, well aware of the distaste with which many perceive the practise of retargeting. "You're going to see ads either way. I don't avert my eyes from London buses because there's advertising on the side, or rip them out of the newspaper. All that the brand is trying to do it to say 'Hey you searched for this, are you still interested?' There's a sensationalist approach to this that it's all evil, but companies are just trying to sell services to the right people."

These points seem fair, but the other side of the coin is that many people don't want to be actively sold to. They don't want to be tracked around the web, with the pair of novelty Christmas socks they glanced at on a whim following them across the digital globe as a persistent reminder that nothing is truly free. Furthermore, an ad on the side of a bus or in a newspaper is passive, but this form of digital advertising has taken data from your browser in order to sell you something.

In short, most people want to be left to make up their own minds, and not be stealthily influenced by large brands with fleets of behavioural scientists, data analysts and digital marketers employed especially for this purpose.

However, most people would prefer the current situation to the alternative, claims Mole.

"We get free services all the time," he begins. "I don't pay for Facebook, LinkedIn, Twitter or Trip Advisor. And then there's the tremendous value we all get from Google. When my washing machine broke down I got a superb new one within 12 hours because companies are advertising deals to us, it's just the way the world works. But if we don't want our data to be so freely available, then these services won't be free any more. How would you like to pay $9.95 each month to use Google, and it's another dollar if you want Facebook?"

And there's the also the irony that even if users across the globe suddenly decided that this is the better option, their privacy would still be at risk because they would have to submit more personal data including financial information to register and pay for these services.

Mole continues, showing that he is at least alive to the privacy concerns, admitting: "Retargeting at its best is good, but at its worst looks creepy. We have no tolerance at all for people who try to abuse data."

Although what exactly he would consider to be creepy in this context is unclear.

One person who is considerably more clear on the ethics of retargeting is Privacy International's Anna Fielder.

"Our view of retargeting is that it should be consent-based. It's fine to do it if people agree to it and are aware that it's going on. I'm not trying to say that there shouldn't be advertising, it's the method, rather than the fact itself," she says.

Mole acknowledges this problem with his industry; that the user is largely unaware of any of it. Part of the issue is that if any of it is admitted at all, it's buried deep within a feature-length terms of service agreement. The sort of document you might irritatedly click straight through when you download a new app.

"If we sat down and read through all the terms of service we receive we'd be there all year. The industry needs to do a better job of helping people to understand what goes on with their data, and the individual should be able to opt out," concedes Mole.

But if you do opt out, you'll see the same number of ads, they'll simply be "insightless not insightful," as Mole describes it.

One perhaps surprising move Acxiom has made in recent years is the launch of Aboutthedata.com in the US. This is a site US citizens can visit, and, once they've logged in using their social security number, check some of the information Acxiom holds on them.

"We felt it was the right thing to do to show how passionate we feel about the right and ethical use of data," says Mole.

But critics say that the site only includes relatively innocuous data, leaving out much of the information which it displays to its clients as evidence of deeper insight and value. Details such as whether someone is likely to inherit a sizeable sum of money, or has an elderly parent, or lives with someone with diabetes, to use a few examples.

Acxiom claims to store around 3,000 data points for every consumer, but there is nothing like that level of details available for users to check. In August 2013 the firm said it would add more detail to the site regularly, however it still only displays a small fraction of the total information tracked for every consumer to date.

On Aboutthedata.com users can not only correct their information, for example adding in any children which may have been born since the last census or questionnaire they filled in, but they can choose to opt out – to have their details removed from Acxiom's databases.

According to Acxiom, far fewer people have chosen this option than you might expect. "We were worried people would opt out, but a very low percentage did. Far more, in fact up to double figures, went in to correct data," Mole claims.

But Fielder is unconvinced this move, suggesting that the choice to opt out would have been made to seem as unattractive as possible.

"These people employ behavioural scientists and they know exactly how to present options to make them appear vital, or to make them easy to ignore," she says. "You would have a completely different design of your webpage if you really wanted to enable opting out. And besides, most of us are trying to live our lives, not worrying about opting in or out of stupid ads!"

Earlier in the conversation Mole had admitted that Acxiom holds data on just about every adult in the UK. When asked why those in Britain are unable to check what data the firm holds on them, Mole stated that the fault is with European privacy laws.

"In the UK you get to a point where in order to see your data, you have to identify yourself by revealing far more sensitive information than we actually hold on you. Things like your credit card or national security number. We don't want to go anywhere near that, we're only interested in marketing," says Mole.

"Acxiom is trying to pull a fast one," states Fielder when presented with this argument. "It's very interesting that there's a lot of misconception about what the data protection regulations in the EU do and don't do."

Fielder likens this to a practise she says is common in financial services. Many banks operate overseas call centres, and the call centre staff use European data protection legislation as way of avoiding certain questions about their operations, claiming to be forbidden from answering questions by the law.

"A lot of it is a myth," says Fielder.

However, firms like Acxiom would appear to be caught between a rock and a hard place. Aboutthedata.com was criticized when launched for what some privacy advocates said is an overly lax identity verification system, which requires the user's name, address, date of birth and the last four digits of their social security number. So in a sense they're damned either way. Fail to demand a detailed list of personal information in order to definitively identify a user and you're considered to be lax. Demand too much data, and you'll be accused of launching just another data gathering exercise.

Fielder adds that the US boasts the highest incidence of identity theft in the world, partly because it has comparatively weak data protection legislation. "Acxiom and others in the industry have a field day in the US as there's practically no data protection at all. But they do have sectoral legislation for things like health and financial services," she concedes.

Despite the lack of overarching data protection legislation in the US, Fielder says that the law in this area is actually "more effective in the US in some ways" because of the way it is enforced.

"It's enforced in the US via the law of misrepresentation. That means it's illegal for a company to say they do something, and then not do it."

Like claiming to protect users' privacy and allow them to opt out, whilst actually doing neither.

"That's how [privacy] activists in the US get companies more often. They watch them, see them claim something, then see them do something else [from what they claimed]. Then they make a complaint, the FTC investigates and if they find that the company lied, they fine them."

And this is precisely what happened in August 2012 when the FTC fined Facebook a record $22.5 million for illegally tracking iPhone, iPad and Mac users by circumventing privacy protections in the Safari web browser.

Jon Leibowitz, chairman of the FTC, said in a statement at the time: "The record setting penalty in this matter sends a clear message to all companies under an FTC privacy order. No matter how big or small, all companies must abide by FTC orders against them and keep their privacy promises to consumers, or they will end up paying many times what it would have cost to comply in the first place."

There can be little doubt that this is an effective enforcement strategy. All companies feel the pain when you affect their bottom line. Fielder explains that the system does not work nearly so well across the pond in the UK.

"That illustrates that in some cases the US enforcement system is more effective [than its counterpart in the UK]. In the UK, we have data protection legislation and other laws, but we have very weak ways of enforcing it. If you know your rights have been infringed under the data protection legislation in the UK, you can complain to [privacy regulator] the Information Commissioner's Office, but they have a backlog of complaints and might look at your issue, and might not."

Fielder also points out that most consumers in the UK have no clue that the ICO exists.

"We did a survey amongst our members, and it revealed that 70 per cent didn't know what the ICO was."

The other method for enforcing your privacy rights in the UK is to take a firm to court directly. But as Fielder states, how many consumers are likely to take that action?

"How many consumers will take a company to court for privacy reasons?" she asks. "It costs money, and you can't prove material damage so easily. That's an ineffective way of enforcing laws. So in the UK, if companies choose not to respect privacy laws, there's little people can do besides complain."

YES BUT SO WHAT!

Ultimately, why should we care about any of this? Does any of it actually matter? So a few firms track us around the web, profile us, package us up and sell us on. Where is the harm?

"The harm can be for example if you have cancer and you visit cancer research and medical sites, you could be profiled and discriminated against by insurance companies because of the way the data is presented," says Fielder.

Another scary prospect is that some financial organizations and insurers are using data profiling to make assumptions about individuals' credit scores. In one famous example American Express reduced the credit limit of Kevin Johnson, a US citizen and one of its customers, to about a third of its previous total because he had been shopping in places frequented by those it considered to have poor credit histories.

Fielder points to 2012's 'Cookie Directive Debate', an issue brought about by EU regulations which stated that internet users needed to be able to give explicit consent to cookies being placed on their computers. They had to be aware of what was going on, and have the choice to opt out if they wanted.

"All that resulted in was some annoying bits of screen appearing when you're on a website telling you we're putting cookies on your PC, then you can either agree or not. It serves no purpose. It tells people that these things exist but they still don't understand what they're for. What would be great would be if you could block all those cookies. You'd still see ads, but you wouldn't be profiled and targeted."

Fielder uses this argument to counter Mole's point that most web services are free, making ads necessary. There's a mantra that's helpful to remember in cases like this: 'If it's free, then you are the product'.

"Google will still make money," she continues. "A lot of the marketing is based on contextual ads, so you see ads based on what you searched for. I don't see a problem with that, but I do have a problem when the ads follow you around the internet and firms build an image of you around your browsing."

There is obviously a wide gap between what privacy advocates would like to see, and what the advertising and marketing industry is prepared to offer. However, despite the criticism it has received, Acxiom's efforts in producing Aboutthedata.com constitute a step in the right direction. It may well be an effort to fend off tightened regulations, like a child who suddenly starts tidying his room to deter harsher punishment when he knows he's about to be told off, but it should be welcomed nonetheless.

Whilst Acxiom claims to have created Aboutthedata.com from the kindness of its heart, which may or may not be true, its inception was presaged by a call for greater transparency in the data brokerage industry from the Federal Trade Commission. In May 2014 the FTC released a report 'Data Brokers: A call for transparency and accountability'. Of the many findings and recommendations made (the report runs to a rather mind melting 110 pages), one telling statistic is that four of five data brokers who sell marketing products examined offered consumers a way to opt out of having their data gathered, analysed and traded. But since these firms have little to no interaction with the public, and hence no one has heard of them, who knows that there is anything to opt out of?

"… it is not clear how consumers would learn about these rights; for example, no centralized portal currently exists for consumers to learn about data brokers and what access rights and choices they provide," says the report.

It goes on to provide some figures on the scale of information held and processed by data brokers, which are either terrifying or impressive or both, depending on your perspective.

Of the nine data brokers examined by the report in total, one boasted a database with 1.4 billion consumer transactions and over 700 billion aggregated data elements. Another's database held data on consumer transactions amounting to one trillion dollars in total. That's a hell of a lot of plasma screen televisions. Another broker surveyed adds three billion new records each month to its databases. And most impressive or worrying of all: one of the brokers has 3,000 data segments for just about every single consumer in the US.

Then there are the decisions the brokers make about each of us, and the categories they fit consumer into. Some are fairly innocuous, as the report states, such as 'Dog Owner', 'Winter Activity Enthusiast', or 'Mail Order Responder'. But there are also more sensitive categories, which would no doubt cause a degree of public outrage should consumers learn into which they had been deemed to fall. Categories which attempt to delineate ethnicity and socio-economic status like 'Urban Scrambler' and 'Mobile Mixers', "…both of which include a high concentration of Latinos and African Americans with low incomes," as the report describes.

What's really concerning about this profiling is that insurers and credit companies use these categories to make decisions about people which affect their lives.

"Other potentially sensitive categories highlight a consumer's age such as 'Rural Everlasting,' which includes single men and women over the age of 66 with "low educational attainment and low net worths," while 'Married Sophisticates' includes thirty-something couples in the "upper-middle class… with no children," it adds.

And still other sensitive categories focus on health-related topics or conditions, such as 'Expectant Parent,' 'Diabetes Interest,' and 'Cholesterol Focus.'

The industry is reluctant to reveal more, however. Marketing firm Epsilon's chief privacy offer and general counsel, Jeanette Fitzgerald, told a panel at an FTC workshop held in Washington in September 2014 that further transparency into what data brokers do with information would be "giving up trade secrets."

Christopher Calabrese, legislative counsel for the American Civil Liberties Union, argued that consumers have the right to know more, regardless of its impact on the industry.

"I think we're woefully inadequate regarding transparency right now," Calabrese said. He conceded that details of how the industry collects data are its "secret sauce", but added: "individual consumers should be able to know what assumptions are being made about them."

There is also the argument that even with the best big data practices available today, companies are still mis-profiling millions of people, with the result that they could be excluded for offers, or denied credit cards or insurance.

"From a statistical perspective if you have a 2-3 per cent error rate – which is good – that means you're wrong 6 million times [using US consumer data]. That's a lot of people that your automated decision-making could be harming," said Jeremy Gillula, staff technologist at the Electronic Frontier Foundation.

But the marketing industry feels that there is already sufficient regulation within the industry itself.

"I think there is already a lot of self-regulation," said Epsilon's Fitzgerald. "There is the DMA [Direct Marketing Association], and the IAB [Interactive Advertising Bureau]. The DMA will enforce those guidelines among members, or get non-members to act in an ethical problem – and then if there is still a problem, they will turn over to FTC."

FTC Commissioner Julie Brill appeared to lend weight to this argument by suggesting that there are existing laws which can be used to target even the newer areas of digital marketing.

"As technologically advanced as we get, there are principles which exist in our law, like discrimination, and targeting vulnerable communities in ways that can harm them, that are fundamental. We are going to be applying those principles even though technology is moving rapidly," said Brill.

Whilst Brill may be correct, that there are laws in place which provide a certain level of protection to consumers, and whilst in the FTC and ICO there are regulatory bodies empowered to examine the industry and at least attempt to keep profiteering corporates in line, the fact remains that the public is largely unaware of what is happening to their data. They're unaware of how it's collected when they visit the supermarket, and how it's harvested every time they use their credit card. They don't understand how it's combined with information from multiple sources in order to build incredibly detailed profiles – which may or may not be accurate, with various consequences either way – then sold on and used to influence them.

Under British law, for a contract to be valid you need there to be what's called a 'meeting of the minds'. Both sides must share a common understanding of what exactly is being transacted. If there is confusion or misunderstanding on either side, then a court can declare the contract invalid. The same principle should apply to people giving up their data. It's true that this data is the payment for otherwise free services offered by firms like Google and Twitter, but if users don't grasp how exactly the data is gathered and used, then there is no 'meeting of the minds'.

And users should have the option to keep their data, and potentially pay for something the old fashioned way, with money. True, few people would probably ever take this option, but at least offering it would cement the notion that there is a two-way value exchange happening. Some services do offer a way to opt out, but they are often hard to find, or even completely outside of the public sphere of consciousness.

References

http://www.theguardian.com/money/2013/jun/08/supermarkets-get-your-data

http://www.telegraph.co.uk/finance/personalfinance/household-bills/10119302/Your-supermarket-is-spying-on-you-and-it-will-cost-you-money.html

http://www.nocards.org/essays/nofakes.shtml

http://www.nytimes.com/2013/09/05/technology/acxiom-lets-consumers-see-data-it-collects.html?pagewanted=all&_r=0

http://www.acxiom.com/resources/consumer-segmentation-drives-successful-launch-luxury-automaker/

http://adexchanger.com/platforms/ftc-big-data-workshop-more-transparency-please/

http://www.ftc.gov/system/files/documents/reports/data-brokers-call-transparency-accountability-report-federal-trade-commission-may-2014/140527databrokerreport.pdf

http://www.ft.com/cms/s/0/7933792e-a2e6-11e4-9c06-00144feab7de.html#axzz3ZSuHwV8i

CHAPTER 4

Google, Apple, Microsoft and the Concept of Evil

When students Larry Page and Sergey Brin first met in summer 1995 at Stanford University in the US, they found one another to be obnoxious. Brin had volunteered to show new students around the campus, and Page, one of Brin's group, spent most of the tour arguing with him at every turn. An inauspicious start for a pair who would in three years go on to found Google.

That Page quickly chose to examine the newly formed World Wide Web for his doctoral thesis will surprise no one. After all Google is today, more than any other firm, synonymous with the web. Indeed its very name is used as a verb by many, meaning to search the web.

But web search wasn't Page's initial area of interest; he preferred to delve into its mathematical secrets, its digital undergarments.

The internet was and is made up of nodes; interconnected computers of various types, be they servers, sensors, routers or laptops. Those connections are mapped out by links on web pages. To a mathematician, the internet is a giant graph. "Computer scientists love graphs," said Page in an interview with Wired magazine in 2005. So Page's doctoral thesis concerned the way the web was interlinked together.

One of his early findings was that it's a simple task to follow links from page A to page B, but far harder to find pages which link back. In other words, page A links to page B, but unless page B also links to A, how do you find A if you start at B?

The internet is the physical infrastructure of interlinked servers and other nodes that allows traffic to flow between computers all over the world. The web is the software layer on top, the websites and interfaces which enable people to send information over the internet.

CONTENTS

CITATION, CITATION CITATION

Interestingly, it is the very tradition of academic publishing which played a big part not just in Google's genesis, but also that of the web itself. When academics write papers, one of the key tasks is to ensure that the work cites as many supporting pieces by other academics as possible. The paper must bring something new to the table, it's not enough just to summarise what has gone before, but nevertheless what has gone before must be acknowledged, and that will form a crucial part of how that paper will be received by the academic community. And if it turns out to be received well, then many papers will cite it in turn in future. In essence, they will link back to it.

Sir Tim Berners-Lee created the 'World Wide Web', as he named it, by joining several pre-existing ideas together: Hypertext (text on a computer with hyperlinks to other texts), Transmission Control Protocol (a way for computers to pass information on to one another), and the Domain Name System (the internet's name and address book). Why did he do it? In part as a way of improving the citation process in academia.

Page understood that the web was basically a huge map of citations. But he wanted more information on backlinks. He wanted to know how many there were for a given a page, and how they worked. Even at this nascent stage of the web's development, it contained something in the region of 10 million documents, with countless more links between them. Obviously the task of mapping everything was not one for a human, so Page built a 'crawler', a piece of software designed to visit every page and document every link. He called this tool 'BackRub'.

It was at this point that Brin got interested. "I talked to lots of research groups" around the school, Brin told Wired magazine, "and this was the most exciting project, both because it tackled the Web, which represents human knowledge, and because I liked Larry." Evidently the early animosity hadn't taken long to wear off.

In March 1996 Page unleashed his crawler on the Stanford University homepage. He didn't have to give it a list of sites to find, it was capable of eventually discovering the entire web from one page, it would just need time and an awful lot of computer power.

Simply mapping out the web, as if not a sufficiently impressive task in itself, was not the only goal. Coming back to academic publishing, it's not just the quantity of citations a paper receives which partly governs its importance, but also the weight of those citations. Receiving a nod from a fellow research student is all well and good, but being cited by a professor of global prominence is far more likely to provoke a stir in the cloisters and libraries of the world. Page's idea was also to map out the relative importance of who linked to whom.

But whilst judging the importance of one academic relative to another is fairly simple – how many papers have they written, what sort of qualifications do they have, what title and position do they hold – how do you judge the importance of a web page? Clearly reading every page and judging its content would be impossible, both for a human who would offer wildly subjective results even if it were feasible in one lifetime, and for an algorithm which would need the sort of artificial intelligence so far only in existence in the pages of science fiction novels. Realizing this, Page hit upon the idea of using the number of links on a page to judge its status. But it gets more complicated as each link also needed its own ranking, based on the rank of the page it was linking from. This is an even trickier problem than it sounds, as you have to count the links on each page, then count the links attached to those links.

Fortunately for Page, this was math prodigy Brin's specialty. The pair teamed up to birth an algorithm, which they called PageRank, to measure the importance web links. PageRank was able to analyze not just the links to a page, but also the links going back to the linking pages.

For example, Amazon is one of the most popular sites on the internet, ranked 6th in the world as of December 2014 according to Alexa traffic rank. Many sites link in to Amazon, from major book publishers to tiny home cottage industries. How might an algorithm determine that the major book publisher carries more weight, in terms of its importance to people who might want to search the web, than the person selling fridge magnets out of their garage? It all comes down to back linking. It's likely that just a few sites at best will link to the cottage industry, and those sites themselves are also likely to sport a handful of links at most. But millions of pages link to Amazon, and many of them will also be linked to by millions of others.

This is again very similar to the way importance is judged in the world of academic papers.

As BackRub generated its results, Page and Brin found themselves looking at an accurate ranking of the world's most popular websites. More accurate than anything else which existed at the time, including the dominant search tools of the day AltaVista and Excite, which only examined text as opposed to links, ranked on key words, and often generated irrelevant results. Only now did the pair see the possibility to revolutionize internet search.

"We realized we had a querying tool," Page told Wired in 2005. "It gave you a good overall ranking of pages and ordering of follow-up pages."

The second thing they realized was that as the web grew, so their search engine would improve; it would scale well. That's why they chose the name Google, a corruption of the word googol, the name given to the number formed by one followed by 100 zeroes.

Using their dorm rooms as a laboratory, an office, and a programming centre, they begged and borrowed what equipment they could to get Google up and running from the Stanford campus. It was so resource hungry that it regularly brought down the entire campus network, despite the fact that Stanford had at the time one of the world's most advanced network infrastructures.

With Google taking off, Page and Brin had to decide whether to continue with their studies, or throw themselves into the frenetic and risky world of corporate start-ups. They weren't keen, with Page in particular wanting to complete his PhD.

In John Battelle's book *'The Search: How Google and Its Rivals Rewrote the Rules of Business and Transformed Our Culture'*, he quotes Brin recalling a conversation with his advisor at the time: "Look, if this Google thing pans out, then great. If not, you can return to graduate school and finish your thesis." Brin replied: "Yeah, OK, why not? I'll just give it a try."

One of their first actions, once they had filed Google for incorporation on September 4th 1998, was to pay the check for $100,000 given to them by Sun co-founder Andy Bechtolsheim into their brand new Google bank account. The investment world was obviously impressed with Google's potential, given that Bechtolsheim was prepared to write a six figure check out to an entity that didn't exist at the time he wrote it. For the first four months Google worked out of the garage of their friend Susan Wojcicki, a former Stanford student herself, and daughter of Stanley Wojcicki, a Stanford professor. She became Google's first marketing manager in 1999, and is, at the time of writing, CEO of YouTube, which Google acquired for $1.65 billion in 2006 following her recommendation.

It was around this time that the company adopted the phrase 'Don't be evil' as its corporate motto. Depending on whom you believe, it was either suggested by Gmail creator Paul Buchheit at a meeting concerning corporate values in 2000, or by Google Engineer Amit Patel in 1999.

Buchheit said that the motto was "a bit of a jab at a lot of other companies, especially our competitors, who at the time, in our opinion, were kind of ex-ploiting the users to some extent."

In their founders' letter produced in 2004, Page and Brin claimed that this 'Don't be evil' culture prevents conflicts of interest and bias towards advertisers in their firm's output.

"Google users trust our systems to help them with important decisions: medical, financial and many others. Our search results are the best we know how to produce. They are unbiased and objective, and we do not accept payment for them or for inclusion or more frequent updating. We also display advertising, which we work hard to make relevant, and we label it clearly. This is similar to a well-run newspaper, where the advertisements are clear and the articles are not influenced by the advertisers' payments. We believe it is important for everyone to have access to the best information and research, not only to the information people pay for you to see," wrote Page and Brin.

But in 2012 the concept of paid inclusion, where companies pay Google to appear adjacent to or even above natural listings, suddenly appeared not to be considered evil any more, as Google began allowing it. It first became apparent in some of the firm's newer products: Google Hotel Finder and Google Flight Search, which take results both from natural search, and from a list of sponsors who have paid to be considered for inclusion when certain search terms are used.

Google argued the case for the change of policy with website Marketing Land at the time. Amit Singhal, a Google executive in charge of search products claimed that it was more about the need for data, than revenue.

"Fundamentally, time and time again, we started noticing that a class of queries could not be answered based upon just crawled data.... We realized that we will have to either license data or go out and establish relationships with data providers."

Google labelled results obtained this way 'sponsored', so at least users would be aware that some of the information returned was the result of some sort of commercial relationship.

The FTC demands that search engines display a "clear and conspicuous" disclosure when listings include results from a paid inclusion programme, but don't go so far as to require these type of listings to be segregated from others, as is the obligation with ads.

The FTC's guidance states that consumers should be able to:

"Easily locate a search engine's explanation of any paid inclusion program, and discern the impact of paid inclusion on search results lists. In this way, consumers will be in a better position to determine whether the practice of paid inclusion is important to them in their choice of the search engines they use."

Searching for things like 'Hotels', 'Flights', or 'Current Accounts' will cause one of these comparison boxes to appear in Google. These boxes display paid inclusion results, but it's currently impossible for consumers to know whether all or some of the results are sponsored. The box includes a pop-up window which when moused over declares: "...Clicking in this box will show you results from providers that can fulfill your request. Google may be compensated by some of these providers."

This conforms to the first part of the FTC's guidelines, in that it is indeed easy to locate the explanation, however how can users "discern the impact of paid inclusion on search results" if they don't know which of the results are paid for, or indeed if they all are?

Google has also been accused of deliberately ascribing a low search result ranking to services which rival its own. In April 2015 the EU accused Google of antitrust violations, basically suggesting that the firm's search algorithms are programmed to prefer its own offerings. This announcement came at the close of a five year investigation. The European Commission released a statement at the time saying: The Commission's preliminary view is that such conduct infringes EU antitrust rules because it stifles competition and harms consumers."

The case is ongoing, but Google could face fines in excess of $6 billion.

HOW EVIL IS 'EVIL'?

But is any of this actually evil? 'Evil' is probably too harsh a term for the comparison boxes, unless we also believe business directories like the Yellow Pages should be similarly branded.

So, do we feel that Google is successful in its mission to not be evil? We can take it as read, given what Buchheit said about the motto being a "jab" at competitors exploiting their users, that shady privacy practices count as evil in this context. Having said that, it's interesting to note that the company's own definition of evil was revealed by Google's then CEO Eric Schmidt (he is now the firm's executive chairman, with Larry Page taking over the CEO role in April 2011) in an interview with Wired magazine:

"Evil is what Sergey [Brin] says is evil."

There's little doubt that Google comes up with extraordinary products. We've covered its search engine at length, but then there are other, no less innovative services like Google Earth, which can show a significant proportion of our planet in good detail right down to the level of individual cars and houses, the Android operating system for mobile devices, and the wearable device Google Glass.

In recent times the firm has gone from public darling to an organization whose motives are questioned, as consumer consciousness of privacy issues grows. Even the products listed above, which were chosen as examples from the many dozens of Google's services for their popularity and level of innovation, each give cause for concern.

GOOGLE GLASS

The most recent of those products, Google Glass, recently discontinued by the search giant, although it insisted the device was "not dead", suggesting that a new version is very much in development, has had its share of critics. US Senator Joe Barton sent a letter to Google in May 2013 asking the company how it would protect not just its users' data, but the privacy of non-users who could be inadvertently (or deliberately) recorded by the device, with tools like facial recognition technology then used to further invade their privacy.

Susan Molinari, Google's vice-president of public policy and government relations, replied that the firm's existing policies would be perfectly adequate to ensure protection for all involved parties, which, if it was an attempt to mollify the Senator, hit some way wide of the mark.

He said in a statement: "I am disappointed in the responses we received from Google. There were questions that were not adequately answered and some not answered at all.

"Google Glass has the potential to change the way people communicate and interact. When new technology like this is introduced that could change societal norms, I believe it is important that people's rights be protected and vital that privacy is built into the device," he said at the time.

Later, Larry Page, by this time Google's CEO (with his co-founder Brin taking the somewhat mysterious title 'Director of Google X and special projects) himself weighed into the argument, claiming that any privacy fears around Glass would simply "fade away".

"People worry about all sorts of things that actually, when we use the product, it is not that big a concern," Page said at an annual shareholders meeting at Google's headquarters in Silicon Valley. He was responding to a concerned shareholder who branded Glass "a voyeur's dream come true".

"You don't collapse in terror that someone might be using Glass in the bathroom just the same as you don't collapse in terror when someone comes in with a smartphone that might take a picture."

Voyeurism aside, the wider fear is that Google has a track record of gathering more information than it admits to, as an analysis of the next product, Street View, reveals.

STREET VIEW

Part of the effort in developing and maintaining the 'Street View' part of its maps product – the part which enables users to zoom right down to view and navigate photos of streets and buildings from road level in villages, towns and cities across much of the world – involved sending specially designed 'Street View Cars' down each of these avenues to take pictures. A mammoth undertaking, and one which began when the firm, in Google's own words: "…packed several computers into the back of an SUV, stuck cameras, lasers, and a GPS device on top, and drove around collecting our first imagery."

But the cars were doing more than just taking photos. After being sued by 38 states across the US (and privacy concerns over Street View are not limited to America, with dozens of countries across the globe raising complaints and investigations), Google admitted that in addition to mapping streets, its cars were hoovering up data from unsecured Wi-Fi networks in people's homes. This data included passwords, e-mail data and other personal information. The company managed to accrue 600 gigabytes of data this way, before it was caught. The story was dubbed 'Wi-Spy' by the media.

Google was later fined $25,000 for obstructing the Federal Communications Commission's (FCC) investigation into the affair – the obstruction was said to include false denials from Google, and the withholding of information. Furthermore, the FCC also discovered that one of Google's engineers had told senior colleagues way back in 2007 that the Street View project was collecting private data including emails, text messages, internet histories and passwords. So the firm was unable to claim that it was all an accident.

Google argued at the time that it has the right to gather even consumers' and citizens' most sensitive data as long as it is transmitted across an open Wi-Fi network.

Google was ordered to delete the data in the UK in November 2010 by the privacy regulator the Information Commissioner's Office. It was given the same instruction again in 2013, when Google admitted that it hadn't quite managed to delete all of it. Google also suffered a $198,000 fine in Germany, and in March 2013 settled a lawsuit from 38 states with a $7 million fine.

ANDROID

Which brings us to Android, the world's most popular mobile operating system with an incredible 85 per cent of global market share as of late 2014, according to figures from analyst firm IDC. "Every day another million users power up their Android devices for the first time and start looking for apps, games, and other digital content," as the software's own home on the internet states.

One of Android's features is its ability to backup users' data and settings. Thus, when they move to a new Android device – which many consumers do at least annually – Google is able to configure the new device very much like the old one, seamlessly via the cloud (which to be fair, other device manufacturers also offer). What most consumers won't be aware of, however, is that the feature also means that Google knows just about every

Wi-Fi password in the world, given Android's install-base. So most data it can't get by driving past in a Street View Car can be accessed anyway thanks to Android.

WHAT DOES ALL THIS MEAN?

Given that Google's business model is based around analysing user metrics and behaviour, and selling that insight on to advertisers, the fact that it has access to so much potentially very sensitive data should be cause for great concern. In fact, the firm is so successful in its mission to advertise at us, that it generated revenues of $50.6 billion in the 2013/14 financial year (well over twice that of its nearest competitor, Walt Disney Company.

But if consumers are largely unaware of many of these issues, are the wider industry, regulators and lawmakers concerned?

Christopher Graham, the Information Commissioner for the UK, says his organization, the the ICO, is working with Google, but states the firm is co-operating well.

"We're working with Google on its privacy policy, which was a game-changer when it came out," says Graham. We want to get them to develop ways of explaining what they do more clearly, rather than expecting everyone to read a privacy policy which is longer than the longest work of Shakespeare.

"They're quite co-operative in terms of coming up with clever ideas to put people in the picture. Consumers are beginning to wake up to this stuff. They don't think well of suppliers who don't treat them as grown-ups," he adds.

Graham cites telecommunications firm Telefonica as an example of a firm which is getting it right – or at least closer to getting it right - in terms of privacy.

"Telefonica's research worked out that customers will not only stay with you, but will engage with you and share more if they're clear what the deal is."

So if customers are prepared to share more information with the company, then they receive an improved level of service, or perhaps additional features. Graham emphasises the point that it's also about consumers understanding what the deal is up front.

"In the early years we weren't asking the right questions, we were like kids in a sweet shop," says Graham, referring to the almost universal delight with which free online services like Google's search engine, and Facebook were greeted, with few questioning why such well developed and marketable products required no fee.

It's similarly arguable however that the organizations behind these services behaved likewise, and in some instances continue to do so. As lawmakers continue to struggle to catch up to technology, and with privacy regulators, especially in the UK, struggling to put out fires with limited budgets, companies like Google are running amok with privacy, filling their pockets with sweets while the shopkeeper's back is turned.

When these actions are illegal, as was the case when Google enabled the privacy technology native to Apple's Safari browser to be circumvented in order to gather user data (a case discussed in the previous chapter), then the regulators act. In that particular case, Google was stung with a $22.5 million fine by the FTC. However, there are many instances where a company's actions are not outright illegal, but they are still harvesting and using private data without users' knowledge or consent, and doing things which users would object to were firms more transparent. In short, there are shady areas.

SHADY AREAS AND CREEPY LINES

"From a rational perspective, everyone knows that if you don't pay for a product you are the product," says Gartner's Frank Buytendijk.

One of the problems is that that the human brain is built to favour short-term gains over concerning itself with longer-term issues, especially if that distant issue is also abstract. So when your brain weighs up the equation of 'getting the shiny thing' now against 'possibly suffering an unquantifiable risk' in future, it's pretty obvious what the result is.

Buytendijk talks about what he refers to as 'the creepy line', beyond which organizations can be considered to be doing something bad with consumers' data. He explains which side of that line firms fall depends partly on the context of their interaction with the user.

"For example [in-car navigation tool] Tom Tom collects traffic data from users in order to come up with better traffic flow information. The intention is to use the data to tell people about traffic jams, which is totally fine. If Tom Tom sells that data anonymously to the 'department of roadworks' so they can use the information to predict whether new street repairs will cause more jams, then that's also fine. But if the police take that data to work out where people are likely to be travelling fast so they know where to set speed traps [which happened in the UK in 2011], then the use of the data is suddenly different from what was intended when it was taken. That's the moment where you say it doesn't feel right.

"It's the same thing with Google Street View collecting Wi-Fi data," continues Buytendijk. "The intent is that the data is available two metres around the house, but when [Google] makes it available [to advertisers] worldwide, suddenly the data is used for something other than intended. It's very shady, and fully crosses the creepy line."

Since this is an ethical discussion, and thus likely to be subjective – you could put these issues to ten people and receive ten different responses back – there is little certainty to be had. Also, since technology in this space is moving so quickly, the boundaries of what firms can do to both harvest and analyse their users' data is expanding rapidly, and they will usually collect data to the full extent of their capabilities, with ethics simply not part of the equation. Where laws are sufficiently vague, or simply not present at all, we are relying on organizations to exercise self-restraint in order to stay on the right side of the creepy line. How can they do that, since it's essentially subjective – barely even a line drawn in the sand?

"The first step," says Buytendijk, "is to think the issues through reasonably, and ask what could possibly go wrong." So if it's possible that your huge database of sensitive customer information could be stolen by a hacker because your security measures are primitive, perhaps you should invest in some better protection."

Privacy advocates would add here that another outcome of this first step could perhaps be to collect less data, or even none at all, although this is likely to provoke at best a roll of the eyes and a choking sound from the marketing department.

"Secondly, and this is the golden rule, think 'what if it was my data being gathered in this way'. Does it feel good or not?" Buytendijk continues.

"Thirdly, we can never think through all the consequences of our actions. There are always unintended consequences, so monitor for them. It's not enough to sit and wait until someone complains and then say 'oops I never thought of that'. It should be an active process."

These are useful measures, which, if employed, would result in firms being at least a little less gung-ho with consumer data. But until the law catches up (and even then we're supposing that the law will actually improve the situation, rather than further muddy the waters which not an uncommon outcome), there will always be problems. Partly this is because without the right regulations in place, companies are caught between the expectation that they should treat data reasonably, and the demand from their shareholders that they do everything possible to maximize value. Whilst it's a popular myth that US corporate law demands that firms maximize shareholder value, (in fact the law does no such thing) most boards and CEOs are measured by their impact on a company's share price. So if something's legal, and it's going to create a saleable asset, ethics are often left in a bloody heap on the floor.

Which brings us to Google's latest privacy terms and conditions referred to as a "game-changer" by Christopher Graham. Amended in 2012, these provisions mean that when a user shares information with one part of Google, that information can be used by any part of the company.

Let's think about the implications of that statement for a moment. It means that anything uploaded to YouTube, or Google's social network Google plus (or Google Apps, Google Art Project, Google Shopping, Google Patent Search, Swiffy, Google Moon, or any one of about 150 other Google products you probably haven't heard of) can be used by any part of the company. Anything you write to a friend using Gmail, anything you type into the search engine, and any data you allow the Android operating system to hold is all fair game.

Here's how Google describes the situation:

"When you upload, submit, store, send or receive content to or through our services, you give Google (and those we work with) a worldwide license to use, host, store, reproduce, modify, create derivative works (such as those resulting from translations, adaptations or other changes we make so that your content works better with our services), communicate, publish, publicly perform, publicly display and distribute such content," states the firm in its policy.

It later claimed that the policy changes gave its customers greater clarity, which suggests it was already sharing data across the entire company, users were just less aware of it before the update.

This policy resulted in a string of lawsuits (which attempted to be brought together as a potential class-action lawsuit – where several people sue on behalf of a larger group) in California from Gmail users who alleged that Google was transgressing wiretapping laws by scanning their emails for information to then feed on to advertisers.

A federal judge rejected Google's request to dismiss the cases, however she also prevented them from progressing through the legal system, claiming that the individual details were too varied to be taken as a unified class.

This wasn't the first time that Gmail's habit of scanning its users to all intents and purposes without their knowledge had caused problems. Indeed in 2009 the firm's then deputy general counsel Nicole Wong (who in 2013 would be given the post of White House chief privacy officer by Barack Obama) found herself testifying before Congress about Google's practise of scanning emails:

"We are using the same technology that scans for viruses and also scans for spam. It is basically technology that looks for pattern text, and we use that not only for the spam blocking and viruses but also to serve ads within the Gmail users' experience," she said.

The Wiretap Law allows email providers to monitor the contents of their users' messages, but only for the purposes of quality control, and not for revenue-generating measures such as targeted advertising.

"Google's alleged interceptions are neither instrumental to the provision of email services, nor are they an incidental effect of providing these services," said Judge Lucy Koh, presiding over the case.

But Google also claimed that its users knew all about its intentions to scan their emails in order to show ads to them as it was all written in the terms of service and privacy policies.

Once again, Judge Koh appeared not to agree, as the policies failed to be sufficiently clear.

"Section 17 of the Terms of Service – which states that Google's "advertisements may be targeted to the content of information stored on the Services, queries made through the Services or other information" – is defective in demonstrating consent for a different reason: it demonstrates only that Google has the capacity to intercept communications, not that it will. Moreover, the language suggests only that Google's advertisements were based on information "stored on the Services" or "queries made through the Services" – not information in transit via email," she said.

And there is also the further argument that if Google is scanning Gmail users' messages, it will by default be scanning their friends and other contacts' messages too. Many of those other people will use email clients from other companies, such as Apple, Microsoft or Yahoo, and will not have agreed to Google's terms of service, however they may have been worded.

Google argued, as it attempted to have the case dismissed, that all email users everywhere understand and agree to the notion that their emails are monitored and scanned.

"As numerous courts have held, the automated processing of email is so widely understood and accepted that the act of sending an email constitutes implied consent to automated processing as a matter of law."

Google's motion continued: "Non-Gmail users who send emails to Gmail recipients must expect that their emails will be subjected to Google's normal processes as the [email] provider for their intended recipients."

The search giant is at least consistent. It believes that if users broadcast Wi-Fi data outside their walls, then the implied message is that it's fine for Google to intercept their data. It believes that if you use any of its services at all, the implied message is that you're fine with your data being harvested and shared throughout the entire organization. And here, it admits to the belief that if you use email at all, you're perfectly happy with whatever it is that Google puts into its Terms of Service agreement, even though you certainly won't have read it.

Fortunately for privacy advocates, Judge Koh once again disagreed.

"Google has cited no case that stands for the proposition that users who send emails impliedly consent to interceptions and use of their communications by third parties other than the intended recipient of the email. Nor has Google cited anything that suggests that by doing nothing more than receiving emails from a Gmail user, non-Gmail users have consented to the interception of those communications. Accepting Google's theory of implied consent – that by merely sending emails to or receiving emails from a Gmail user, a non-Gmail user has consented to Google's interception of such emails for any purposes – would eviscerate the rule against interception."

Since we know that Google is determined not to 'be evil', and that evil is 'whatever Sergey Brin says is evil', it follows from the above example that making huge assumptions about what users' will find an acceptable way to treat their personal data is not evil.

Also apparently not evil is the way Google treats Microsoft, one of its principle rivals. In late 2014 Google began disclosing so-called zero-day vulnerabilities in various versions of Windows, Microsoft's flagship operating system, responsible for powering over half of the world's desktops (as of December 2014), according to data from netmarketshare.com.

Zero-day vulnerabilities are basically security flaws which no-one knows about yet. There is an industry built around discovering them. Hackers (and here we're referring to so-called 'black hat' hackers, who have malicious intent, as opposed to 'white hat' hackers who seek to improve products or security via their efforts), an increasingly well-funded and organized bunch, want to find them so they can slip their malicious code into lots of computers, for various nefarious reasons which we'll come to in chapter 6. Bug-hunters want to find them so they can sell the details on to third parties, who pay handsomely to find coding errors before the bad guys (and the largest pay-outs are often offered by the US government, which is always on the lookout for ways to hack its rivals, outright enemies, and indeed its own citizens). And of course the software firms themselves have engineers on the lookout for vulnerabilities, because their customers being hacked due to flawed software isn't great for business.

The security industry likes to paint itself as enjoying a slightly more Musketeer spirit than most, with the idea of solidarity against the bad guys often taking precedence over individual firms' selfish concerns. There is to be fair a greater degree of collaboration than you'll find in some sectors. Anti-virus firms, for instance, will share data on many new threats they find with their rivals, with the result that all of their customers are better protected. Security researchers in particular are a fairly tight-knit bunch. So they won't think of it as Kaspersky calling McAfee to share threat information, it's just Igor calling Dave. Having said that, there are plenty of companies who exist to research and find exploits and then sell them on to the highest bidder, with no thought given to the intentions of that bidder, or the likely consequences of the sale.

Google though decided to buck the trend of collaboration between the big firms, and in January 2015 went public on no fewer than three separate occasions about security holes in Windows 7 and 8.1, without waiting for Microsoft to produce a patch fixing the vulnerabilities. Worse, Google didn't simply release information about the bug, it included with it proof-of concept code to show the world exactly how the vulnerabilities could be exploited. This is the equivalent of your neighbour – with whom you've had an admittedly fractious relationship – telling everyone not just when you're going to be on holiday, but that you also hide your keys under the mat.

Google's explanation was that they had revealed the flaw's existence to Microsoft in October 2014, and set the information on a 90-day countdown until its release. Microsoft had planned to release a fix to its customers before the deadline, but cited "compatibility issues" in its decision to push the change back a couple of weeks to February.

Google went ahead and released the information anyway. In case it's not already clear, this is a big no-no in security circles.

"Of course, in an ideal world, Microsoft shouldn't have had the security bugs in the first place," wrote security researcher Graham Cluley on the blog pages of Lumension, a security firm. "But I find it difficult to see how its response hasn't been appropriate. Microsoft clearly wants to fix bugs, but it wants to make sure that the fixes work. Google, meanwhile, appears to have adopted behaviour which I would find more common in a schoolyard.

"Isn't it about time they grew up, and acted responsibly for the safety of internet users?"

And it's not as if Google's products are entirely free from zero-day vulnerabilities themselves (a fact which it is admittedly fairly open about, and even has a bug bounty program where it pays researchers for data on its vulnerabilities). Its mobile operating system Android has had more than its fair share, as has its web browser Chrome, so the company can't claim the high moral ground that it is simply outraged that such vulnerabilities exist.

Not that Microsoft is particularly angelic itself. In 2012 it set up a website which it called 'Scroogled', designed to attack Google and its products. It attacked

Google Shopping, a price comparison service, claiming that all shopping results were paid ads. It lambasted Gmail for its practise of scanning users' emails in order to better target them with ads, and, somewhat oddly, criticized Google's Chromebook range by claiming pawnshops wouldn't accept anything incapable of running Windows or Office.

Leaving aside the logic of whether consumers purchase technology intending immediately to sell it on to a pawn shop for a fraction of its value, these are all transparent attempts to convince consumers to switch to Microsoft products. But the difference is that Microsoft doesn't attempt to set itself up as a paragon of virtue. Its most recent motto is the banal but at least non-sanctimonious 'Be what's next', rather than 'Don't be evil'.

However, in April 2013 the firm launched a new campaign titled 'Your privacy is our priority'. In a triumph of bad timing for Microsoft, a couple of months later reports emerged claiming that its remote video conferencing platform Skype secretly sends its users' communications to the NSA. The service was investigated by Luxembourg's data protection authority, but later cleared of any wrongdoing, which would probably have surprised Edward Snowden, from whose document trove the initial suspicions arose.

But what's Google's side of the story, how does it defend the business practises outlined in this chapter? Unfortunately we don't know. Upon hearing the title and subject of this book, the firm refused to speak to the author. Credit should be afforded to Acxiom, who in the face of fierce media criticism and regulatory concern are still prepared to engage in conversation and to answer difficult questions. As for Google, readers are invited to draw their own conclusions.

APPETITE FOR INFORMATION

One of the other targets of Microsoft's Scroogled attacks was the Google Play store, which contains apps for Android devices. The attack centred on Google's practise of handing its users' personal information to app developers. But sucking in personal data is what apps (and not just Android apps, but programs on all mobile platforms) are all about.

When you download an app to your phone, it will usually request a raft of permissions to let it access information on the device. Few people question why a simple game needs to know the contents of their address books, and since the permissions box is in the way of their quick blast of entertainment, it is seen as something to skip through rather than read. But the range of information that these innocuous apps can hoover up is vast. It includes phone and email contacts, call logs, internet, calendar and location data, the device's unique ID, and data on how the app is used.

There is no need for a link between the information an app can access and its function. The cat, bird or monkey bouncing around the touchscreen doesn't require your personal data in order to play out its story, but it makes a good living for someone, somewhere. And that someone could be the app developer, the app store owner – most likely Google or Apple – or an advertiser or ad network. And it doesn't stop there, there is nothing to prevent them selling that data on once again to whomever else will pay for it.

How many users understand that this is the deal when they download Angry Birds or Candy Crush? In fact, let's take a look at these apps – two of the most popular in the world – to see how they treat personal data.

Security firm Veracode performed an analysis on Angry Birds using an Android device in 2014. They found that it accesses unique device identification information, like the phone number and IMEI. It retrieves SIM card data, including its serial number and the provider network with which is connects. It gathers data around the brand and model of the device it's installed on, and the version of the operating system. It monitors the device's location and tracks it. It identifies and retrieves information about users' mobile service providers. It monitors the device's status including battery life, signal strength, network traffic and CPU performance. It also listens out for key and touch presses. You would be hard pressed to find many users who are aware of that level of activity as they fling a variety of avians at green pigs.

The story is similar with Candy Crush, which has been described by news service Bloomberg as one of the 'leakiest apps' (for its poor security in addition to its overcollection of data). And it's not just ad networks which see the data these apps retrieve, some of the documents released by former NSA contractor Edward Snowden reveal that the NSA and its UK-based counterpart GCHQ have sensors at key internet junctures to capture this information too – so the spy agencies are taking advantage of the situation to harvest even more data.

These factors caused Michael Sutton, vice president of security research at California-based Zscaler to tell Bloomberg: "Privacy is dead in the digital world that we live in. I tell people, unless you are comfortable putting that statement on a billboard in Times Square and having everyone see it, I would not share that information digitally."

The behaviour of apps towards user data has actually improved slightly in recent years thanks to a public outcry in 2012 over the way personal diary app Path was found to handle its customers' data. A hacker (in the sense of someone who likes to play with and modify code, rather than someone looking to illegally obtain data) discovered that Path uploads the entire contents of users' address books to its developer's servers, without asking for permission or even notifying consumers that it could happen.

The story blew up and created something of a storm amongst smartphone users, and other hackers and developers started to get interested. What they found was that many popular apps were taking data either partially or wholly without permission or notification. It was soon uncovered that location and discovery service Foursquare uploaded all email addresses and phone numbers from users' contacts with no requirement for consent. Photo-sharing network Instagram, and social networks Facebook and Twitter behaved similarly, though these three at least allowed a warning message to pop up first. Twitter also later admitted to storing users' IP address, browser type, pages visited, mobile carrier, device and application ID and search terms used on its servers.

The makers of these services often argue that their products need access to their users' contacts. After all, if you're offering yourself up as a social network, it's quite useful to know who your users' friends are so you can tell them if they're available to hook up with. But where this argument falls down is in the concept of 'hashing'. This is a method of anonymizing data by replacing the plain text of address book contacts with code. They can still offer all the same features, the difference is that they're not able to see those contact details for their own benefit.

Many of the apps mentioned above released patches to either stop harvesting the data, or to at least provide warnings before it happened shortly after the furore over Path broke. But whilst the situation improved somewhat, there is still an almighty disconnect between what a user thinks is happening when he or she downloads an app, and what actually happens.

So whose fault is this? Shady app developers? Poorly governed app stores? Ill-educated and naïve users?

The answer is all three. Mobile operating systems need to be architected in such a way that developers are forced to ask for permission before harvesting and transmitting their data. It's important to note that this isn't a question of a few more paragraphs of legalese in the terms of service, but the need for proper permissions to be hard-coded into mobile operating systems. The Path story, and the apps mentioned as part of it were all operating on Apple's iOS software. At the time Apple's terms stated that apps need to be up front about their behaviour towards user data, but clearly without a working means of governance or enforcement this is at best a small nod towards the need for privacy and at worst complete dereliction of duty.

Apple's App Store could learn something here from Google and Microsoft, whose own stores list the data apps will use clearly in the information provided before the app is downloaded. This is preferable to a simple dialogue box flashing up on screen notifying users just before data is taken, as if there's one thing modern life has taught computer users, it's never to read terms of service.

YOSEMITE WHAM BAM THANK YOU SAM

Apple has also been found wanting when it comes to protecting its customers' privacy with the 'Yosemite' update to its OSX operating system for its desktop and laptop computers, released in October 2014. The software has been found to log users' locations, and send that information, together with lists of all internet search terms used to Apple's servers, calling it 'usage data'.

The data is anonymized, and transmitted securely using HTTPS, so whilst you could argue that Apple doesn't need to have all of this information all of the time (though it can be legitimate – for example its maps function won't work well if it doesn't know your location), it has at least taken steps to ensure the data doesn't fall into the wrong hands. However, not all of these steps are especially effective. In the age of big data, it's a trivial matter to identify individuals from supposedly anonymized data, as we'll explore more thoroughly in chapter 9.

The bigger problem is once again that it happens without proper notification and consent from the user. This is compounded by the fact that it all happens by default – users have to delve into their settings in order to opt-out, something you wouldn't expect many to do if they aren't even aware that it's happening.

Yosemite also sports a useful feature that automatically uploads documents to Apple's iCloud Drive service every couple of seconds. Previous iterations of the operating system automatically saved documents locally, on the user's hard drive. Saving documents to the cloud allows users to switch devices on the fly and keep working on the same document, and provides added resilience in the event of drive failure. But the problem is that once again it doesn't make users aware of what it's doing; it happens secretly, and by default. If you didn't want that data in the cloud, tough luck.

This encapsulates much of the problem with the issues discussed in this chapter. Some of the issues are downright creepy – like Google's data harvesting Street View cars – and some is perhaps just ill-considered, like Yosemite's automatic cloud saving feature. The fundamental problems are the same though. Users aren't aware of what firms are doing with their data, and aren't being given the opportunity to opt in or out, at the right time. And the right time is when they have a clear and thorough understanding of the transaction. Download this app, hand over this data. Use these search terms, have them added to your profile. Write a document, watch it replicate itself in the cloud.

The situation continues, and arguably even worsens when you start using social media, as we'll see in the next chapter.

References

http://infolab.stanford.edu/~backrub/google.html

http://archive.wired.com/wired/archive/13.08/battelle.html

http://www.google.com/about/company/history/

The Search: How Google and Its Rivals Rewrote the Rules of Business and Transformed Our Culture, *by John Battelle*

http://blogoscoped.com/archive/2007-07-16-n55.html

https://ico.org.uk/media/about-the-ico/documents/1042994/roscoe-lecture-script.pdf

http://www.google.com/maps/about/behind-the-scenes/streetview/

http://developer.android.com/about/index.html

The Shareholder Value Myth: How Putting Shareholders First Harms Investors, Corporations, and the Public, Lynn Stout

http://www.nytimes.com/interactive/2013/10/02/technology/google-email-case.html?_r=0

http://blog.lumension.com/9721/dont-be-evil-google-discloses-yet-another-zero-day-vulnerability-in-microsoft-code/?utm_source=GCHQ+-+Graham+Cluley%27s+Security+Newsletter&utm_campaign=c9e8549a01-GCHQ&utm_medium=email&utm_term=0_8106850f4a-c9e8549a01-61701177

http://www.techrepublic.com/blog/it-security/guess-whos-buying-zero-day-vulnerabilities/

https://www.onguardonline.gov/articles/0018-understanding-mobile-apps

https://nakedsecurity.sophos.com/2013/06/25/google-gets-35-days-to-wipe-its-wispy-data/

https://www.veracode.com/blog/2014/01/how-angry-is-that-bird

http://www.bloomberg.com/news/2014-01-29/nsa-spying-on-apps-shows-perils-of-google-candy-crush-.html

http://marketingland.com/once-deemed-evil-google-now-embraces-paid-inclusion-13138

http://www.telegraph.co.uk/technology/news/8480702/Tom-Tom-sold-drivers-GPS-details-to-be-used-by-police-for-speed-traps.html

CHAPTER 5

Social Media and the Dangers of Over-Sharing

Launched in February 2004, Facebook today boasts just under 1.4 billion active users. Facebook's population rivals that of China, the most populous country on Earth. Showing its partners' ads to those users helped it to pull in $3.85 billion revenue in the fourth quarter of 2014. So if you have an active Facebook account, you're worth something in the region of $11 to the firm per year. Facebook is free to use, and we know from the aphorism we quoted in the last chapter, if you don't pay for the product, you are the product.

Today Facebook makes its money by tracking everything you do on its service. When you log in, how long you log in for, where you log in from, and of course all of the information you throw at it voluntarily, including photos, videos, status updates and messages.

Most firms have to work hard for your data. They have to provide an extremely complicated web search service for example, or a robust and reliable email client, or any one of thousands of other methods, all designed to give you just enough of a reason to hand over your data. But few of them manage to convince users to hand over their data so willingly, gleefully and often as Facebook.

Like Google, Facebook has its origins in a US university campus. Only this time we swap Stanford for Harvard, and Page and Brin for Mark Zuckerberg.

Like Google, Facebook didn't appear from nothing. Where Google's precursor was Backrub, Facebook's was Facemash. In late 2003 Zuckerberg banded together with classmates Andrew McCollum, Chris Hughes, and Dustin Moskovitz to launch a 'hot or not' game on the college network. The game worked by showing pictures of two random Harvard students side by side, inviting the user to define which was the more physically attractive. The pictures were taken from dormitory 'facebooks', online catalogues of students' names and faces designed help students find friends and identify people.

Even at the time, Zuckerberg appeared to acknowledge the tacit unpleasantness of the idea, writing in his blog:

CONTENTS

"Perhaps Harvard will squelch it for legal reasons without realizing its value as a venture that could possibly be expanded to other schools (maybe even ones with good-looking people...). But one thing is certain, and it's that I'm a jerk for making this site. Oh well. Someone had to do it eventually..."

Facemash didn't take long to find its way onto several campus servers, but Zuckerberg was right to be concerned about the university's response. Harvard shut the site down in days, and Zuckerberg himself was charged with infringing copyright, breach of security and violating students' privacy by publishing their pictures without permission.

This is precisely the same issue as we covered in the last chapter, where information (in this case photos) was given for one purpose, then used for another. The students allowed their pictures to be used in dormitory facebooks so that their friends could look them up, but when those pictures were then used in a way which encouraged their peers to judge their physical and sexual appeal, that went way beyond their intended use. Here, it's easy to put it down to a simple student prank, but as we'll see later in this chapter, it's a situation Facebook (as in the global social network which would spawn out of Facemash) would find itself in again in later years.

The Harvard authorities evidently also regarded Facemash as a simple prank, as all of the charges against Zuckerberg were soon dropped. Facemash was eventually sold to an unknown buyer for $30,201 in October 2010, but for now, let's go back to January 2004, when Zuckerberg began coding the site he called 'theFacebook'.

LAUNCHING THEFACEBOOK AND DROPPING THE 'THE'

Coding took little more than a week, and theFacebook was launched on February 4 2004. It was in essence a standard Harvard dormitory facebook, but with a little more information and a feature that allowed students to find their friends by searching for others on their course, or living in a particular part of the campus. The University was also working on a broader facebook for all of its students at the time, but like all innovators Zuckerberg was impatient, as he told Harvard Universtity news site 'The Crimson'.

"Everyone's been talking a lot about a universal facebook within Harvard," Zuckerberg said. "I think it's kind of silly that it would take the University a couple of years to get around to it. I can do it better than they can, and I can do it in a week."

Interestingly, perhaps burned by his experience with Facemash, Zuckerberg now spoke of privacy as one of his chief concerns, describing how the various ways of searching for students could be restricted if users didn't want to be found.

"There are pretty intensive privacy options," he told The Crimson. "You can limit who can see your information, if you only want current students to see your information, or people in your year, in your house, in your classes. You can limit a search so that only a friend or a friend of a friend can look you up. People have very good control over who can see their information."

Later in the same interview, he added that the purpose of theFacebook was not to make money.

"I'm not going to sell anybody's e-mail address," he said. "At one point I thought about making the website so that you could upload a resume too, and for a fee companies could search for Harvard job applicants. But I don't want to touch that. It would make everything more serious and less fun."

But theFacebook was about to become a whole lot more serious.

Within 24 hours of its launch to the Harvard campus, theFacebook had around 1,500 registered users. It soon expanded to allow students from other US-based universities including Stanford, Columbia and Yale to sign up. Before long it had spread to most universities in Canada and the US, and by October 2005 it had registered students in most universities in the UK too. By August 26 2008 it hit 100 million users, having opened up to the wider world, not just dorm rooms.

Facebook (the network dropped 'the' from its name in 2005) was a good idea, certainly a popular idea, but was it Zuckerberg's idea? It wasn't the first social network, having been preceded by Friendster, SixDegrees.com and MySpace, amongst others. But ownership of the very idea of Facebook was brought into question less than a week after its launch when three Harvard seniors, brothers Tyler and Cameron Winklevoss and their associate Divya Narendra, alleged that Zuckerberg had stolen the concept from them after initially agreeing to work for them as a coder. The case was eventually settled in 2008 with the complainants receiving a total of $20 million in cash and $45 million in Facebook stock.

SOCIAL MEDIA: BOTH A BLESSING AND A CURSE

Whilst much of the above relates little to privacy, it serves to give an ethical background to the company, and some of the characters behind it. But we perhaps shouldn't read too much into it. Just because someone is allegedly prepared to steal intellectual property from another party, it doesn't necessarily follow that he or she is going to steal information from others.

We know that Facebook and its many of its peers take their users' data and sell it on to advertisers, and for the most part users are aware too. But the problem is two-fold. Firstly that not all users are aware, and secondly that even the relatively clued up users aren't aware of the full-scale of the data mining that goes on.

Facebook captures around 600 terabytes of data every day from its users. To give an idea of exactly how much data that is, the entire printed collection of the US Library of Congress amounts to about 50 terabytes. So stack 12 of those on top of one another, and you've got roughly the amount of information Facebook users give the company on a daily basis.

And Facebook shares much of that information with the applications it allows to run on its platform. Applications like Candy Crush saga, Farmville and Clash of Clans boast up to something in the region of 60 million daily users on Facebook, and the network gives them permission to access just about all of the information about those users that the users themselves can access. Adrienne Felt, a Ph.D. candidate at Berkeley in the US, explained that Facebook exercises no control over what information an application is able to access, and entirely fails to police how the data is used once gathered.

"If a user wants to install an application, she must grant that application full privileges," Felt wrote in a blog. "Privacy settings can be applied to friends' applications, but one standard is set for all applications. There's no way to say, 'X gets my hometown but Y only gets my favorite music.' The principle of least authority, a security design principle, states that an actor should only be given the privileges needed to perform a job. In other words, an application that doesn't need private information shouldn't be given any."

She performed a study of the top 150 Facebook applications and found that 8.7 per cent didn't need any information; 82 per cent used public data (including name, network and list of friends); and only 9.3 per cent needed private information (like email address and birthday).

"Since all of the applications are given full access to private data, this means that 90.7 per cent of applications are being given more privileges than they need," she concluded.

On top of the consent and data sharing issues, social media like Facebook also have the potential to create employment problems. This is a privacy concern, but the blame really lies more with the user or the employer rather than the social network in this case. Many firms examine current and prospective employees' social media footprints in order to make key decisions about their careers – especially in making a verdict as to whether to offer a job. The individual is unlikely to be told this is happening, and probably would not give consent if asked – besides LinkedIn most of us see social media as a personal rather than professional space. This sort of activity is illegal in the states of California, Maryland and Illinois, but nowhere else, although Title VII – part of the US Civil Rights Act 1964 – also prohibits discrimination during any aspect of employment, including recruitment, and has been said to extend to social media.

In fact, some employers even ask for prospective employees' Facebook user-names and passwords before offering a position, so they can really have a good rummage into their personal lives. The practice became sufficiently widespread that by early 2014 12 US States passed legislation to expressly ban the activity.

Frank Buytendijk, research VP at analyst firm Gartner advises consumers to use different social media for different purposes. So for example create a professional persona on Google Plus and give that link out to professional contacts, and keep Facebook for drinking buddies and other people unlikely to be perturbed at photos of you behaving oddly in the small hours.

Whilst that will help the employment issue, it doesn't tackle the underlying problem that sites like Facebook fundamentally don't appear to believe in the concept of privacy, or at least they believe it has changed, and indeed their business models depend on it.

CHANGING THE NORM TO SUIT YOURSELF

In January 2010, Zuckerberg declared that privacy is no longer a "social norm".

"People have really gotten comfortable not only sharing more information and different kinds, but more openly and with more people," he said, speaking at the Crunchie awards (awards given to Silicon Valley firms from several technology blogs) in San Francisco. "That social norm is just something that has evolved over time."

Zuckerberg intimated that public attitudes have changed over the last few years, with the result that privacy no longer matters, or at least matters less than the burning need to share personal information.

"When I got started in my dorm room at Harvard, the question a lot of people asked was, 'why would I want to put any information on the internet at all? Why would I want to have a website?' Then in the last five or six years, blogging has taken off in a huge way, and just all these different services that have people sharing all this information."

This is an extremely dangerous pattern of thought. Here, Zuckerberg is attempting to turn the entire privacy debate on its head, claiming that his firm is simply following consumer whim, rather than effectively defining what constitutes normal.

At a conference on digital privacy and data protection in the NHS, the UK's health service, in February 2015, an executive from consultancy McKinsey cited consumers' propensity to share information on Facebook as an argument for questioning their need for privacy around their health data.

"There's been a huge focus on data privacy concerns [in the health sector]," she said. "Is this such an issue for patients who are already sharing private things about themselves on Facebook?"

The response came a few minutes later at the same conference, from Sam Smith of health industry privacy campaigning group med Confidential. "People choose what they put on Facebook and what they do with it, whereas [UK government medical data sharing programme] care.data was done to them by the system."

The point is that what Zuckerberg was saying is dangerous. His firm defines what people come to accept a 'normal' when it comes to privacy, and it doesn't take long for it to start to applying in all sorts of dangerous areas, like healthcare.

And there's a further point that when users upload information to Facebook, they're doing so in order to share information with their friends. The fact that they have chosen to do so does not mean that they are no longer entitled to privacy.

So Zuckerberg claiming to follow consumer whim is at best a misunderstanding, but more likely an attempt at obfuscation. Popular services like Facebook define the norms in privacy, and for it to remove safeguards and make data publically available by default without repercussion from regulators erodes the very concept of personal data.

Zuckerberg's announcement was also very convenient for Facebook. His declaration came about a month after the site changed its privacy settings to make status updates and other data public by default, unless the user specifically tags them as private. Today this sounds like a small issue but at the time it was big news.

Privacy campaigning group the Electronic Frontier Foundation (EFF) called the change "ugly" at the time.

"These new 'privacy' changes are clearly intended to push Facebook users to publicly share *even more* information than before," wrote the EFF on its blog. "Even worse, the changes will actually *reduce* the amount of control that users have over some of their personal data. Not to say that many of the changes aren't good for privacy. But other changes are bad, while a few are just plain ugly."

The fact that this particular privacy change today sounds relatively inconsequential starkly illustrates the point that society's perception of what's acceptable is changing rapidly, and it is being driven by firms with a vested interest in its reduction.

Furthermore, users have little choice when platforms like Facebook decide to change their privacy settings. They don't have the option to stick with the existing policy, they can either accept the changes or stop using the service (which does not, incidentally, mean that Facebook stops holding and trading their data). This is an ultimatum, not a choice.

In his speech at Crunchie, Zuckerberg pressed his claim that the situation is exactly the opposite; Facebook merely mirrors society's attitudes rather than drives it.

"A lot of companies would be trapped by the conventions and their legacies of what they've built," he said. "Doing a privacy change for 350 million users is not the kind of thing that a lot of companies would do. But we viewed that as a really important thing, to always keep a beginner's mind and what would we do if we were starting the company now and we decided that these would be the social norms now and we just went for it."

It's an interesting use of language, the description of sticking with the earlier privacy policy of allowing users' updates to be private by default as being "trapped" by convention and legacy.

What's also interesting is that this was something of a turning point for Facebook in terms of its approach to privacy. This was the point where most information which users give to the site, excluding their email address, was made to default to publicly visible. And this from a firm which spent its earlier years trading on its penchant for privacy – Zuckerberg's 2004 interview with The Crimson where privacy and security were touted as cornerstones of the service set the tone for the next six years.

Privacy is "the vector around which Facebook operates," Zuckerberg told technology blog Readwrite in 2008.

"I don't buy Zuckerberg's argument that Facebook is now only reflecting the changes that society is undergoing," wrote industry commentator Marshall Kirkpatrick on Readwrite in 2010. "I think Facebook itself is a major agent of social change and by acting otherwise Zuckerberg is being arrogant and condescending."

Barry Schnitt, director of corporate communications and public policy at Facebook in 2010 (and head of communications at rival social network Pinterest at the time of writing), attempted to justify the changes to Readwrite by saying that Facebook discarding its earlier strategy of prioritizing limited exposure in order to encourage a greater degree of sharing was due to the world changing. But how was the world changing?

"Tens of millions of people have joined Twitter," Schnitt replied. "That's wide open. So is MySpace." And when asked if the rise of reality television was another example he said: "Frankly, yes. Public blogs instead of private diaries, far more people commenting on newspaper websites than ever wrote letters to the editor."

Quoting this interview, Readwrite's Kirkpatrick said: "Do they really expect us to believe that the popularity of reality TV is evidence that users want their Facebook friends list and fan pages made permanently public? Why cite those kinds [of] phenomena as evidence that the red hot social network needs to change its ways?

"The company's justifications of the claim that they are reflecting broader social trends just aren't credible. A much more believable explanation is that Facebook wants user information to be made public and so they 'just went for it'."

Kirkpatrick goes on to argue that Facebook users – some 350 million of them in 2010 – signed up to the service in the belief that their data would be shared only amongst their friends. For the firm to then turn around and label that accepted and agreed contract as "being trapped by convention or legacy" is both alarming and telling.

It's also dishonest. Both Zuckerberg and Schnitt attempted to pass the changes off as being beneficial to users, and reflecting changing attitudes. In reality, the changes happened because they benefited Facebook.

More recently, in early 2015, Facebook changed it privacy policy again. One of the amendments allows the company to share its users' data with partner sites and apps, in much the same way that Google exchanged its users' data amongst its entire ecosystem. This change is designed to allow the platform to deliver targeted ads on external websites and on mobile, and it alarmed Germany's privacy regulator Johannes Caspar.

"I think it's problematic that Facebook wants to exchange user data between all of its various units, including WhatsApp and Instagram. I will coordinate with my various European colleagues to see what action may be needed," he said.

What's slightly ironic here is that in March 2014 WhatsApp's founder and CEO Jan Koum wrote a blog discussing his childhood in KGB-controlled Russia, and declaring that his firm would only ever collect the minimum amount of data possible from users, irrespective of its deal with Facebook.

"Respect for your privacy is coded into our DNA, and we built WhatsApp around the goal of knowing as little about you as possible... If partnering with Facebook meant that we had to change our values, we wouldn't have done it," wrote Koum.

"I guess things change over time, eh?" commented security firm Sophos on its blog.

21ST CENTURY ETHICS

So is this unethical or just the way the modern world works? Or perhaps both?

Gartner's Buytendijk believes that from an ethical perspective, it's all about the real intention behind a company's actions. He says that if a firm truly intends to redefine privacy because it believes its way will lead to a better way of life for everyone, then it doesn't matter if the result is public outcry, media vilification and court cases, it's not unethical – provided you subscribe to the notion that ethics are personal, rather than absolute.

"But if your intent basically is that you don't give a hoot (fill in your favourite word here) about privacy, and you just want to collect and sell as much data as you can because it benefits you, what you do can be considered unethical."

But how can it be unethical if the users ultimately don't mind? After all, 'I have nothing to hide' is a common response from consumers to the privacy advocate's arguments.

Buytendijk suggests that this response is naïve.

"It is not for you to decide what is there to hide, others will determine that in [their use of the] information. Also, times change, and what is nothing to hide today becomes a problem tomorrow. This is all just conceptual however, so people don't take it into account, until there is a real issue. Those issues could include not getting a job because of photos from the past, or getting into trouble with the police, because your innocent behaviour fits a certain suspicious pattern."

There is a further problem when users post updates or pictures of and about their friends for the wider world to see. You may not mind your immediate social circle seeing the photo of your embarrassing dancing, wardrobe malfunction, or late night behaviour, but when that post suddenly defaults to being published to search engines everywhere, you may feel differently.

This is an extension of the issue mentioned in the first chapter, with the example of the man standing in a bar shouting something ill-considered to his friends.

"In general we are programmed to realise that most of what we do and most of what we say in the grand scheme of things doesn't make a difference, it has limited reach," explains Buytendijk. "However, if someone decides to post what you say on Twitter, it is out there, in an environment where we don't feel safe. Or even more, we think we are safe in the comfort of our own home when we post something, and just don't realise what the reach is, as we posted it in the spur of the moment.

"Is it our own fault? Certainly. Can we be blamed? Not entirely. Social media do not have an in-built feedback mechanism that provides us with a safety context to what we are saying, like real life. Social media need to figure that out."

So this is partly something users need to get used to as social media become more embedded into the daily routine – the concept that what you type online is there forever in some form, and won't necessarily be judged within the same context as it was originally meant. A risqué joke between close friends can look very different to work colleagues or employers in the cold light of day. But it's also something that the social networks themselves need to help users get to grips with in Buytendijk's opinion.

We are some way off the sophisticated artificial intelligence required for your phone to be able to pipe up 'Are you sure you want to post that?' just at the right time, and similarly a warning popup message appearing before every up-date is allowed to be posted will be both irritating and ignored.

So what should the social networks do? One approach which would at least help would be to permit permanent deletion. Whilst Twitter does indeed allow users to delete tweets they've previously made public, it caused an outcry in November 2014 when it made all tweets ever posted since its creation in 2006 suddenly searchable (previously only a far shorter timeline was made publicly available).

Facebook however currently does not offer any form of account or update dele-tion. Whatever you share (including all the information you don't deliberately share but Facebook captures anyway) with the site is logged forever, however embarrassing, thoughtless or regrettable.

So should we lobby for change here? The problem with demanding that your information be deleted is that it's effectively asking to reduce your value to the network. And if Facebook is going to be denied value from offering you access to its services, since you don't pay for it, why should it bother running servers and paying for staff? Again it comes back to the principle that if it's free, you're not the customer, you're the product.

"We don't pay for most social media, and they make money by creating cus-tomer profiles, and selling them to advertisers," says Buytendijk. "So this is the reason why 'the right to be forgotten' is so controversial for social media. It limits the value of the product."

The fundamental disconnect with social media is that both the users and the social network providers believe that the data belongs to them. The law, so far as it has anything to say about such 'new' fads, sides with the providers, as long as the terms of use governing data ownership is available to users before they sign up. It doesn't need to be clearly written (and in fact it almost never is), and it can be buried on page 87, but as long as it's there somewhere, it's binding.

This is an area ripe for disruption, either from legislation, or new businesses looking to offer some different ideas. Social networks could allow users to own and control their own data without harming their revenue streams. And far from damaging firms like Facebook, such a change could in fact end up benefiting both sides.

"From a consumer perspective, [owning their own data] makes perfect sense," says Buytendijk. "The sides don't have to oppose one another. In all the data collected [by social networks] there is a lot of noise; outdated and plain incorrect information. There are also a lot of false positives; conclusions based on patterns of behaviour which don't actually match reality.

"If you allow people to see their own [hidden] profiles, manage them and delete where they want, what you keep is far more targeted, rather than broad. You would also have much more buy-in from consumers as well. There would be a more direct relationship between data they share, and the commercial consequences. I think the two positions can be synthesised for both consumer and business value."

He mentions a further point, that as consumers become more tech savvy and concerned about their data, some will become sufficiently motivated to adopt what he calls 'obfuscation services', where a social media account is made to behave irrationally, and entirely out of kilter with the user's genuine habits in an attempt to mess up the profile and the data analysis going on behind the scenes.

"If this happens, no one wins," he adds.

So what should users do in the short term? A simple solution is to use separate social media for personal and business use, don't add both your friends and business colleagues to Facebook, for example. Check privacy setting regularly. As we have seen in this chapter, social network providers are not above making sudden changes with little warning, and what you once knew to be a relatively safe corner of the internet can suddenly be very public. If you feel strongly enough then calling your Congressman or Member of Parliament in the US and UK respectively to lobby for increased regulation would be a step in the right direction. Or, rather more dramatically, Buytendijk adds - perhaps with his tongue firmly in his cheek - a final option of going to war against social media itself.

"Become a digital expert, and arm yourself. Use encryption, firewalls, the TOR network [a virtual network designed to enable anonymous use of the internet], your own personal cloud on your own servers, and then use obfuscation.

Continuously post messages in languages you don't speak, about places where you have never been, and find other ways to mess up the profiles."

Anyone especially keen to try this out is welcome to post the following to their preferred network: "An diesem Morgen habe ich ein stück Kuchen in Reykjavik wirklich genossen!"

That's "Really enjoyed a slice of cake in Reykjavik this morning!" in German. Although its effect will be reduced if you are actually German, and currently travelling though Iceland. It may also confuse friends and relatives rather more than Facebook's analysts.

So how long do we have to wait for a social network to wake up to the realisation that they don't have to own all the data and keep it forever in order to make money? The answer is no time at all, because in fact some new services are already doing just that. One in particular goes much further, and even went so far as to publish this 'manifesto':

"Your social network is owned by advertisers.

"Every post you share, every friend you make and every link you follow is tracked, recorded and converted into data. Advertisers buy your data so they can show you more ads. You are the product that's bought and sold.

"We believe there is a better way. We believe in audacity. We believe in beauty, simplicity and transparency. We believe that the people who make things and the people who use them should be in partnership.

"We believe a social network can be a tool for empowerment. Not a tool to deceive, coerce and manipulate — but a place to connect, create and celebrate life.

"You are not a product."

The network in this instance is Ello, a service launched in March 2014 which at its peak was processing over 30,000 account requests per hour, although according to some reports levels of interest had dipped sharply by the end of the year. However, given that the service is still currently in Beta, there is still time for it take off.

As is apparent from its manifesto, it uses privacy as its selling point. So is this the social network privacy advocates have been waiting for? To answer that, it's necessary to look beyond the manifesto, which at its heart is a marketing document. Any social network entering the market today has to compete with well entrenched incumbents like Facebook and Twitter. Even Google Plus (which in March 2015 the firm announced would be broken up into separate parts around its video calling feature Hangouts, photos, and a new social feed called streams), with the weight of Google's brand and marketing budget behind it failed to make much of a dent in Facebook's user base, so to encourage users to abandon existing services you need to make some noise.

So once you're inside Ello, is it a marketing-free zone? Well it's certainly not free from marketers, advertisers and PRs, who are often the first to flock to any new network to check it out as a way of reaching new and existing customers. But is it at least free from corporate accounts, allowing only actual humans to populate its servers with profiles actually about themselves and their interests? Again, no. In fact, Ello's founder Paul Budnitz owns a bicycle shop. And this shop, Budnitz Bicycles, has its own profile on Ello, used to market its products.

However, it's still a marked step up from most of its peers in privacy terms. The commitment to not harvesting and selling user data to advertisers is a bold one, and should be applauded. Ello is relying on increasing user disquiet with modern marketing and advertising practices, and only time will tell if that disquiet is sufficient to make users give up their existing homes on the internet and migrate en masse. After all, a social network only functions if its users are actually able to find the people they want to network with. But even if Ello ultimately fails, or perhaps carves out a minority niche of privacy enthusiasts, the fact that it exists is proof that existing practises amongst mainstream networks are viewed very dimly in some corners. It's a cast-iron certainty that Facebook and its kin will have noted Ello, and will be monitoring it closely. If they start losing significant numbers of users – or 'product' in their parlance – to services like Ello, we should expect a sudden about-face in Facebook's privacy policy, reverting more towards its original stance of protecting personal data. And no doubt this will again be sold as reflecting societal norms.

Ello isn't the only privacy pioneer within the social networking world. There's also Swiss messaging app Threema which promises "true end-to-end encryption". But this alone shouldn't be seen as much of a differentiator, given that the industry leader in this space, Whatsapp (bought by – as mentioned earlier – Facebook in February 2014 for a cool $19 billion), which boasts over 500 million users and is still growing, introduced encryption to its service in November 2014.

Whatsapp uses an encryption system called TextSecure, developed by non-profit group Open Whisper Systems. But according to Threema, this just isn't good enough.

"Many manufacturers of messengers claim that their product encrypts the messages that users exchange. However, with most of them the server operator can still read the content of the messages," claims Threema on its website.

It goes on to explain that services like Whatsapp use transport encryption only, which means that only the connection between the mobile device and the server is encrypted. So users' messages cannot be usefully intercepted whilst in transit, but get access to Whatsapp's servers, where messages are decrypted, and everything will be laid bare. This of course also means that Whatsapp and by extension Facebook can also read, digest and analyze users' messages.

"Threema uses end-to-end encryption and enables users to verify the public keys of their conversation partners offline. Of course there is also a separate transport encryption layer to protect the header information (whom a message should be delivered to etc) in transit over the Internet," Threema's site continues.

Like Ello, Threema is a niche service for now, but just as mainstream social media help to define consumers' privacy expectations, the more new services which spring up offering something different, the greater the opportunity for the global conversation to change.

So do all these privacy violations amongst social media just mean that we see more advertising, or that yet more firms make a shady buck or two at our expense? Unfortuantely no, they also enable something far more dangerous.

IDENTITY THEFT

'When I was little my mother told me I can be whoever I want to be. Turns out that's called identity theft,' goes the well-known joke.

The dangers of social media don't stop at having personal data harvested and sold on. According to recent research published in USA Today, the economic damage of identity theft is now overtaking 'normal' physical theft, which is a frightening prospect. And besides the economic damage, feeling of violation and disruption it causes, it's also an incredibly hard thing to fix once it has happened.

"Most organizations have no way to turn back the consequences of identity theft," says Buytendijk. "Police have issues fixing their systems, so people, even when cleared, still get into trouble. And just about every commercial organization has an issue. The challenge I often pose is to figure out what one's core processes are, and ask the question whether they can handle a phone call from a customer who claims he or she didn't sign up for a mortgage/subscription/product/service or whatever it is the firm offers. Is it the customer's problem to prove? Can it even be rolled back? The answer is often 'no'."

Court records are filled with examples of identity theft, many of which involve the criminal filing false tax returns and claiming large rebates under the profiles they've stolen. The IRS lists hundreds of such cases each year on its website, even stating in some cases that the criminals managed to obtain victims' details "from the internet".

And the problems can go well beyond your taxes, financial records, or credit score. In 2003 Malcolm Byrd was at home with his children when three police officers knocked on his door. Despite his protestations that he was innocent and that they had the wrong man, Byrd was cuffed and put in jail, where he remained for two days while the legal machine processed his information and eventually uncovered that they had indeed got the wrong man. For Byrd, this was the latest in a long-running saga of unwelcome police attention since his identity had been stolen by a criminal five years earlier.

"This is the ultimate humiliation, the ultimate nightmare if you ask me," Jim Doyle, president of Internet Crimes Inc., and co-founder of the New York City Police Department's Computer Investigation and Technology Unit told NBC News at the time. "And it falls on the victim to clear up the criminal record."

Byrd's case was seemingly simple. In 1998 a man arrested on drugs charges identified himself as Malcolm Byrd. Reading about the incident in his local newspaper, the real Byrd went to the police to rectify the issue, and the newspaper even printed a correction. But despite those rapid attempts to fix the issue, Byrd was still being hounded by the authorities five years later.

If you wanted to design a tool designed to facilitate identity theft, you'd come up with something remarkably similar to a social network. Something which encourages people to freely tell the world not just where they live, work, shop, play and travel, but when, how and why. They'll include photos and even videos of themselves doing all of these things too, often unwittingly geo-stamped with precise locations too because it sounded fun when the feature first became available and they've never thought to go back and turn it off.

Geo-tagging adds a small packet of data to a file – often a photo – giving the precise location of the device at the time the file was created. It can show when you're not at home – useful information for burglars – or if you're posting a picture of valuable property inside your home, it can show where you live. Social network Foursquare in fact is based purely around telling friends (and potentially the whole world) where you are.

An app called 'Girls Around Me' appeared in early 2013. Almost unbelievably, its sole purpose was to show the locations of nearby females (males were also an option, but the default was women). Once activated, the app, after showing a tacky screen with silhouetted women appearing to pole dance in various stages of undress, displayed a map of the user's location, then populated it with points of interest. But rather than restaurants, or tourist attractions, those points of interest were women, their locations taken from Foursquare, and their details and photos lifted from Facebook. Again, if you were to design a service tailor-made for stalkers and rapists, this would be it.

The law has very little to say about this sort of activity. The app was doing nothing wrong, simply taking readily available Application Program Interfaces (APIs) from Facebook and Foursquare, and bundling the data into one form. Not only did it break no laws, it didn't even break the developer agreements with the mobile platforms for which it was created.

In fact Foursquare quickly blocked the app's access to its API data, thanks to the public outcry generated by various media stories at the time. The developers, i-Free, removed it from Apple's Appstore shortly thereafter, telling Apple news website Cult of Mac that it is: "…unethical to pick a scapegoat to talk about the privacy concerns. We see this wave of [negativity] as a serious misunderstanding of the app's goals, purpose, abilities and restrictions."

However, this response is hard to rationalise with the following statement about the app, which was displayed on i-Free's website when the app was live.

"In the mood for love, or just after a one-night stand? Girls Around Me puts you in control! Reveal the hottest nightspots, who's in them, and how to reach them… Browse photos of lovely local ladies and tap their thumbnail to find out more about them."

The app allowed users to find women in their area, perhaps in a local bar, and see their, name, interests, photos, school history and family details. It's not hard to imagine people using that information to pass as an old friend from school, and strike up a conversation about faked interests in common, with the victim unaware that the meeting is entirely planned and based on online stalking.

The fact that it existed at all demonstrates both the dangers of oversharing on social media, and the need for regulation.

In a further example of the dangers of sharing location information, photo sharing network Instagram enabled a violent burglary in Arkansas according to Sgt. Mike Blain of Pulaski County Sheriff's Office, speaking to US news channel THV11 in February 2015. "Someone had posted a photograph on Instagram, look at what I have," said Blain. "Look what I got for Christmas. And that post unfortunately led to a residential burglary where an altercation occurred and someone was harmed."

The very accessibility of this sort of data led to the creation of pleaserobme. com, a website which took data from Foursquare and Twitter to show vacant or temporarily unoccupied buildings potentially ripe for burglary. The website owners' intentions, so they claim, were not to incite crime, but to raise awareness of the dangers of oversharing. Whatever their original purpose however, the public outcry led to the site's functionality being removed, and instead it is now used to publish and link to articles related to online privacy.

One of the fundamental traits of social networks is that they allow people to connect to their acquaintances. That means that an aspiring identity thief or hacker can see who their potential victims' friends are, and what sort of relationships they have with them – friendly, romantic or professional.

Most people know enough not to post their bank details, social security number (in the US) or National Insurance number (in the UK) to social media, but many of the details they do willingly give up – often at the behest of the service itself – are equally valuable to identity thieves.

Information like:

- Full name
- Date of Birth
- Photo
- Address
- Relationship Status
- Education and career history
- Names of pets
- Interest and hobbies, including lists of favourite films and musicians

This is all gold dust to the identity thief. For a start it's potentially a great help in guessing what a user's password is for their social media account, or even their online banking application. 'But my banking service is protected by a series of security questions' you might think. And that's often true, but what are the answers to those security questions? Often they're your date of birth, home town, name of first school, or most recent pet. It's hard to imagine how much easier those guilty of over-sharing on social media could make it to be hacked, or to have their identities stolen.

It also leads to a hacking technique known as spear-phishing, which in turns leads us neatly into the murky world of hackers, and cyber crime.

References

http://www.statista.com/statistics/272014/global-social-networks-ranked-by-number-of-users/

O'Brien, Luke (November–December 2007). "Poking Facebook"

http://www.thecrimson.com/article/2010/11/19/according-facemashcom-photo-through/

http://www.thecrimson.com/article/2004/2/9/hundreds-register-for-new-facebook-website/

http://www.nytimes.com/2010/12/31/business/31twins.html?src=me&ref=homepage&_r=0

https://gigaom.com/2012/08/22/facebook-is-collecting-your-data-500-terabytes-a-day/

http://www.careerbuilder.com/share/aboutus/pressreleasesdetail.aspx?id=pr691&sd=4/18/2012&ed=4/18/2099

http://www.theguardian.com/technology/2010/jan/11/facebook-privacy

https://www.eff.org/deeplinks/2009/12/facebooks-new-privacy-changes-good-bad-and-ugly

http://techcrunch.com/2014/09/25/ello-ello-new-no-ads-social-network-ello-is-blowing-up-right-now/

http://contentmarketinginstitute.com/2015/02/ello-really-means-content-marketers/

http://www.cultofmac.com/157925/girls-around-me-dev-we-didnt-do-anything-wrong-statement/

http://www.eonetwork.org/octane-magazine/special-features/social-media-networks-facilitate-identity-theft-fraud

http://www.cs.virginia.edu/felt/privacy/

http://www.washingtonpost.com/news/the-intersect/wp/2014/10/29/almost-as-many-people-use-facebook-as-live-in-the-entire-country-of-china/

CHAPTER 6

Security, Spear Phishing and Social Engineering

The human brain actually works in a fairly rigid and defined way, certainly in adults. Whilst children's brains exhibit a certain amount of plasticity, that is the ability to learn and adapt to new situations and experiences, once a person reaches adulthood, the scope for variation has vastly diminished. And by and large that's a good thing, as it allows us to focus at being good at a few tasks.

"As you age, it changes who you are and how your brain works," explained security researcher Pete Herzog at the RVASec conference in Richmond, Virginia, in July 2014. "When you're tiny you have tons of connections and few neurons. When you get older you have loads of neurons and fewer connections. You get specialised. You get really good at one, two or three things. That's why you become the 'crotchety old man'. You just want to stay at home. You don't want to try new things. Basically you lose neural plasticity, and it gets harder to learn."

But more adaptable and 'plastic' thinking is very helpful in safeguarding your data, and thus your privacy, when confronted by a hacker, or group of hackers, who may attempt to manipulate you.

Herzog gave the example of a standard test which he said can be used to determine someone's ability to 'think outside the box', adding that it is often used as a recruitment exercise.

CONTENTS

PLASTIC THINKING TEST

You are in a room. There is a light bulb in front of you and it is on. There is a switch on the wall behind you. List 10 ways to shut off the light.

Try this test now, before reading on to see the answers. There is no right and wrong. Some people are more able to think differently and attack a problem from multiple angles than others. Fortunately, companies, and more broadly society, need all types of thinkers.

Herzog had the benefit of an entire audience full of security professionals to come up with some answers, like those listed here:

1. Switch off the light.
2. Get someone else to switch off the light.
3. Close your eyes.
4. Break the bulb.
5. Unscrew the bulb.
6. Don't pay your bill and wait for the electricity to be cut off.
7. Throw something over the bulb.
8. Cut the electricity cord.
9. Wait for the bulb to burn out.
10. Put it next to much brighter light source.

Although arguably the best answer, given by a member of the audience, was: "Get a bunch of marketing people in the room and redefine what 'light' means!"

"It's about thinking beyond," said Herzog. "Think how things are connected. Engineers talk about disrupting the photons, and there are a lot of different ways to shut off a light. Some people however just can't think beyond the regular, and they stop at two. It comes down to how you learn and think, how self-aware you are, and also your situational awareness, which itself comes down to whether you can be manipulated."

Ask a group of security professionals, law enforcers or possibly insurance investigators if they believe that they could be manipulated or defrauded, and they're all likely to say yes. That's because they all come into contact with hackers, con artists, scammers and other types of trickster, and have learnt that it's actually rather easy to predict or even drive someone's behaviour once you have a basic grasp of how the human brain works. But the ordinary person on the street doesn't usually have this experience, and so few believe themselves to be easy to defraud. According to Herzog, they are at 'amateur level'.

And he adds that the 'experts' can be easily defrauded, even when they know to be on their guard, once they are distracted. Pickpockets often operate in groups. One or two people act as lookouts, one person actually picks the target's pocket, whilst the final person is the distraction. This could be someone 'accidentally' walking into or otherwise bumping the target, then apologising, rather too profusely, and for rather too long. Whilst the target is making puzzled faces at the stranger mumbling on and on about how sorry he is, the crime is taking place entirely without their knowledge.

"You are not designed by default to be security aware," said Herzog. "You are not aware or even in control of your thoughts. You are a bag of hormones and disease making wants and needs."

Strong stuff. But hang on, we're not even in control of our thoughts now? Herzog is talking about the brain's 'autopilot' system, where certain familiar actions and processes happen by default.

"Have you ever driven to work and not remembered how you got there?" he asked the audience. "It's a default, you get distracted and you just don't remember it. This autopilot exists for everything you do. You have to stop to make a conscious decision. You have to think through options to know you're actually making the decision yourself, and even then sometimes the brain decides for you."

His point is that we are not in true command of our own minds, but rather – and without wishing to get too philosophical – our consciousness exists in a compartment of the mind. For instance, you can 'scream' silently in your own head. Some people might even feel their stomach muscles tighten as they do so. Or you can imagine the colour red, or the emotion love.

"How is this possible?" asked Herzog. "It happens because it's something you remember how to do. You watch a movie and you cried. It happened because something triggered you. It perhaps triggered a memory, and you were affected by that."

To illustrate the point further, here's another test. Picture a playing card, in full detail. Imagine the colour to its maximum possible extent – it's a bright, vibrant card. Picture the card, and remember it.

Many people will have pictured the King of Hearts. Or if not that specific card, the vast majority would have pictured another red face card – that is the Jack, Queen or King of Hearts or Diamonds. This is because of a manipulation technique called 'priming'. A few moments ago we mentioned the colour red, and the emotion love. Then the reader was asked to pick a card. Having pointed it out, the ruse is now obvious – but hidden amongst the distractions of trying to make sense of a fairly complicated philosophical point, it's all too easy to miss.

And it's this sort of manipulation that proves useful to groups who may exist on different sides of the law, but are nonetheless both very interested in your data. Hackers, and marketers.

"The truth is that if I'm a marketer and I only need one per cent of you to buy my product, this technique works very well. It works because you are not in control of your brains, you're influenced by your environment," said Herzog.

NOT A UNIQUE SNOWFLAKE AFTER ALL

In comedy group Monty Python's 1979 film 'Life of Brian', false and reluctant Messiah Brian tries to tell his followers that they don't need him, or indeed any leader, because they can fend for themselves.

"You're all different!" Shouts Brian. "Yes, we're all different!" Parrots the crowd, clearly still very much following him and happy to repeat whatever he says. "I'm not," claims one man, with his hand up.

It turns out that the man with his hand up was right, according to Herzog. "You are not unique or special," he said at RVASec. "You are like one of huge groups of people who all act the same way and fall for the same things. You are screwed," he added for comedic effect.

"You're going to say 'No, I'm special, my mom told me!' he continued. "But there are hundreds of thousands of years that make you not special, because all of those [evolutionary] changes leads to where you are now, compared to [a few decades of your life which might make you different]."

A good example is the game 'rock paper scissors'. Most people who could be classified as 'followers', which is a very significant proportion of the population, are likely to start a game with scissors. This group is people who have a favorite sports team, singer or band.

"It happens to be a correlation of the mind-set," explains Herzog. "People who band together or follow something almost always pick scissors first."

This fact that we have evolved to be so broadly similar also enables mind reading, after a fashion. This enables the horoscope industry, for one. There are many traits, habits and fears that are common to almost everyone. Herzog explained that you can name an aspirational trait (you are progressing well in your career), use a little flattery (you are more intelligent that most of your peers realise), and add a little piece about insecurity from which we all suffer (you're not always happy with the way people perceive you), and you can pretend to 'read' just about anyone.

Unfortunately, the fact that we are all so similar in many ways does not lead to good team working.

"You are not able to work well with others," said Herzog. "You like to think you can. You are designed primarily as a social animal, but despite that fraternization is the most mentally complicated thing you do."

There is nothing more tiring for the brain that being around and interacting with other people, especially at work.

"Your brain is always in high gear making sure you don't say the wrong thing to the wrong person," he added. "Sales people have it really tough as they have to be so careful about what they say and how they say it."

The problem is exacerbated by people's natural tendency to socialize when on a break. When you go for your coffee break, you chat to colleagues. If you're sitting, bored, at your desk, you chat. Herzog explains that this all contributes to mental fatigue, which most suffer at work. And he adds that the problem is worst of all in the US.

"Way too many American companies are actually being manipulated, attacked and defrauded. Part of problem is that America has one of the greatest number of overworked information workers. There's no way you work a standard 40-hour week. When I take a job here in the US, it's 60 or even 80 hours [per week] at first just to show how dedicated you are."

And it's impossible for workers to be able to combat hackers and fraudsters who already understand how to manipulate others, if they're too exhausted to spot the signs and make safe choices.

So what have we learnt so far? That it's surprisingly simple to get people to do what you want them to do, that people have limited control over their thoughts and actions, are running on autopilot much of the time, and to top it off, are mentally tired most of the time that they are at work.

It sounds like a 'perfect storm' – a confluence of phenomena - which together create a situation ideal for hackers and scammers. Let's have a look at some examples of how it works in real life.

TARGET BY NAME...

"Fazio Mechanical is... Refrigeration." That's the motto of the Pennsylvania-based firm Fazio Mechanical, which designs, builds, installs and maintains refrigeration units for large supermarket chains. Keeping fish fingers and other perishables cold is as much about energy saving as it is about maintaining the correct temperature as far as supermarkets are concerned. Electricity costs can be huge for large stores, so ensuring that systems and machines are running at optimal efficiency – day and night - is paramount for supermarkets which typically run on tight margins, and can ill-afford unnecessary expenditure, especially in the current climate of price wars between leading brands.

So firms like Fazio Mechanical don't just build and install refrigeration, they actively monitor the systems remotely, to ensure that they're only using as much power as absolutely necessary, and to get advanced warning of any potentially costly malfunctions. And the company doesn't just deal with frozen items, it also manages the heating and air conditioning systems for its clients.

The company is an expert in an industry known as HVAC – Heating, Ventilation and Air Conditioning.

In chapter three we found out just how much information the supermarkets know about us. In this chapter, we'll learn just how vulnerable that data is in their hands, and expand upon the massive cyber breach at US retail chain

Target mentioned earlier in this book. We'll also explain why we're briefly so interested in air conditioning.

On December 19th 2013 Target announced that it had suffered a data breach in which millions of customer records were stolen. It later transpired that the thieves had maintained access to Target's servers between November 27th and December 15th 2013, during which time they had downloaded details of around 40 million credit and debit cards belonging to the super-market's customers. Other information was taken too, including 70 million customer records containing names, addresses, email addresses and phone numbers.

For Target, this was catastrophic. In August 2014 it announced that it expected the breach to cost the company in the region of $148 million – still significant despite overall sales revenues of $72.6 billion for the year. On top of the financial loss, the firm also lost its CEO and Chief Information Officer (CIO), who were both sacrificed to appease investors and show the markets that the firm had 'taken action'. And on top of even that, there's the reputational damage to the Target brand, which has suffered enormous negative publicity follow-ing the breach, with a resultant erosion of customer trust (which was perhaps at least partly behind the firm's 46 per cent year on year drop in profits in the fourth quarter of 2013).

But how did it happen?

What's interesting is that the breach is now thought to have been entirely preventable, and that's not always the case in cyber security. Corporations, governments and even individuals are engaged in a constant, high-stakes game of cat and mouse with hackers, whether they're aware of it or not. Hackers – using the term broadly to cover everything from teenage boys in their bedrooms to well-funded state-sponsored professionals – use networks of compromised machines, known as bot-nets, to send out almost unthink-able quantities of spam (for example over 200 billion spam messages were sent in March 2014 according to Cisco), and also to 'rattle the front doors' of websites and corporate servers to test their security. They have vast numbers of other techniques too, but describing all of them would fill several vol-umes. The ultimate aim for most of their efforts though is to find out whose security is weakest, at which point they can break in and deface the site, take it offline for no reason beyond their own entertainment, steal information if there's anything valuable, or ignore it if it seems unlikely to hold anything of worth.

This is hacking at its most basic level, and the aim for those potentially being attacked is simply not to be the 'low hanging fruit'. In other words; don't be the softest target. Have at least some security measures, be it a correctly configured firewall, spam-filter on your email server, or properly set up identity and access management systems, and you'll largely escape from the mass trawling of the internet perpetrated by this sort of low-grade opportunistic attack.

What keeps Chief Information Security Officers (CISOs) and others in charge of corporate security awake at night is the other sort of attack – the specific, targeted kind. The prevailing view amongst cyber security professionals is that once a well-funded or skilled hacking group has decided that it wants to get inside your servers, then there's basically nothing you can do to stop them, besides locking the door, barring the windows, unplugging the internet and basically going out of business.

Fortunately most non-state hacking is financially motivated, as it was in the case with the Target attack. In this instance it's not necessary to attempt to make cyber intrusion impossible, just financially unviable. If it costs a hacker more in terms of effort and investment than the likely return will be once the desired information has been captured and sold on, then they'll give up and move on to a softer target.

There is another form of targeted attack, or rather, another source, and that's a targeted attack from another nation state. Perhaps the most well-known example was the 'Stuxnet' cyber-attack on Iran's nuclear programme, discovered in June 2010. The computer worm, designed to attack industrial programmable logic controllers, caused around a fifth of Iran's nuclear centrifuges to spin out of control and damage themselves, putting the nation's nuclear programme back several years. Stuxnet is thought to have been designed by Israeli and US teams, although at the time of writing no group has confirmed ownership for obvious political reasons.

The Windows flaw which allowed Stuxnet to function (which involved the way Windows handles the loading of DLL files) was swiftly patched by Microsoft in August 2010. However in March 2015 it was revealed that the patch failed to fully plug the vulnerability, when Microsoft released another patch to address the vulnerability. Assuming this fix actually works, that's at least five years during which Stuxnet was known and its operation not fully blocked.

It's tempting to cast this sort of state hacking to the side in the belief that it only affects the bad guys, and consumer privacy is unaffected by it, but that's a fallacy. For instance the Flame malware, discovered in 2012, attacks computers running Windows, and is used for cyber espionage purposes. It can record audio (including conversations over Skype), take screenshots, record key presses and network traffic. It can also turn infected machines into Bluetooth beacons which try to download contact data from other local Bluetooth-enabled devices. It was described by security firm Kaspersky Labs as "20 times more complex than Stuxnet".

The point is that governments are aware of the security holes via which these forms of malware (and there are many more which we don't have the time to go into here) operate, but they choose not to notify the security industry so that their malware continues to work. This leaves vulnerabilities out in the open for anyone to exploit, and creates an environment in which everyone with a device is insecure.

Back to the assault on Target, this was a targeted attack, but from a hacking group rather than a state. Had its network proved sufficiently resilient, the group would most like have moved on, and the company might never even have noticed the attempt. In fact, this is precisely what should have happened (although strictly speaking a diligent company should be monitoring attempted hacks too).

Six months before it was breached, Target invested $1.6 million on a sophisticated new security tool from a vendor called FireEye. This tool is designed to protect against advanced malware and other forms of cyber-attack, and also to notify network administrators once attacks have been caught. If set up properly, it could have automatically detected the malware used to infiltrate Target's network, and deleted it before any harm was done. The fact that it didn't is now believed to be because that functionality had been deliberately turned off by Target's security staff, as they weren't yet familiar with the new system, and didn't feel comfortable using all of its features.

If you were wondering why the CIO, the person with ultimate responsibility for technology within the company, was fired after the breach, then look no further. Having to admit that the network had been breached because the expensive and shiny new software designed to protect it hadn't yet been switched on must have been the low-point in Beth Jacob's 12 years at the retailer. In fact, what surprised most observers was that it took six months for Jacob to go.

The tool Target purchased is the same as that employed by organizations like the CIA and the Pentagon. Networks don't come with more stringent security requirements than those. The FireEye software is slightly different from certain other anti-malware solutions, in that it can react to new and unknown suspicious software in real-time, rather than relying on the more common practise of comparing suspected viruses with a database of known malware looking for matches. The problem with that technique is that a hacker need only make a very subtle alteration to a commonly available piece of malware in order for it to look new to an anti-virus database. Security vendors update these databases very regularly, but they are still essentially reactive, and all but useless against determined attackers.

Instead, FireEye creates a completely new and separate virtual network which mirrors the real system on which it is installed. When traffic arrives knocking on the door from the internet, it is shown in to the virtual network, rather than the actual live one in use by the organization. This means that the tool can look to see how the software behaves once it's let loose. If it turns out to be a plain old PDF with nothing nasty lurking within, then it can be released to its intended recipient. But if it starts writing directly to the servers' registries or attempting to get access where it shouldn't and send data back out to the internet, the administrators are notified and the software is kept well away from the real network.

Back to Fazio Mechanical. It was access privileges supplied to the HVAC firm which were used to gain access to Target's network. So one of the world's largest corporate hacks of all time was down to a refrigeration company.

After the breach, once Fazio's involvement became apparent, many sources reported that it was the firm's remote monitoring activities which had been behind its network access. However, the firm released a statement in February 2014 declaring that its network access was for billing, amongst other activities.

"Our data connection with Target was exclusively for electronic billing, contract submission and project management, and Target is the only customer for whom we manage these processes on a remote basis. No other customers have been affected by the breach," it reported on its website.

The fact that access details given out to Fazio Mechanical were stolen and subsequently used in the Target breach illustrates the security maxim 'you are only as secure as your supply chain'.

On 30th November 2013 the FireEye tool captured the first evidence of malware from the hackers, uploaded using the Fazio Mechanical credentials to gain access. The hackers proceeded to upload around five samples of malware in total, all of which were captured, with alerts sent to Target's administrators. The alerts were ignored. Again, it wasn't the systems to blame, but the people.

And the opportunities for responsible staff to notice and stop the breach before anything important was taken didn't stop there. Target also had Symantec Endpoint Protection, an anti-virus tool, installed on its network. It too detected the malware and sent alerts to administrators. These too were ignored.

In a third layer of protection, the company also had a team of security specialists in Bangalore actively monitoring its networks, looking for threats and suspicious activity. They too spotted the malware and sent the alert through to Target's own security team based in Minneapolis. Yet again, Target failed to respond.

The attack started slowly – and it could afford to, with all the notifications being ignored - with the hackers initially uploading their card-stealing software to just a few Target cash registers, and testing that it worked properly.

"By the end of the month — just two days later — the intruders had pushed their malware to a majority of Target's point-of-sale devices, and were actively collecting card records from live customer transactions," wrote security expert Brian Krebs on his blog.

The hackers managed to collect over 11 GB of data from 1,797 Target stores. Federal law enforcers discovered evidence of the breach on servers the hackers were using to transfer the data out of the US and across to Russia, and notified Target on 12th December. Three days later, Target made the breach public.

In its statement, Fazio Mechanical described the attack as a "sophisticated cyber-attack operation." But rather than being truly sophisticated, it appears from everything we now know about the breach that the malware itself wasn't especially well engineered; rather the breach happened because nobody at Target bothered to stop it.

In fact Bloomberg quoted McAfee director of threat intelligence operations Jim Walter as describing the malware as "absolutely unsophisticated and uninteresting."

In short the breach happened because Target was careless. And being careless about its security effectively means that it was careless with its customer data.

But there's still a piece of the jigsaw missing. We know that the hackers managed to get access to Target's network by stealing credentials from one of its sub-contractors, but how did they make that first step towards the eventual breach?

Whilst that information hasn't yet been made public, and the FBI, who investigated Fazio Mechanical in the wake of the breach certainly aren't telling, reports have surfaced suggesting that an email malware attack was carried out on the HVAC supplier several months before the Target breach. Krebs suggested on his blog that the malware in question was Citadel, a fairly common hacking tool designed to steal network passwords.

With the Target breach serious enough to arouse the interest of the FBI, it's unsurprising that Fazio itself went on the defensive, and made a statement that its "system and security measures are in full compliance with industry practices."

However, Krebs cites investigators in the case who apparently said that the firm had nothing more sophisticated protecting itself from cyber-attack than the free version of Malwarebytes Anti-Malware. Whilst this particular tool can scan for threats when manually requested by the user, it doesn't provide protection in real-time, and is actually prohibited from corporate use by the terms of its license agreement.

If that's true, then Fazio's systems and security measures were entirely inadequate, and certainly not in compliance with industry practices.

So that's how the hackers obtained initial access to Target's network, probably via its external billing or project management system. But getting to sensitive data like customer credit card information from there is quite a leap, especially given that it's good practice to segregate a network according to the sensitivity of the data it handles, for precisely this reason. Having access to the external-facing partner billing system shouldn't also allow access to the point of sale systems. So either Target's network was very poorly or not at all segregated, the hackers obtained additional access credentials from somewhere else, or they managed to escalate their access privileges via Active Directory (a Microsoft directory service which handles authentication and security policies for Windows-based networks).

The point of all this is that we already know how supermarkets play fast and loose with customer data in an attempt to encourage them to spend more money in their stores; now we see how vulnerable that data is to anyone with half a mind to go and grab it for themselves.

The further problem is the overcollection of data by supermarkets. By collecting and holding more of our data than they actually need, they do us even more of a disservice when they fail to adequately protect it.

And what happens to the data once it's in the nefarious hands of the cyber criminals? Usually it gets sold on in shady cyber markets to the highest bidder (or indeed simply anyone prepared to meet the asking price). According to reports, the hackers made in the region of $53.7 million from selling around 1-3 million of their haul of customer cards (apparently the average price for a viable stolen credit card at the time was $26.85). The rest of the cards were cancelled by their respective banks before they could be used for fraud, but by any measure, a return of nearly $60 million must count as a wildly successful job for the hackers.

Whilst we're discussing the financial impact of the heist, it's worth mentioning that it also cost banks over $240 million to replace the stolen cards, though the banks would have been able to recoup at least some of this from Target. And Target's costs don't stop there, ousting their CEO, Gregg Steinhafel – who 'stepped down' according to the official line – cost the firm another $55 million.

All in all, a lot of people were left wishing someone had switched on the shiny new security software.

PHISHING, WITH OR WITHOUT A SPEAR

All of this massive tsunami of financial loss started with some simple malware sent by email to Fazio Mechanical. It's likely that this was part of a large-scale spam campaign from the hacking group, hoping for a high value target to click on their link, or download their attachment. Luckily for the criminals, someone did.

Hackers motivate people to open their messages by posing as legitimate organizations, or people. Anyone with an email account will be familiar with the tide of spam that fills their junk folder, purporting to be from their bank, mortgage provider, or even online gaming network. The best examples of these messages are very hard to distinguish from the real thing, since it's not terribly hard to copy and paste an organization's logo into an email, use appropriate language, and obfuscate a link. The last point is crucial, since many consumers are not sufficiently savvy to realise that what appears to be www.bbc.co.uk actually directs the user to www.yourebeinghacked.com. The canny user will know to 'mouse over' the link, which in most browsers will reveal the actual URL that the link will direct it to, however this functionality doesn't exist in most mobile browsers. Given that internet traffic is rapidly migrating from laptops and desktops to mobile devices (with around 60 per cent of web traffic now coming from mobile devices as of June 2014 according to Comscore), this failsafe is becoming less effective.

This technique of faking a legitimate email is called Phishing. It started on US media firm AOL, with hackers attempting to pass themselves off as support staff in order to steal passwords and account information from other users.

For example: 'Hello, this is the AOL helpdesk. Please enter your username and password below in order to verify your account' is the sort of message they might have sent.

Once they'd successfully hacked into an account, it would then be used to commit fraud, or to send out spam. It became so prevalent that in the mid-1990s, AOL added a subscript to all instant messages which stated: "No one working at AOL will ask for your password or billing information", a message which is common in most corporate communications to consumers today.

Phishing got its name from the common HTML tag '<><' which appeared in almost all early AOL chat transcripts. Hackers at the time used those characters to replace terms like 'hacking' 'spamming' or any other words likely to be filtered by AOL's security staff in order to find criminal activity. Since '<><' appeared naturally in every transcript, it was completely unusable as a search term. Phishing's stylized spelling came from the term 'phreaking', where hackers learnt how to abuse the intricacies of telecommunications networks to obtain free long-distance calls, among other things (a practice enjoyed by no lesser luminaries than Apple founders Steve Jobs and Steve Wozniak in their youth).

The basic format of email malware is plain spam, for example it could be an email asking you to click a link for access to cheap Viagra. Phishing, being slightly more sophisticated, purports to come from a legitimate source, with the more advanced examples being hard to distinguish from the real thing, and the cruder variants being poorly spelled and thrown together.

Today phishing is used to do everything from spy on you, to harvesting your details, by both individual hackers and nation states. The phishing attempt could be embedded within a Word document, a PDF file attached to a message, a malicious link, remotely loaded image, or from a faked website. The ways in which you can be infected by malware are seemingly endless, and are still growing.

RSA SECURITY DISCOVERS IT'S NOT VERY SECURE

If there's one industry which definitely doesn't want to be very publicly hacked, it's the cyber security industry itself. Even more so that the finance industry, which of course trades on trust and reliability, the security experts have no business model to speak of if they can't even protect themselves.

Unfortunately for RSA Security, a division of storage firm EMC but a major security firm in its right, a famous example of a successful phishing attack, and one which also involved aspects of social engineering, happened at its expense in March 2011. A hacking group sent phishing emails with the subject "2011 Recruitment Plan" to two specially selected groups of employees. That's a nice generic title which could appear relevant in just about any corporation. Most firms run security training as standard for their employees, and one of the first rules is don't open email attachments if you're not completely sure you know who the sender is. Unfortunately for RSA, that's exactly what one of the employees did.

Is this surprising? Given what we know about humans running on autopilot and being mentally tired purely by being at work, we have to say: no. However, you'd be right to expect better from a security firm.

The email sending address was obfuscated, or 'spoofed' in hacking parlance, to appear to come from a "web master" at Beyond.com, a recruitment website. The message itself contained just one line of text: "I forward this file to you for review. Please open and view it."

It also had an attachment, an Excel file, which on the face of it isn't terribly suspicious. However, when opened, the spreadsheet triggered an embedded Adobe Flash player exploit – a previously unknown or 'zero day' vulnerability in fact – which then installed a backdoor known as 'Poison Ivy' on that user's machine.

With the machine successfully under his thrall (most hackers being male, we're going to assume this wasn't an exception for now), the cyber criminal was then able to install further malware without anyone at RSA noticing. This enabled him access to more of the machine's systems and files, which allowed him to gather usernames and passwords for several other company tools, which in turn gave him access to other employees with access to more sensitive corporate data.

The final stage of the attack was to copy the data over to the hacker's own servers, which is harder that it sounds, with most large corporations actively monitoring for unusual patterns of data movement both within and without the organization's boundaries. However, that's exactly what the hacker did, uploading the sensitive data to another compromised machine at a hosting provider, and then on to the hacker's own system from there.

A couple of weeks after the attack, RSA Security uploaded a blog to its website giving its version of events, some of which genuinely gave us more insight into what had happened, whilst other parts simply attempted to justify the breach.

What's interesting in the blog is where it discusses the use of social media in determining the right targets at RSA, and how to persuade them to open the malicious file.

"The first thing actors like those behind the APT [Advanced Persistent Threat] do is seek publicly available information about specific employees – social media sites are always a favorite. With that in hand they then send that user a Spear Phishing email. Often the email uses target-relevant content; for instance, if you're in the finance department, it may talk about some advice on regulatory controls."

This illustrates both sides of the blog. It explains a little more around how the attackers managed to get inside such a well-protected network, but also describes the malware used as an APT.

If you asked ten different security experts to define APT, you'd probably end up with around 12 different explanations. But the gist is that it's a network attack where the hacker maintains the breach for a length of time, with the intent to steal data rather than simply deface a website or otherwise cause damage.

It's a marketing buzzword, designed to make technology budget holders believe that there's a good reason to get their corporate wallets out when the security firms come calling. In this instance it's designed to make us believe that there is little or nothing that RSA could have done to avoid the breach, so sophisticated and ingenious was the attack.

The blog continues: "When it comes to APTs it is not about how good you are once inside, but that you use a totally new approach for entering the organization. You don't bother to just simply hack the organization and its infrastructure; you focus much more of your attention on hacking the employees.

"One cannot stress enough the point about APTs being, first and foremost, a new attack doctrine built to circumvent the existing perimeter and endpoint defenses. It's a little similar to stealth air fighters: for decades you've based your air defense on radar technology, but now you have those sneaky stealth fighters built with odd angles and strange composite materials. You can try building bigger and better radars, or, as someone I talked to said, you can try staring more closely at your existing radars in hope of catching some faint signs of something flying by, but this isn't going to turn the tide on stealthy attackers. Instead you have to think of a new defense doctrine."

Whilst it's true that as security technology has improved, the human element has become the softest target in many cases, not everyone agrees that this particular attack was really so unique and special.

Jeremiah Grossman, founder of WhiteHat Security, said on Twitter at the time: "I can't tell if this RSA APT blog post is actually being serious or an April 1st gag. The content is absurd either way."

This attack employed elements of social engineering, a technique which goes beyond phishing in terms of both its complexity and success rates, and it involves using the very information we talked about in the last chapter – the information we give out freely over social media.

If your goal is to entice someone to visit your website, where you'll download malware onto their machine, imagine how much more success you're likely to have if you can convince that person that you're a friend or acquaintance. It's actually not that hard in most cases, but it does involve more effort than the standard spam message rolled out in its millions.

In the last chapter we discussed 'Girls Around Me', which allowed the sort of people desperate enough to download an app to help them con a potential partner into going home with them to find out all manner of personal details about their prey to enable the trick. This has much in common with social engineering attacks.

A hacking group might decide to target an individual responsible for server administration at the firm whose data they're interested in. After tracking that person on social media for a few days, they can build up a pretty accurate picture of his or her likes, dislikes and habits, as well as map of their recent activities. It's then a fairly simple job for someone to approach the target and pass themselves off as a casual acquaintance. For example they could refer to a recent golf tournament in which they know the target participated, claiming perhaps to be a friend of a friend met at the event. They would know the target's interests, and should, with a little social skill, be able to strike up a rapport. This could all happen in person or even over email or social media, over days, weeks or even months.

Once the target's confidence has been gained, the scam moves on to the next level. Early on in the relationship our hacker would have claimed to work for a supplier, partner or customer, perhaps even faking up a LinkedIn account, or other social media presence to legitimise the lie. Then the hacker calls the target discussing some urgent problem, asking for access to a certain system to solve it. And it would be a system which the hacker would legitimately have a need to access, if he really did work the organization he claimed to, and it wouldn't sound like an unreasonable request to the target, who has no reason to be suspicious of his or her new friend.

So the hackers obtain their access, worth potentially millions of dollars, depending on the nature of the information the target firm is guarding, and all it has cost them is a little time.

In his book 'Social Engineering: The Art of Human Hacking', penetration tester Christopher Hadnagy describes how he used social engineering techniques to hack his way into the servers of a printing firm who had employed him to test its security. The CEO of the company was confident that he at least would be impervious to any attempts to mine him for information, saying that "hacking him would be next to impossible" since he "guarded his secrets with his life."

Evidently the CEO hadn't attended a presentation by Pete Herzog, otherwise he'd be aware of absurdity of that claim.

In the book Hadnagy describes the CEO as someone who thought of himself as "never going to fall for this." "He was thinking someone would probably call and ask for his password and he was ready for an approach like that," he added.

Hadnagy performed some fairly simple internet searching, and quickly found server locations, email and physical addresses, IP addresses and various other types of data on the company. But this wasn't enough information to be able to pass himself off as someone with an existing relationship with the firm, and from there to go about conning someone into giving him server access.

But that changed when he learnt from social media that a member of the CEO's family was in remission from cancer. This was the breakthrough he had been waiting for.

Hadnagy called the chief executive and claimed to be raising cash for a cancer-related charity. He had already discovered the CEO's favorite sports team and restaurant from Facebook, and used that information in the ruse – offering vouchers for those restaurants and tickets to see that team as prizes as part of the fundraising. It was the perfect way to hook the target and reel him in.

With his emotional triggers successfully pulled, the CEO sensed nothing awry. He gave Hadnagy his email address so he could send him a PDF with more information on the fundraising, even going so far as to give out his exact version of Adobe reader: "I want to make sure I'm sending you a PDF you can read," Hadagny told him.

If you want to send a piece of malware to someone which exploits a loophole in part of the Adobe suite of software – as in the RSA Security breach – then knowing the version they're using is incredibly helpful, it means you know exactly which piece of malware will work.

The CEO opened the file, the malware was installed, and as simply as that, Hadagny had access to his machine. The unhackable CEO had been hacked.

"He felt it was unfair we used something like that," said Hadnagy. "But this is how the world works. A malicious hacker would not think twice about using that information against him."

YOU ARE SCREWED

Herzog was fond of adding the line 'you are screwed' to his statements in his presentation, and given what we've seen in this chapter about the frailties of the human mind, and ingenuity and persistence of hackers, we could be forgiven for agreeing with him.

Our private data is held by countless firms all over the world, gleaned from more sources than we could guess at. Many of these firms have poor security technology and practises, and as we've seen, even those whose very business is security are still unable to keep out the determined hacker.

And on top of that, many of us freely give up much of this information over social media, which can itself be used against us to trick us into unlocking what few secrets both we, and the organizations we work for have left.

So what can do? What can organizations do to protect themselves, and help us to help them?

One answer is to improve corporate security awareness training. In most firms this training, where it happens at all, constitutes an hour in a meeting room within the first month of employment and that's it, forever. A security person will tell staff not to open suspicious emails, maybe hand over a mouse mat branded with 'I'm secure!' or similar on it, and the lesson will be forgotten by the time the employee has had his or her next coffee break.

A better solution is to make security training a regular activity, with frequent tests and exercises given to staff. And these don't even have to be security-related tests – a brain teaser is a good start. It just needs to be something to engage the employee's mind, and make force that person to come out of autopilot.

Some organizations go further, and send out phishing emails of their own to their staff. When someone opens the compromised attachment, instead of installing malware onto their machine, it makes a message pop up telling them about their mistake and reminding them of their cyber duties.

Herzog recommends that firms allow their staff to report suspicious activity anonymously, as people will inevitably make mistakes, and could be reluctant to report the potentially disastrous results for fear or incriminating themselves.

"Firms need a way [for staff to] anonymously contact security departments to say something is wrong, with no reprisals. They went on a site they shouldn't, they took a call they shouldn't, they opened an attachment they shouldn't. They need to be able to tell you that something went wrong."

After all, if a firm is facing a security breach which will quickly cost it hundreds of millions of dollars and destroy its reputation, what's more important? To find and stop the breach, or to shout at a member of staff?

As for consumers, a good start would be to share much less information on social media, and to regularly check privacy settings. Does the whole world really need to know every last detail about you?

If the answer to that last question is 'yes', then you might just have to resign yourself to a lifetime of risk. Or you might believe that you're perfectly well protected by the law. If you'd rather not be disabused of this notion, you might want to skip the next chapter...

References

http://krebsonsecurity.com/2014/05/the-target-breach-by-the-numbers/

http://krebsonsecurity.com/2014/02/target-hackers-broke-in-via-hvac-company/

http://bgr.com/2014/03/13/target-data-hack-how-it-happened/

http://blogs.cisco.com/security/spam-hits-three-year-high-water-mark

http://blog.credit.com/2014/02/target-data-breach-cost-banks-240-million-76636/

http://www.usatoday.com/story/money/business/2014/05/05/ousted-target-ceo-to-collect-millions/8719471/

http://www.comscore.com/Insights/Blog/Major-Mobile-Milestones-in-May-Apps-Now-Drive-Half-of-All-Time-Spent-on-Digital

https://blogs.rsa.com/anatomy-of-an-attack/

https://www.schneier.com/blog/archives/2011/08/details_of_the.html

Social Engineering: The Art of Human Hacking, Christopher Hadnagy

https://www.youtube.com/watch?v=gz3UHYKTxq0

CHAPTER 7

Privacy and the Law

The law has a tough time with privacy. For a start it's not entirely sure that it knows what the term means. In his 1878 work 'A Treatise on the Law of Torts or the Wrongs Which Arise Independently of Contract', Judge Thomas Cooley defined privacy as: 'the right to be let alone'.

Almost a century later, in 1973, the Younger Committee (set up by the UK government in order to consider whether legislation was needed to protect individuals and organizations from privacy intrusions) report refused to define the term at all, arguing that any legal definition would be too specific, and therefore limiting.

"Law can have an effect in influencing behaviour in a particular direction over and above its function in penalising breaches of the law. Its declaratory function would be particularly important in an area like that of privacy, where pragmatic considerations are likely otherwise heavily to influence journalists and broadcasters in particular. It must in fairness be recorded that the British Council of Churches, in its evidence, considered that there was a danger that once the right of privacy is legally defined, society's conception of it may thereby be limited to what comes within the legal definition and assume that what falls outside the scope of the law is necessarily to be tolerated."

And then in 1990 the Calcutt Committee on Privacy and Related Matters (so-called because it was chaired by Sir David Calcutt QC, the Committee was created following UK MP's calls for curbs on press freedom, and increased press regulation) concluded that: "nowhere have we found a wholly satisfactory statutory definition of privacy."

Campaign group Privacy International defines privacy as "a fundamental right, essential to autonomy and the protection of human dignity, serving as the foundation upon which many other human rights are built." It continues: "…privacy is an essential way we seek to protect ourselves and society against arbitrary and unjustified use of power, by reducing what can be known about us and done to us, while protecting us from others who may wish to exert control."

CONTENTS

This is further than the law has ever gone (at least in the UK and US) to define it, however, the need to protect privacy by law has long been recognized.

In 1981 the Council of Europe Data Protection Convention, which amongst other influences came out of the recommendations of the Younger Committee, established a consensus which included the automatic handling of personal information, and contained guidelines for the safeguarding and control of data stored and processed digitally. It also made the processing of sensitive personal data (relating to topics including race, politics, health, religion, sex life, and criminal record) illegal, in the absence of proper statutory safeguards. "Particularly important was the way in which the Convention dealt with cross-border transfers for information," writes the Centre for Information Rights Law on its website. "It provided that only countries with data protection laws equivalent to those set out in the Convention could ratify the Convention. Data could be transferred freely between ratifying countries, but could only be transferred to other countries under restrictions. The Convention also enshrined the individual's right to know that information is stored about him, and the right to have it corrected where necessary," it adds.

This in turn caused the UK government to introduce the Data Protection Act in 1984, as it feared that without new legislation it would fail to meet the standards as set out by the convention, and thus would be unable to transfer certain types of data.

This Act gave individuals the right to know if an organization was processing their personal data, and to be able to request a copy of that information. It also established the office of the Data Protection Registrar (now the Information Commissioner's Office), with the job of enforcing the legislation.

Many other countries around Europe developed their own data protection legislation around the same time, often with very different rules and ways of enforcing them. This prompted the European Commission to produce a draft directive in 1990 in an attempt to harmonize rules across the EU, and facilitate the free movement of data across the region. Unfortunately, few things in the world move slower than Brussels-based bureaucrats, and the draft directive didn't find formal approval until 1995, with member states permitted a further three years to put it into practise. This resulted in the UK replacing its 1984 legislation with the Data Protection Act 1998.

Whilst newer privacy-related legislation has been enacted since then, this Act, 17-years old at the time of writing, still forms the basis of privacy and data protection law in the UK. In 1998, the internet was still in its infancy and largely consisted of brochure-ware, public data collection was largely performed by census and questionnaires, and mobile phones where the size of bricks and used almost exclusively for talking.

It's small wonder that many complain that the law is no longer fit for purpose. Speaking at an event given by the Royal Society in London entitled 'Can our online lives be private?', Christopher Millard, Professor of Privacy and Information Law and head of the Cloud Legal Project in the Centre for Commercial Law Studies, Queen Mary University of London, said: "The law is a bit of a mess. By the time it gets to data, it's completely obsolete. The same principles are used today as in the 1970s. The core principles are sound, but a bureaucratic nightmare has evolved around them."

So that's the rather sorry picture in the UK, what about the US, how has it historically approached privacy?

In the US privacy concerns grew out of an increasing fear of media intrusion – the very same anxiety which gave rise to the Calcutt report across the pond. In 1884, Eastman Kodak, a firm which we may know better simply as 'Kodak', introduced the first cheap, mass market camera, the Kodak Brownie. The fact that reporters, and indeed anyone, could now take clandestine photographs of people in public places, together with the growing sensationalist and tabloid press at the time, was the catalyst for change. In 1890, Samuel Warren and Louis Brandeis, both young, ambitious lawyers, wrote an article for the Harvard Law Review entitled 'The Right to Privacy'.

In it, they explained the need for explicit privacy laws.

"The press is overstepping in every direction the obvious bounds of propriety and of decency. Gossip is no longer the resource of the idle and of the vicious, but has become a trade, which is pursued with industry as well as effrontery. To satisfy a prurient taste the details of sexual relations are spread broadcast in the columns of the daily papers....The intensity and complexity of life, attendant upon advancing civilization, have rendered necessary some retreat from the world, and man, under the refining influence of culture, has become more sensitive to publicity, so that solitude and privacy have become more essential to the individual; but modern enterprise and invention have, through invasions upon his privacy, subjected him to mental pain and distress, far greater than could be inflicted by mere bodily injury."

Legal scholar Roscoe Pound later said that it did "nothing less than add a chapter to our law". Its influence has proved to be enduring; in 1966 legal writer Harry Kalven described it as the "most influential law review article of all", and in 2001 it was even cited by both sides in the Supreme Court case of Kyllo v. United States.

Indeed, reading the Brandeis and Warren article today, there is much which is still relevant, perhaps especially this sentence, which now seems startlingly prescient:

"Now that modern devices afford abundant opportunities for the perpetration of such wrongs without any participation by the injured party, the protection granted by the law must be placed upon a broader foundation".

You could utter the same sentence today at a conference on law, techno-logy and privacy, and elicit a tidal wave of sage nodding and intelligent frowning.

So the law has been slow to adapt to modern times, we'll come back to that point shortly. But how does the current outmoded legislation get put into prac-tise? The task of enforcing it in the UK falls on the Information Commissioner, Christopher Graham, and his 383 staff.

Perhaps surprisingly, Graham's greater concern is implementing law across in-ternational boundaries, rather than worrying about outdated rules.

"The basic Data Protection Act framework is fine, we don't have problems with the principles, it's all in the implementation," he says.

"We have to try to make things work in the face of global companies and technologies delivering global services. I'm hot on finding points of contact and leverage between the US and European legal systems to make things work for citizens and consumers. For example we work with the FTC, so that although the law is different, we can get points of leverage between the two systems."

Graham adds that with the US better equipped legally to hit companies where it hurts – in their pockets - he likes to bring in his American colleagues in in-ternational cases.

"I remember hearing Peter Fleischer from Google [the firm's global privacy counsel] a couple of years ago saying that what keeps him awake at night is EU regulations and US enforcement. We shamelessly bring in FTC who can impose eye-watering fines, which has major effect in protecting privacy. Boy do they make you pay!"

He describes a recent settlement made with photo-sharing service Snapchat, which in 2014 was found to be storing its users images without their consent, following a breach.

"Snapchat will now be audited for 20 years on pain of massive fines. The most I can fine anyone for the most serious breaches is half a million pounds. Whilst that's quite a lot, if you're dealing with Google, Facebook or Apple they don't take too much notice of that, it's neither here nor there. The FTC wouldn't cross the road for half a million pounds or dollars."

COMPARING THE US AND UK PRIVACY LAWS

So we've established that firms are liable to be hit with larger fines should they infringe privacy laws in the US, than the UK, but how else do the two systems differ?

Andrew Dyson, partner at law firm DLA Piper explains that the UK operates under legislation which governs basically everything, where in the US the laws are divided by sector, and even by state.

"The formal regulatory regimes are quite different [between the US and UK]," says Dyson. "The UK adopts a comprehensive privacy framework under the Data Protection Act which seeks to regulate all forms of personal data, with enhanced protection offered to certain categories of particularly 'sensitive' information like health, criminal record, religious belief, and political allegiance. By contrast, US privacy laws regulate information collected and used in particular sectors (for example healthcare, financial services and children), regulate particular types of marketing (such as telemarketing, text, fax and email marketing), and around broader legal principles of consumer law protection. On the other hand, the US regulates information security and security breach notice more extensively than does the UK."

And the approach is mirrored in the enforcement models adopted by the two countries. The Information Commissioner's Office enforces the Data Protection Act in the UK, and it is able to fine firms up to £500,000 (around $746,000), though the actual penalties are often significantly lower. However, where the breach involves an organization regulated by the Financial Conduct Authority – which means it's likely to be a financial institution of some form – fines can be larger as the FCA has no such cap to its levies.

"We have seen a handful of fines in the order of £2m or more in recent years," adds Dyson.

In the US there are various different enforcement methods, though violations are generally handled by the FTC, State Attorneys General, or the regulator for the industry in question.

"Civil penalties can be significant," explains Dyson. "In addition, some privacy laws (for example, credit reporting privacy laws, electronic communications privacy laws, video privacy laws, call recording laws, cable communications privacy laws) are enforced through class action lawsuits for significant statutory damages and attorney's fees. Defendants can also be sued for actual damages for negligence in securing personal information such as payment card data, and for surprising and inadequately disclosed tracking of consumers. The FTC has used this authority to pursue companies that fail to implement minimal data security measures or fail to live up to promises in privacy policies. For most FTC enforcement actions, there are no monetary penalties for a first violation, but the company is required to establish a privacy governance structure, to avoid similar violations in the future, and to submit to compliance audits over a 20 year period."

THE NEED FOR COLLABORATION

Of course there are many other jurisdictions in the world, most of whom have their own privacy laws, regulators, and methods of enforcement (though one of the reasons that the EU data protection and privacy laws are so important is that they are widely followed and therefore set the global norms).

Graham emphasises the need for these various data protection authorities around the world – not just in the UK and US - to work together. There is an international enforcement co-ordination effort going on out of the public eye which is attempting to put a framework in place to enable this collaboration. It found some success in late 2014 when a Russian website was found to be live-streaming broadcasts from consumer web-cams around the world. Consumers were purchasing web-cams and installing them either with no password protection, or simply leaving the devices with the factory-installed security settings, which to even a basic hacker is functionally the same thing. Without a co-operating framework in place, it would have been next to impossible for the privacy enforcement authorities to stop the activity, because so many different territories were involved. Basically, they would have been so bound up in red tape as to be utterly ineffective.

"There was a Russian website live-streaming from unprotected webcams that was registered in Australian territory, with a domain name bought in the US, which was streaming the very private business of consumers. The [UK-based] ICO, the Canadian Privacy Commissioner, the FTC and the Australian authorities worked with authorities in Hong Kong and Macau to have the whole operation stopped by working effectively together."

IS THE EU "MAKING A FOOL OF ITSELF"?

It's comforting to hear that the privacy enforcement bodies of various nations are getting together to adopt a pragmatic approach to their work. But nevertheless, that doesn't change the fact that the law badly needs updating, in the EU especially. Although he describes himself as comfortable with the basic data protection framework already in place, Graham is still frustrated at the pace of the reforms, though he does concede that the process is finally picking up pace.

"It hasn't happened quickly enough," he states. "We've been up a blind alley for much of past three or four years with very theoretical debates about rather obtuse fundamental rights, but it is getting a move on now. Having said that, even if the reforms are completed by end of year, they won't be implemented until 2017 so it's still not happening quickly. There needs to be a sense of urgency or the EU will make a fool of itself."

Graham was speaking to the author at the end of 2014. At the time of writing – mid 2015 – the reforms were still not complete. Given that member states will be given three years to implement the necessary changes, and usually they take every available month on offer to push through such legislative reforms, the law won't be updated until late 2018 at the earliest.

The reforms were actually close to being finalized in 2013, but were paused and then severely delayed by the Snowden revelations, which necessitated a broad re-think. Then, around the same time, German chancellor Angela Merkel believed that her phone had been bugged by security agencies (as a result of a claim made in a document allegedly from the Snowden trove, though doubts as to its authenticity have subsequently emerged), and made many public statements about the need for privacy. Ironically, her government and various EU leaders decided to pass on finalizing the new data protection laws at almost exactly the same time.

Even the EU itself appears to recognize the need to hurry. On January 28th 2015, which was the 9th annual European Data Protection Day in case that event wasn't marked in your calendar, it released a statement which included the following: "We must conclude the ongoing negotiations on the data protection reform before the end of this year. By the 10th European Data Protection Day, we are confident that we will be able to say that the EU remains the global gold standard in the protection of personal data."

The reform is twofold. It consists of a draft Regulation which provides the basic framework for data protection, and a draft Directive whose purpose the EU describes as: "…protecting personal data processed for the purposes of prevention, detection, investigation or prosecution of criminal offences and related judicial activities."

It was first proposed in January 2012, so it had already taken three years just to get to what are hopefully now the final round of discussions between the two EU co-legislators, the European Parliament and the Council of the EU.

Information Commissioner Christopher Graham continues to discuss the nature of some of the proposed rules, as he feels that they give him too little room to exercise his judgement – especially the proposal that every single breach of data protection regulations should be met with a fine, however small.

"I don't like the prescriptive nature of the legislation in terms of the process for Data Protection authorities [such as the ICO]. It's not helpful to decree that I must issue a fine for every breach, I need discretion to take risk and proportionality into account. I've personally been told by the European Commission that I only actually need to fine one Euro, but that's ridiculous! We'll be tied up in knots, and organizations will challenge us legally. It's a misapplication of our resources, there ought to be a risk-based approach. We should put our effort into making sure that everyone understands the rules, then jump on the breaches which cause the most damage, or where people have been behaving badly."

So besides spending years debating with one another over the minutia of legal reforms, how do governments decide how to update legislation in complex areas like data protection? One way is by consulting with industry.

There are two schools of thought around this methodology. One holds that of course governments and the EU must consult industry around the rules that will be imposed on them. That way they stand more chance of being practical and enforceable. Industry will also be more prepared to buy in to the regulation if they've been involved in its conception.

The other line of thinking is that of course industry wants to be involved in the rule-making; so that it can ensure it's as broad and unrestricting as possible. And the rule-makers have proved themselves in the past to be highly susceptible to demands from business, even going so far as to copy and paste changes to data protection laws directly from the recommendations of Amazon and eBay, amongst others. Privacy pressure group Lobbyplag was initially set up to track this activity and make the public aware of it, and in March 2015 it was involved in the leaking of many classified EU documents which revealed the extent to which various governments are attempting to weaken the new data protection legislation as it crawls through Parliament.

Lobbyplag found that 132 of 151 (87 per cent) changes by EU member states lowered privacy requirements. Germany was revealed to be leading the field in terms of seeking weaker privacy rules, despite its many strong public statements to the contrary. Berlin had proposed 73 amendments, only 11 of which are pro-privacy. Next in the hall of shame is the UK, which has tabled 49 anti-privacy proposals.

This torrent of anti-privacy activity watering down EU data protection laws is a direct result of lobbying by huge, well-funded technology corporations.

Green MEP Eva Lichtenberger called it "one of the biggest lobby wars of all times". Commissioner Viviane Reding, who initially proposed the legislation, described the lobbying as "absolutely fierce – I have not seen such a heavy lobbying operation". Another Green MEP, Jan Philipp Albrecht, described the pressure as coming from "a wish list of companies that do not pursue harmonization of data protection in the EU, but complete deregulation."

But what's the story from industry's side? One firm heavily involved in discussions with the EU about the new rules is data broker Acxiom. Dr Sachiko Scheuing, European privacy officer at the firm, explains that her company has been involved in advising European legislators in the current discussions.

"We try to engage ourselves in dialogue with lawmakers and with regulators," begins Scheuing. "They are specialists in law, but detached from what's really happening on the ground, or what's happening on the computer of a data scientist. We go to the lawmakers to explain what we do and how, and in this way we help to shape the law so that it's going to be relevant and effective."

The scale of Acxiom's involvement in the current proposed legislation is either comforting or concerning, depending on your perspective.

"We've been involved in the [upcoming] EU privacy regulations, ever since the initial consultations in 2008," says Scheuing. We're a one of the discussion partners of the European Commission not only as Acxiom, but also on behalf of the interactive marketing industry of Europe. We're also board members of various data protection officers associations, and I personally also work very closely with different data protection authorities, and the Article 29 Working Party [a group set up by the European Commission to advise on matters of data protection]. We also have direct communication with government delegations from each member country."

She adds that the direct and interactive marketing sector, of which Acxiom is a part, is the only sector in Europe which has its code of conduct approved by both the European Commission, and by the Article 29 Working Party. This causes the industry to be slightly more under the microscope of the regulators than others, who must ensure that it actually adheres to the code they have approved, but also, in Scheuing's view, gives them a right to be involved in the legislative process.

She goes on to state that the privacy debate is bigger than Acxiom's commercial concerns.

"The point is we are talking about fundamental human rights. I can represent the interests of my industry, but at the end of the day I'm more interested in the future of myself, my children and the generation to come. The law is not written for the online marketing field, it covers anything and everything."

Scheuing is evidently aware that many would be critical of a firm arguably at the forefront of the industry which privacy advocates would say is most in need of regulation, getting cosy with the lawmakers and regulators. It's certainly a hard sell to claim that this activity is done out of a sense of altruism for future generations, but Scheuing argues that privacy is a more important issue, admitting that "without marketing data, nothing is going to die".

She makes a more compelling point by comparing the current situation with its alternative. If the organizations being regulated were entirely left out of the debate, the risk is that the law would be unworkable, and given how long it takes for the rules to be agreed in the first place, that would be in no one's interests.

"One needs to have continuous dialogue otherwise the law will not just be ineffective, but practically unimplementable," she says.

"The other thing is, it's very important to understand the reason we have laws; it's that there are bad characters in our industry. There are people who don't give a damn whether it's illegal, or harmful. So creating the right laws is in everyone's interests, not just ours but our clients. Imagine a huge supermarket chain, they use us or our competitors, and then realise that they are dealing with an industry full of bandits. It's in our collective interests to ensure that we continue our dialogue so the people making the law know the realities we're facing."

Information Commissioner Christopher Graham sees nothing untoward in Axciom's involvement with regulators and lawmakers.

"In any parliament you get a lot of public affairs activity, and it's the same in Westminster. I think it's a bit naïve of [people] to whine saying it's not fair. The industry side would say the privacy activists are all over it. We elect MEPs [Members of the European Parliament] to choose between various courses of action put forward, and I think it's a sign of an immature parliament that they can't cope with being lobbied. That's what democracy is, everyone who's involved all want to put their case forward. I don't see evidence of one side having more influence than another, you might say that the draft parliament developed was very much influenced by civil liberties campaigners. The LIBE committee [a group responsible for the protection within the EU of citizens' rights, human rights and fundamental rights] were more inclined to listen to the fundamental rights argument than business and job creation arguments. So unless there's a corrupt deal going on, I expect MEPs to be grown up and to withstand blandishments."

So if Graham is comfortable with the manner in which the new rules have been created, is he happy with the outcome as it currently stands? He gives a mixed answer, arguing that some of the changes will mean that the regulators are so busy auditing firms that they'll have no time or resources left for actual enforcement.

"Even if I have the power under the new regulations to impose eye-watering fines, the rest of regulation is so much about new obligations on data protection authorities to check that data controllers have done their jobs properly, that we'll be less fleet of foot than we are now. My staff will be devoted to endlessly checking up on data controllers [defined by the EU as 'the people or bodies that collect and manage personal data'].

"The ICO has in its evidence to the justice committee said that this policy was overdoing it some years ago. We said it's a system that cannot work and which no one will pay for. It's not clear whether any of the EU governments have an appetite to fund data protection authorities to the level necessary to carry out all these obligations under the proposed regulation, and I'm inclined to say 'show me the money'.

"If you want to create massive data protection authorities then I might believe it. But I fear they'll pass legislation and everyone will feel good about it, but then the enforcement will be patchy because the data protection authorities won't be able to the see the wood for the trees."

This is a worrying assertion. The new regulations are supposed to bring the law up to date with modern technological and societal changes in order to make it easier for the data protection authorities to understand what to do and how to do it, with the ultimate goal of better protection for consumers. But as the proposals currently stand, the regulators will have such steep workloads thanks to new tasks to check up on data controllers.

But there is still time for amendments, and Graham expresses his wish for a conversation with the European Parliament (a directly elected Parliamentary institution, and one of the two chambers of the legislative branch), Council (the other chamber) and Commission (the executive body of the EU responsible for proposing legislation, implementing decisions, upholding EU treaties and running the organization day-to-day) so that these problems can be "ironed out".

He describes the current proposals as a "shopping list of every best practice idea anyone ever had, and that's not quite how you do best practice."

WHAT ARE THESE NEW RULES ANYWAY?

The legislation, as described earlier in this chapter, consists of a general data protection regulation which will apply in the same way to all 28 EU member states. This is the ruleset which will cause the UK to revise its data protection act to conform.

The other piece, the directive, will apply to law enforcement agencies, police, the judiciary and border control and customs, amongst others. Member states will be able to adapt this legislation to suit their needs.

Privacy International's Anna Fielder explains why it's taking so long to debate.

"Every country has its own opinion," begins Fielder. "Germany for instance has strong laws already and doesn't want its laws changed or weakened. But the UK doesn't have such strong laws and wants to maintain the strength of the amendments, so there's a dispute going on."

The new legislation once in force will strengthen data subjects' rights, which is to say yours and mine. It provides improved rules on deleting out of date information, the so-called 'right to be forgotten'.

"This is nothing to do with being forgotten," says Fielder, "but the right to delete information that's no longer valid. At the moment you can't delete your Facebook account. You can exit Facebook but it keeps your information forever. Under the new regulation you'll be able to tell Facebook to delete your data and they'll really have to delete it. It's about the right to object to your information being collected."

It also governs privacy notices, which as currently written often rival Shakespeare's Hamlet for length, and are even so much as glanced through by only a tiny fraction of a percentage of users.

"Privacy notices will have to simpler and written in plain English so people can understand them. It will also strengthen consent provisions, so there will need to be explicit consent to data being captured, not just implied consent. There has been a lot of controversy around ad tracking, profiling and targeting, it mostly goes on without your knowledge. But the strengthening of the rules around that area puts the media industry up in arms. They say 'we'll have to shut down, this is what's financing us. If you want free stuff you need to put up with being targeted'," says Fielder.

Acxiom's Dr Scheuing agrees, adding that education as well as legislation is needed. "Is it really effective to show people a privacy policy which just requires you to say 'yes' and then you get a free service?" she asks. "In reality people just don't read them. The industry needs to work with governments to educate people. I can't believe we don't have a mandatory curriculum in schools where we learn about data protection, and how our private data will be used. We need to pass a test before we're allowed to drive a car, but we don't get a minute of education on privacy before we register for Facebook or Twitter."

Fielder also argues that there are still compromises to be reached between advertisers, privacy advocates and legislators, especially around the concept of anonymous data.

"Yahoo for instance say that where they have no direct relationship with the consumer [in other words where they have bought data on someone via a third party], they do their tracking purely based on an IP address. They watch it surf around the internet and that target ads purely to that number, without knowing who you are and where you live. Their argument is that it's not personal information, simply a proxy used to target people - it doesn't identify them personally.

"But the privacy community argues that that's rubbish, you can easily identify individuals from that data if you want. There's a lot of to-ing and fro-ing over this. The politicians need to reach a decision based on the fact that the industry makes a lot of money out of this sort of data, so how do we balance that need against people's rights?"

Scheuing says that the situation is complicated because the lawmakers struggle to really understand the different characteristics of sensitive data, or even sometimes which data should fall under that category.

"In data protection circles we talk about sensitive data. Names and addresses and contact details are generally considered to be harmless. But credit agencies can use names and addresses to define the credit-worthiness of an individual. Using simply an address we can see the value of a property, and how it's being financed, so names and addresses are becoming extremely sensitive."

More worryingly, for privacy advocates at any rate, Scheuing goes on to argue that data brokers and analysts should be allowed to work with as much data as possible at first, in order to later intelligently trim that data down to the barest essence of what they need.

"You can also think about the different ways that analysts and data scientists, use data that's collected for other purposes [than specified to the consumer at the point at which it is collected]. When you attempt customer segmentation, the first stage of working with the data is called the explorative stage. It doesn't matter if the data doesn't come with an identifier. Analysts don't care if you can't find that person's name and address, but you want to have as many variables as possible so you can discover different groups of people.

"The techniques used for this phase are things like cluster analysis and actor analysis. You need lots of data and it doesn't matter whether it's anonymous or not, you just need a lot of data, that's what marketers need. Once you have an understanding of your customer segments, you realise that the only variables that matter in real terms is age, income and level of education. All of a sudden, because we carried out the explorative research that big data enables, we can slim down the amount of data that we need to use for customer segmentation to just three variables.

Privacy advocates would be extremely alarmed however at the prospect of so much data being collected up front, irrespective of what happens to it later. Scheuing talks about the prospect of later deleting data as 'data minimisation'.

"This is what we call data minimisation. It's the principle which says you shouldn't use or collect more data than you absolutely need. To realise that in the big data era, you first need the entire lot of data. These analytical methods which we have available today need to actively sink into the minds of legislators, so for that we need a dialogue. Let's face it lawyers were never good at maths! Analytics is a scientific process, so the scientific and literary brains need to come together and learn from one another."

Acxiom's desire to conform to data minimisation principles should be applauded, but Scheuing's definition is perhaps misleading. Data minimisation is about the collection part of the process. If you initially collect data you don't need, then you are not practising data minimisation.

This initial hoovering up of all data may prove to be too steep a price to pay for legislators and lobbyists both. She says that the data can be anonymous, but in the era of big data which she invoked herself, anonymization is far from an absolute concept. With the amount of information that is out there about all of us who participate in the information age, coupled with the power of modern analytics, it is relatively trivial to de-anonymize data (various studies have indicated that a person can be accurately identified from just three or four points of anonymous data). We'll return to this point in more depth in chapter 9.

Coming back to the reforms, one of the stated aims is to build consumer trust in online services through the protection of personal data, and to protect their rights. That's a great intention, and the way the EU intends to deliver it sounds reasonable enough at first glance; to write data processors' data security obligations into the law itself.

But this is unworkable, according to Kathryn Wynn, senior associate at law firm Pinsent Masons.

Most obligations around data protection currently fall on data controllers. They may at times hire outside bodies to handle some or all of the data in collaboration with them, and these organizations are defined as data processors, and traditionally have had less responsibility under the eyes of the law. Before we progress with this point, a quick exploration of the difference between data controller and data processor is necessary, as that in part determines their legal duties.

The EU Data Protection Directive 95/46/EC defines data controller as "the person or entity that determines, alone or jointly with others, the purposes and the means of the processing of personal data". A data processor is "the person or entity that processes personal data on behalf of the controller."

So an outsourced payroll company is a data processor, because it handles data purely on behalf of a company for a specific service, and is not permitted (at least for the purposes of this explanation) to use the data for any other purpose. Your social network provider is a data controller, because it entirely controls your data and can do – pretty much – what it likes with it.

The problem with making data processors more responsible for data security is that it potentially blurs the lines of liability. Whereas currently the situation is clear: the controller has the overall responsibility, and is required to specify the correct data security standards in their contract with the data processor; under the new proposals both are potentially liable in the event of a data protection failure, which could result in "legal wrangling… and a blame culture," says Wynn, writing on her firm's website.

"The way the new regime would be implemented would lead to a blurring of the responsibilities of data controllers and processors, difficulties in establishing liability for breaches of personal data and confusion for data protection authorities – all while delivering no benefit for consumers," she adds.

The requirement for an exacting contract between data controllers and processors will still exist, but since processors will now be liable for breaches, they will be far more keen on specifying the limits of their responsibility, explains Wynn.

"In practice this will mean that outsourcing agreements between data controllers and processors will become prescriptive and much more technical in detail on data security arrangements. There could be gaps in expectations and in the willingness of data controllers and processors to take on certain data security responsibilities. This could lead to a complete breakdown in the negotiation of contracts," she adds.

Wynn continues: "Where agreements are forged, the technical language could make their interpretation difficult. Disputes could arise over where respective liabilities lie, and where a breach occurs data protection authorities could find it difficult to identify which party in the agreement is at fault or how to otherwise apportion blame, making it difficult for them to follow through with enforcement action.

"Currently the legal position is clear. Data controllers are ultimately liable for non-compliance with data security rules under EU data protection laws even if the problem stems from activities carried out by data processors."

Given that the debate over the legal minutia of the current EU reforms has at the time of writing persevered for over three years, there are clearly many more issues and bones of contention than have been presented in this chapter. However, this is an overview of the most salient points.

Reforms from Brussels are not the only driver for legal change in the UK, shocking world events can also result in reforms – and not always the reforms we would like.

IN THE WAKE OF JE SUIS CHARLIE...

The Charlie Hebdo shootings in Paris in January 2015 shocked the world with their brutality. In the UK, the coalition government used them as an opportunity to attempt to push through legislative reforms to allow government intelligence agencies greater powers to monitor internet users.

The reforms were driven by concerns from spy agencies that as major technology firms like Google, Yahoo and Microsoft introduce end-to-end encryption in their services (largely as a result of the Snowden revelations), their capacity to track individuals around the internet diminishes.

Prime Minister David Cameron vowed to increase government surveillance powers should his party – the Conservatives – win the 2015 election, which they subsequently did. Speaking at an event in Nottingham, he said that technology firms should give the government access to private communications data in order to help combat terrorism and other crimes.

"Are we going to allow a means of communication where it simply isn't possible to do that? My answer to that question is 'No we must not,' he said.

"If I'm Prime Minister I will make sure it is a comprehensive piece of legislation that makes sure we do not allow terrorists safe space to communicate with each other."

This amounted to the government's third attempt to push through the controversial Data Communications Bill, otherwise known as the 'Snoopers Charter'. Critics of the proposed legislation have described its design to enable government agencies to store and access the digital communications of all UK citizens without any requirement for a warrant as a breach of privacy rights.

A further criticism of the bill came from the Open Rights Group, with a spokesperson pointing to the restriction of free speech promised by the proposed powers.

"While it may be tempting to acquiesce to government demands, we don't protect our civil liberties by limiting them further. Mass surveillance treats us all as suspects, reverses the presumption of innocence and has a chilling effect on free speech," the spokesperson said.

Christopher Graham describes himself as "very concerned" when Snowden revealed that the NSA has been colluding with the big technology firms and leaving backdoors open (and directly and illegally accessing their servers) to aid the surveillance of their customers.

"At same time governments are worried about extremism, terrorism, cyber warfare and industrial espionage," says Graham. "As fast as I tell people to adopt strong passwords and use encryption, then government agencies are saying 'you're making it too hard we can't see anything'. It would clearly be wrong to rush to make changes to policy on the strength of one or two ghastly terrorist incidents, so we need to think it through calmly.

"I wrote to the Intelligence and Security Committee [ISC, an organization designed to oversee various UK government defence and security agencies] explaining my concern, and asking what to do about the encryption issue. The committee has still not reported on that question. There needs to be a rational debate about what we do. The solution to the challenge of finding a needle in haystack can't be to build a bigger haystack. When the ISC's report into the Lee Rigby case [where a soldier was beheaded in a public street by extremists] indicated that the authorities had been aware of these guys but [no action had been taken], and the situation had been the same in France apparently [with the Charlie Hebdo shootings], so it's a very big price to pay to say none of us have privacy anymore in order to deal with the terrorist threat. The security authorities don't have the resources to comb through every email there ever was, so it needs a sensible debate. It cannot be right for citizens not to have any secrets from governments, that's very 1984 [the novel by George Orwell]."

So ultimately whilst there is good, if slow, work happening in Brussels to improve privacy across the EU, there are concerns both about how close industry is to the reforms, and about the reforms themselves. Voters also need to be wary of opportunistic attempts from the government to erode privacy in sudden sweeping moves like the Communications Data Bill.

Whilst the Information Commissioner is happy to comment on the glacial pace of European reforms, his job is more to explain and enforce the law than help in its creation.

"Technology is always moving faster than legislation," says Graham. "We're in a situation where the Data Protection Act 1984 is out of date, the 1995 EU directive is out of date, and the 1998 Act too is well out of date today. It's very important that the latest EU reforms proceed at a pace as we've got a lot of catching up to do. I think there's a very important role for data protection authorities like mine to explain what the law says to companies and to the public, then to use our power against organizations that fail to comply.

"I don't think it's for me to fret about what the law should say, but my major job is to explain data protection to data controllers, whether that's commercial companies, public authorities or the government, and also explain to citizens and consumers what their rights are, how to exercise them and how to look after them themselves. We need to keep thinking about the challenges, but there is still some very basic work to be done."

So that's an overview of the situation in Europe, but what of US law?

ACROSS THE POND

On 12 January 2015, President Obama announced a raft of wide-ranging additions to US privacy laws. These reforms were taken as a response to the Snowden revelations and the increasing threat and volume of cyber-attacks on US firms and government agencies.

These attacks included events like the Sony pictures hack of December 2014, with large amounts of private data about celebrities and Sony staff being released to the general public.

And in an embarrassment for the US government, the US military's Central Command (which leads US military action in the Middle East) was hacked shortly after President Obama's speech announcing the new proposals. In that attack, the military's Twitter account was inundated with pro-Isis posts, some using the hashtag #CyberCaliphate. The government later admitted that its account had been "compromised". President Obama described these issues as "enormous vulnerabilities", and used them to justify his privacy reforms.

Speaking in 2012 as he unveiled what he called the 'blueprint' for his Privacy Bill of Rights, President Obama explained that if consumers don't feel safe online, then ultimately businesses will fail.

"American consumers can't wait any longer for clear rules of the road that ensure their personal information is safe online," said President Obama. "As the Internet evolves, consumer trust is essential for the continued growth of the digital economy. That's why an online privacy Bill of Rights is so important. For businesses to succeed online, consumers must feel secure. By following this blueprint, companies, consumer advocates and policymakers can help protect consumers and ensure the Internet remains a platform for innovation and economic growth."

And the President has research on his side. A survey from the Pew Research Center from November 2014 entitled 'Public Perceptions of Privacy and Security in the Post-Snowden Era' revealed that 91 per cent of Americans believe that consumers have lost control over how personal information is collected and used by companies. The survey also examined attitudes to privacy and data in the wake of the Snowden revelations, and suggested that 64 per cent of Americans believe that it is up to the government to regulate the way advertisers access data.

President Obama's changes fall into four major sections.

A Consumer Rights Bill

This describes the steps firms need to take to tell consumers what data they're gathering, and what the intend to do with it, on top of suggesting various ways they should allow people to opt out. It also mandates that organizations give people information about how they store their data, for long, and to give consumers access to that data.

Tackling Identity Theft

The introduction of the Personal Data Notification & Protection Act which intends to establish a single, national standard for reporting data breaches, and to mandate the report of any such breach within 30 days of the date of its occurrence.

Safeguarding Student Privacy

The Student Digital Privacy Act is intended to ensure that data collected from students is used only for educational purposes. It also aims to prevent organizations from selling student data to third parties for purposes unrelated to education.

Protecting Electricity Customer Data with a Code of Conduct

The Department of Energy has developed a new voluntary code of conduct for utilities firms, designed to protect electricity customer data (including information relating to energy use). As more firms sign up, the government hopes to raise consumer awareness will, which should improve choice.

CRITICISM OF THE REFORMS

But almost as soon as they were announced, President Obama's reforms were widely criticized, with many commentators suggesting that they would do little to help consumers, whilst giving organizations too much freedom to determine how they gather, use and share personal data. Furthermore, they apply only to US citizens. So what about non-Americans, whose data is being collected and stored by US companies? The inference is that they have no rights to speak of.

An article in the New York Times in March 2015 described the draft bill: "... only vaguely reflects those ideas [of consumer protection] and is riddled with loopholes." It added that the draft appeared to be written more to benefit internet giants like Google and Facebook, and data brokers like Acxiom than consumers. Could it be that industry lobbyists are too close to the lawmakers in the US, as they arguably may be in the EU?

Privacy groups and even some Democratic lawmakers have also criticized the draft, with no fewer than 14 US-based privacy groups banding together to write an open letter to President Obama outlining the detail of their concerns (see fig) (https://www.dropbox.com/s/qja4udboxycqlqd/Consumer%20 Privacy%20Groups%20Letter%20to%20the%20President%20-%20FINAL. pdf?dl = 0). Amongst their issues is the opinion that the bill fails to define what sensitive information is, and also that it misses large categories of personal data including geolocation.

And Ed Markey, Senator for Massachusetts and a member of the Commerce, Science and Transportation Committee also stated that he felt the bill falls short of the necessary provisions to adequately protect consumers.

"Instead of codes of conduct developed by industries that have historically been opposed to strong privacy measures, we need uniform and legally-enforceable rules that companies must abide by and consumers can rely upon," he wrote on his website in late February 2015. "I am concerned that this proposal includes a provision that could preempt strong state laws that already are protecting the privacy rights of consumers. And I am especially concerned that companies and data brokers could be able to deny consumers the right to say no to selling their sensitive information for marketing purposes.

"Next week, I will introduce legislation that will allow consumers to access and correct their information to help ensure maximum accuracy. The bill also provides consumers with the right to stop data brokers from using, sharing, or selling their personal information for marketing purposes. We need to put in place a system of rules that puts consumers in control of their information, not corporate interests and data [gatherers]."

If the bill is passed as it currently stands, organizations will be permitted to create their own codes of conduct defining how they collect, use and share personal information. These codes would still need to be approved by the FTC, but these approvals would not amount to much since the amendments would make it very difficult for the regulator to throw out codes it doesn't like. Furthermore, the fact that companies would be required to tell individuals about the data they collect on them is a step in the right direction, but since they is still no requirement for consumers to give their permission, it seems like lip service rather than a genuine attempt to improve individual privacy.

Then there's the ability for consumers to see the data that has been collected about them. Again, this is superficially a progressive move, however it is totally undermined by the out-clause given to businesses. If the organization determines that the requests are "frivolous or vexatious", then it can refuse the request without consequence. As the article in the New York Times states: "This is a fairly low bar for the legal departments of thin-skinned, easily vexed corporations to meet."

The reforms also limit civil fines against firms which breach the new laws to $25 million, which isn't a grave sum if you're Google, Apple or Microsoft. And worse, firms aren't liable for the first 18 months of their data gathering activities, effectively giving them free reign to behave badly.

But even the firms around whom the bill appears to have been written aren't happy. The Internet Association, which speaks on behalf of firms including Amazon, Google and Facebook, released a statement saying that the bill still needs works.

"Today's wide-ranging legislative proposal outlined by the Commerce Department casts a needlessly imprecise net. We look forward to working with

Congress and the Administration to ensure that this proposal does not create a drag on our economy and inadvertently mark a shift from 'permissionless' to 'permission slip' innovation."

The existing US system is well-buttressed by effective state privacy laws. As Privacy International's Anna Fielder explains, this often makes for better protection than most Europeans enjoy.

"The way they enforce laws in the US is very different from the UK, and it's more effective is US in some ways. The US doesn't have gen data protection laws except sectoral legislation around children, financial services, and health. But the state laws are much more comprehensive. For example California has far more comprehensive privacy legislation than you'll find at the federal level."

The problem introduced by the new bill is that it would overrule most state privacy laws, ultimately eroding consumer privacy rather than increasing it.

A QUICK FIX

Obviously with something as complicated as legislation, there is never going to be a simple solution. But DLA Piper's Andrew Dyson believes that accepting a risk-based model would be the best possible start, rather than attempting to prescribe for every potential privacy failing and then enshrining its corresponding punishment in law.

"The draft EU Data Protection Regulation to some extent attempted to deal with this through its focus on conducting privacy risk assessments, and the FTC strongly recommends use of privacy by design safeguards to address privacy risks in the product design and development stages," says Dyson "If an organization thinks about potential risk at the outset of a project and works through the potential impact it is more likely to put in place mitigations that support compliance without causing detriment to the underlying project needs. Requiring organizations to adopt this simple governance in the process of developing new products and services will put privacy risk on the radar as something that needs to be thought through at a principle level, and through having it documented it is more likely to result in a balanced outcome."

References

Cooley on Torts, 2d ed., p. 29

http://lawresearch.northumbria.ac.uk/cirl/sources/dpa/history/?view=Standard

http://hansard.millbanksystems.com/lords/1973/jun/06/privacy-younger-committees-report

http://www.gresham.ac.uk/professors-and-speakers/professor-sir-david-calcutt-qc

Samuel Warren and Louis D. Brandeis (1890), "The Right To Privacy"

http://europa.eu/rapid/press-release_MEMO-15-3802_en.htm

http://ec.europa.eu/justice/data-protection/article-29/index_en.htm

"Public Perceptions of Privacy and Security in the Post-Snowden Era" - Pew Research Centre, 12 Nov 2014

http://www.out-law.com/en/articles/2015/march/data-security-rules-for-data-processors-fail-stated-aim-of-eu-data-protection-reforms-says-expert/

http://www.hunton.com/files/Publication/8fe272d1-d29c-4abd-85ae-17843d084da3/Presentation/PublicationAttachment/6d1be60b-be7d-413c-bd6f-6ee37c02c631/Treacy_controller-processor_distinctions.pdf

https://www.whitehouse.gov/the-press-office/2012/02/23/we-can-t-wait-obama-administration-unveils-blueprint-privacy-bill-rights

https://www.whitehouse.gov/sites/default/files/omb/legislative/letters/cpbr-act-of-2015-discussion-draft.pdf

https://www.dropbox.com/s/qja4udboxycqlqd/Consumer%20Privacy%20Groups%20Letter%20to%20the%20President%20-%20FINAL.pdf?dl=0

http://www.markey.senate.gov/news/press-releases/markey-white-house-privacy-bill-of-rights-needs-to-go-further

http://internetassociation.org/022715privacy/

https://euobserver.com/justice/127961

http://lobbyplag.eu/lp

CHAPTER 8

Privacy and Health

On the face of it, technology and health are made for one another. Hospitals are flooded with technology, from hugely expensive CT (Computerised Tomography) Scanners (which alone can set a health authority back in the region of $300,000), to more prosaic kit like networking infrastructure, desktop computers and X-ray viewers.

Even relatively recently, hospitals offered patients little beyond a warm, clean bed and a regular supply of food and water. In his 2012 TED talk 'How do we heal medicine?' doctor and writer Atul Gawande referenced 'The Youngest Science', by another doctor and writer, Lewis Thomas. In the book, Thomas described his experiences as a medical intern at Boston City Hospital in 1937, before the widespread use of penicillin.

"It was a time when medicine was cheap and very ineffective," said Gawande. "If you were in a hospital, [Thomas wrote], it was going to do you good only because it offered you some warmth, some food, shelter, and maybe the caring attention of a nurse. Doctors and medicine made no difference at all."

Today however, largely thanks to technological advancements, almost all human ailments can at least be treated, if not outright cured.

One of the principal ways in which technology has enabled more efficient medical care is in the sharing of information. Understanding a patient's medical history is often crucial to diagnosing and treating their condition. Having access to such information is even more important where the patient is unable to communicate.

But the health industry has struggled for decades to get its collective heads around information sharing. Speaking at event called 'Electronic health records and IT in the NHS: data protection, care.data, and implementing Personalised health and care 2020', Lord Turnberg, chair of the All-Party Parliamentary Group on Medical Research said that how to share medical records has been a tricky question since he started his career in medicine.

CONTENTS

"We've been struggling with the business of what to do with medical records since I started fifty years ago. We used to have a leaky system with paper records being wheeled around hospitals and half of them used to get lost. We've never had a good system, but it's only since we've had electronic records that we've decided quite rightly that we need a better system."

He explained that the problem with health records is less one of people trying to hack or steal them, and more one of negligence and accidental loss.

"There is very little malicious use of health data compared with the likes of Google and others who use our data with gay abandon. We need a safe and secure way to use the data we have, and that will require much more public information, education and understanding, backed up by the reassurance given by protection and governance mechanisms."

NHS Connecting for Health, an agency within the UK government's Department of Health which is tasked to oversee and develop NHS IT infrastructure, tried to improve the situation when it assumed responsibility for the ill-fated NHS National Programme for IT (NPfIT). NPfIT was designed to implement a single, centrally-managed electronic care record for every patient, and to connect around 30,000 doctors to 300 hospitals, all of whom would have secure access to those records. In September 2011 it was announced that the programme had been scrapped, having already run up costs of £12 billion (almost six times its original £2.3 billion budget), whilst running over four years behind schedule, and likely to deliver only a fraction of its originally-scoped benefits. After the project's closure, some media reports suggested that the final cost to the UK taxpayer had been closer to £20 billion.

Without diving into the tale of mismanagement and poor planning which resulted in NPfIT's failure (which could fill a large book in its own right), it serves to illustrate the difficulty of implementing a nationwide electronic care records system.

But the UK government didn't give up after NPfIT. In March 2013 NHS Connecting for Health was effectively closed down, with some of its responsibilities assumed by the Health and Social Care Information Centre (HSCIC), which describes itself as "…the national provider of information, data and IT systems for commissioners, analysts and clinicians in health and social care."

CARE.DATA

Just a few weeks later, HSCIC announced care.data, a programme designed to take data from GP surgeries and upload it into a centralized database. Every UK citizen who was registered with a GP was informed (or at least, that's what the HSCIC intended) that their health data was going to be shared in this way, with an opt out available by informing their doctors. Data on patients who didn't opt out – and doing nothing in this case counted as opting in - was to be anonymized then shared within the NHS, with medical researchers, managers and health planners, and outside the NHS, with academic organizations and even commercial bodies.

Unsurprisingly, this caused an uproar. Few patients understood or had even heard of the programme, and the methods and details of opting out were criticized for being both unclear and unnecessarily complex. NHS England (a public body within the Department of Health which oversees the budget, planning, delivery and operations of NHS commissioning in England) produced a leaflet which was described by Med Confidential as "…one of the most disingenuous pieces of literature in the history of the NHS, full of ambiguity and misdirection."

A survey conducted by *Pulse*, a magazine targeted at GP's, revealed that 40 per cent of the 400 doctors who responded said they would not allow their own personal health information be uploaded to the care.data database. Both GPs themselves, and the British Medical Association voted overwhelmingly to demand an opt-in be given to patients for care.data.

Speaking at the Local Medical Committees Conference in 2014, British Medical Association GPs committee chair Shaand Nagpaul described why he and his peers felt that care.data should be stopped.

"…whatever mud is slung, let us not forget that the sanctity of the interaction between GP and patient in the privacy of the consulting room has remained unchanged for decades," began Nagpaul. "We're let in to the world of our patients, confiding in us secrets not even known to their loved ones.

"General practice remains a great job, indeed the best job in medicine. And it's rooted in the trust that defines the GP patient relationship. Trust that cannot be taken for granted, and which once lost will not be regained.

"And which is why we must reject, oppose and challenge any system that threatens it, from perverse schemes that crudely incentivise GPs to deny patients care, systems that contaminate the consultation with conflicts of interest, or anything that threatens the confidentiality of the personal information that patients provide to us.

"And this is at the heart of why GPC called for a halt to care.data - because we want to ensure that patients trust the security of their personal information held by their GP, and what happens to it," he concluded.

The care.data programme was eventually put on hold for an initial period of six months in February 2014 (and it's still on hold at the time of writing – Summer 2015), but only after many months of furious criticism from privacy advocates, pressure groups and GPs themselves. During all of that time, the original privacy status of the programme was unaffected; if a patient does nothing, their data is uploaded.

Dr Neil Bhatia, a GP based in Hampshire in England and a Caldicott Guardian (a role which takes its name from Dame Fiona Caldicott, the UK's National Data Guardian tasked to be the patients' champion on security of personal medical data, and described on HSCIC's website as "a senior person responsible for protecting the confidentiality of a patient and service-user information and enabling appropriate information-sharing") explained that patients wouldn't necessarily have been against the plans, had they been approached differently.

"Many might be happy to allow information from their GP record to be shared if they were asked first, if their data was anonymized before upload or if only anonymized information about them was ever released, if their data was only used within the NHS, and if their data was only used for the purpose of medical research. But… care.data respects none of those."

The fact that HSCIC is able to extract patient data without prior consent is thanks to the Health and Social Care Act of 2012. This legislation enables the assumption that every NHS patient opts in to schemes like care.data. This means that health information, arguably the most sensitive data of all, is shared by default in the UK.

"Under the Health and Social Care Act 2012, GP practices have no choice but to allow the HSCIC to extract this information," Bhatia stated.

"The Act removes any requirement to seek the consent of either patients or GPs before extracting and uploading the data," he added.

The care.data programme has so far cost the British taxpayer something in the region of £1.5 million, a bill which is likely eventually to rise to £50 million – small potatoes compared with NPfIT, but a substantial sum nonetheless. Technology integration and consultancy firm ATOS is receiving eight million pounds over five years to provide the infrastructure underpinning the project.

HSCIC specifically, rather than individual GP surgeries or the NHS as a whole, will own and administer the data, once captured. It hopes to use the information to find better ways of preventing and treating illness, and to anticipate risks of certain diseases occurring. It also says that the programme will help it to make decisions around how to best align NHS resources to carrying out its objectives.

Few patients will find much to disagree with there, and taxpayers may even agree that £50 million is not an outrageous sum if the programme is to deliver on its stated goals. Where it falls down though is in the way it has been handled, and the way its public perception has been created. Back to the leaflet campaign, which saw two missives delivered to letterboxes across England throughout January 2014. Med Confidential said that they was designed to make the reader think that nothing extraordinary was going on, whilst in its opinion, events were far from ordinary.

"The leaflet, which many patients may never actually see [residents who had used a Royal Mail service to opt out of junk mail didn't receive the leaflet, and thus somewhat perversely missed the opportunity to opt out of care.data], is a study in evasion and omission, failing to mention rather significant pieces of information like the name of the scheme itself – 'care.data' appears just once in the leaflet as part of a URL at the bottom of the last page; it doesn't appear at all in the first leaflet – and, more crucially, the new leaflet doesn't contain an opt out form," explained Med Confidential.

"That's because this is about consent," it continued. "Or rather it's about manufacturing consent."

Many people would not have received the leaflet, or would have ignored it, because it appeared to be junk mail and was not addressed to specific individuals. And arguably worse, a patient who did manage to receive, read and understand the leaflet, and then decided to get out of the scheme was instructed to "speak to your GP practice" in order to opt out. In fact this was never necessary, opting out could be done via a form (which could and arguably should have been provided with the leaflet) or a letter, without wasting valuable GPs' time.

"NHS England's leaflet campaign is a deliberate and shameful attempt to make it as awkward for you to opt out as it can," continued Med Confidential. "And if this is how they are (begrudgingly) going about 'informing' the public about care.data, can the scheme really be trusted? If it can, then what have they got to hide?"

But opting out of care.data was about to get even trickier and more shrouded in uncertainty. In April 2014 the HSCIC produced a third opt-out form, to sit alongside the two existing opt out codes which patients could ask their GPs to add to their records. This form was either thrown together carelessly, or constructed in a deliberate attempt to blackmail patients. Readers can make up their own minds as to which of those traits they find more terrifying in a body charged with championing public health.

The HSCIC this time added an extra section to the form which bore no relation to care.data. It related to a different system called National Health Applications and Infrastructure Services, and if a patient had completed that section – and most people are prone to fill in everything when working on long, complicated and far from riveting forms – they would have been de-registered from their local GP and not be called in for necessary screening services, like cervical smear tests for instance.

A blog post from Med Confidential reveals an exchange between UK Parliamentary Select Committee member Barbara Keeley MP and HSCIC Chair Kingsley Manning, which gives a sense of how this addition was viewed by the Committee:

Barbara Keeley MP: But it's the way its [sic] phrased, it just looks like a threat. If you opt out…

Kingsley Manning: No, I agree, I agree…

Barbara Keeley MP: …your GP will drop you, and you'll never have any screening.

Kingsley Manning: …I entirely agree.

And the problems with the care.data opt out sadly do not end there.

In January 2015 the HSCIC submitted written evidence to the Parliamentary Health Select Committee admitting that it had made a mistake with one of its opt out codes. What it classed as 'Type 1' objections, which prevents data flowing from the GP record to the HSCIC, was apparently fine and working. But 'Type 2' objections, which stop data flowing out from the HSCIC was seemingly problematic.

The HSCIC suddenly realised that this form of opt out also precluded patient data from being disseminated to support direct care. This was not clear from the way the opt out had been originally worded, and it's perfectly possible that someone would have ticked that box because they didn't want to have their data sold on to commercial firms for profit, but would want their data to be shared if it would support their actual healthcare. It was, in blunt terms, a cock up.

To rectify the situation the HSCIC said it would send individually addressed letters (as opposed to junk mail) to everyone who attempted to opt out via this code again, but since it had not acted on those objections, and since it had resumed releasing patient data over six months previously, it appears likely that that particular group of people would have had their data shared anyway, despite their attempt to opt out. HSCIC is at the time of writing unable to confirm whose data it has released.

Another factor about the programme which if not actively malicious, then at least was not initially made clear, is that the programme itself is not about information sharing between healthcare professionals. It's not about making patient records more easily transferrable between organizations within the NHS.

It is instead about "data extraction, linkage and analysis: in other words, data mining" says Bhatia.

SELLING YOUR HEALTH RECORDS

The information gathered under the care.data programme can be sold to third parties for money. HSCIC and its forebears have a long history of doing just this. Identifiable data in the form of Hospital Episodes Statistics (described by the HSCIC as "a data warehouse containing details of all admissions, outpatient appointments and A&E attendances at NHS hospitals in England"), has been sold by the organization for years. In June 2014 it was revealed that an internal review by the NHS information centre (a body subsequently replaced by the HSCIC) had found evidence of 588 data releases to 178 private-sector organizations between 2005 and 2012. Those organizations included technology firms, healthcare consultancies, insurance companies and pharmaceutical giants AstraZeneca and GlaxoSmithKline.

The HSCIC however describes its activities as "cost recovery" rather than profiteering. But the commercial bodies with which it transacts will very much be expecting to make a profit in some way from those health records, so the distinction, as far as the patient is concerned, is perhaps moot. Furthermore, some of the firms who pay for health data also purchase a commercial reuse license, enabling them to sell potentially billions of medical records on perfectly legally to just about anyone.

How many patients are aware, or have consented to this?

The prices the HSCIC charges for patient data is published on its website. A section of aggregated data costs up to £1,200 ($1,785), pseudonymized data up to £1,800 ($2,680), whilst extracts of certain types of confidential personal data can cost as much as £12,000 ($17,850).

Speaking at the time the review came to light, the HSCIC's non-executive director Sir Nick Partridge said: "The public simply will not tolerate vagueness about medical records that may be intensely private to them. We exist to guard their data and we have to earn their trust by demonstrating scrupulous care with which we handle their personal information."

The more personal and identifiable the data gets, the more the body charges for it. This seems slightly odd for a body which is merely covering its costs. Does the retrieval of sensitive data somehow necessitate more of its resources than say, aggregate data?

The justification for the NHS is that the data when sold on cannot be used to identify individuals. Thus, the nightmare scenario where a citizen is denied health insurance, or perhaps suffers increased insurance premiums, because the insurer has bought their dataset and doesn't like what it sees, is supposedly averted.

Except it isn't. Once a patient's data has been uploaded to the HSCIC under the care.data program, it can be released to outside organizations in four different formats:

Aggregate Data

This data summarizes entire groups of people, and cannot be used to identify individuals. The data is often expressed as numbers or percentages.

Anonymized Data

Whilst certain obvious identifiers such as NHS number, data of birth, and name and address are removed or at least heavily cut down, in the age of big data, it can be relatively trivial to re-identify individuals with as little as three other points of information.

UK Member of Parliament David Davis argued that he could be easily identified from pseudonymized data if it were to be cross-referenced with other information in the public domain, such as his age and the fact that he's broken his nose five times. "That takes it down to about 50... even if they take out all postcodes, there will be other things in the public domain, which have been in the newspapers," he told Computing magazine in late 2014.

Faced with a barrage of criticism, the care.data programme was temporarily stopped in May 2014. Five months later, in October that year, six health bodies from different parts of England were chosen to participate in a "pathfinder" programme (in other words a trial) involving 265 GP surgeries with 1.7 million patients.

Pseudonymized Data

Data is pseudonymized when the fields most likely to identify an individual, such as name, address, or social security number, are replaced in the database by a sequence of numbers, or some other form of arbitrary identifier.

However, like anonymized data, pseudonymized data is far from a guarantee of anonymity. It could be used to identify individuals "especially if it contains very large amounts of information, or very detailed and rich information – just like care.data does," explained Bhatia.

Psuedonymized data could still contain information like a patient's zip code or post code, depending on which side of the Atlantic you are, or data of birth. It's not hard to see how with just a small amount of data from elsewhere, a person could easily be identified from this.

However, using different data sets to re-identify individuals from pseudony-mized information can be illegal, according to Kathryn Wynn, senior associate at law firm Pinsent Masons.

"If there is evidence of re-identification taking place, such as reconstructing individual profiles using fragments of data from different data sets - the ICO is likely to take regulatory action, including potentially imposing a fine of civil monetary penalty of up to £500,000 or take enforcement action if the data was collected through re-identification process without knowledge or consent of the individual," she told Computing magazine in 2015.

Whilst patients may draw some comfort from the fact that this activity is against the law, in practice it would be an extremely hard crime to detect with-out a whistleblower within the offending organization. Furthermore, the ICO would have no remit to act if the re-identification took place off-shore, outside its jurisdiction.

Clearly Identifiable Data

This, it hardly needs stating, is data from which it is trivial to identify an indi-vidual. The information held by GP surgeries in the UK is an example of clearly identifiable data.

It is this latter category which describes the nature of the data uploaded from GP's surgeries into HSCIC's systems, there is no way for patients to consent to some of their data being uploaded, or perhaps only aggregated or anonymized data. It is the full deal, or nothing. Some have suggested that there is noth-ing new here, that GPs habitually share patient data with other organizations, and this is partly true (although that data has never been held in a centralized database before). GPs in the UK do indeed share their patients' personal data concerning their medical history to other bodies within the NHS when required for the patient's direct care. They can share more limited data where they deem it necessary for the protection of others – for example they might share infor-mation about a parent with social services where that information may help to protect a child. They share certain types of information when is then aggregated and used to ascertain outcomes of various treatments or progress of certain ill-nesses, or for medical research. They can even share data with external organiza-tions, even insurers, but only, and this is the key part, with the patient's explicit consent. There has never been a policy of assumed consent, until care.data.

PRIVACY FEARS CAN KILL

A recent study by the British Journal of cancer found that one in five cancer patients waits at least three months before visiting their doctor after noticing symptoms. Another study, from women's healthcare specialists Balance Activ, found that a third of young women would prefer to Google their ailments than visit their GP, especially if it concerns something they feel is embarrassing.

Bhatia, himself a GP, points out that he and his peers are concerned that patients might stop visiting surgeries for fear of the details of their embarrassing ailments being released to third parties.

"GPs are quite rightly concerned that patients might begin to refuse to attend their surgery for essential investigations, monitoring and management of medical problems, both new and ongoing, out of fear that the subsequent information collected will be uploaded in an identifiable format under care.data," wrote Bhatia.

"And in all honesty, such information will be uploaded as part of care.data unless you do opt-out," he added.

The prognoses for certain illnesses, and many types of cancer specifically, significantly worsen the longer they are allowed to progress untreated. Deterring patients from visiting doctors with potential ailments because they fear that they will subsequently be unable to preserve their privacy not only worsens the outcome for those patients, but also places an additional cost burden on the health provider, as more advanced illnesses generally require longer, more intense treatment, with an increased likelihood of surgery and in-patient hospital care.

CAN YOU HAVE TOO MUCH PRIVACY?

The other side of the argument is somewhat surprisingly given by Dame Fiona Caldicott herself when she talks about the risks of not sharing patient data.

"Patient data is sometimes not being shared, organizations err towards confidentiality," she says.

As part of her role as the UK's National Data Guardian she was asked by the government in 2012 to look into information governance in health and social care. She described the task as "trying to find the right balance between sharing and protecting data."

"We tried to redress the balance by saying that the duty to share information can be as important as the duty to protect confidentiality. The imposition of fines by the ICO made clinical staff nervous about taking decisions [about data sharing], so we put in place recommendations aimed to address that balance. But I don't think the balance has been addressed to much of an extent in the two years since we did that work."

At Caldicott's request the government set up the Information Governance Alliance (IGA) in July 2014, a body designed to be a "single authoritative source of information and guidance for the health and care sector," as it states on its website. The IGA is made up of representatives of the Department of Health, NHS England, the HSCIC, Public Health England and the ICO, amongst others.

The IGA is tasked to provide resources and guidance to health workers around best practice and law, so that in future that balance between patient confidentiality and effective treatment can be found more effectively than it has been up until now. Whilst it's still in its infancy as an organization, its principles are sound, and the fact that it has been set up at all is encouraging.

"Consent management is an important area," continues Caldicott. "Identifiable data can be used if a patient agrees that it's fine but not where the exact nature of that consent is unclear. There is no legal definition of implied consent. Implied consent is assumed when a patient is referred on from a GP, and a lot of things are assumed when a patient visits a hospital. We think the public wishes to have more clarity about the information sharing that goes on, which has been part of general clinical practice for a long time, but it doesn't have the clarity around it we think the public would wish it to have."

Caldicott continues, explaining that the rules on data sharing must be made more clear to clinical staff.

"The culture in health and social care must be changed, the new duty to share must be more clearly evident to front line staff, and should require continuing professional development. As staff become more senior, they need to know more about the rules and not keep turning to the Caldicott guardian in their organization."

She adds that staff need to remember that the ICO has never fined an organization for the inappropriate sharing of information, but rather only for cases involving security breaches.

"We want clinicians to share information appropriately. They should use clinical judgement on sharing decisions, not leaving it to colleagues in technology," says Caldicott. "It's important that we have as much clarity as possible about the consent – and its extent - that patients or [health] service users give. There must be no surprises for members of the public, so all of the information in this area is clearly available, and everyone has access to their electronic records."

Although Caldicott was commenting – at an event discussing privacy around data sharing in the NHS – on privacy and information sharing principles generally, it's clear that much of her content applies directly to the care. data programme. This was made more evident as she concluded her speech: "Care.data was paused because it was not helping us move in a positive direction."

Caldicott's speech wraps up care.data's problems in a nutshell. Patient consent was assumed rather than explicitly sought, and the extent of that consent was never questioned. Furthermore, it was difficult for patients to understand the full extent of the consent that wasn't even being properly asked of them, because very few of them knew that the programme was happening, and of those that did, even fewer understood is full extent.

Also speaking at the event was Dawn Monaghan, Strategic Liaison Group Manager, Public Services, at the ICO. She emphasized that privacy needs to be built into healthcare systems, rather than considered only as an afterthought.

"Patients don't yet fully understand what their medical records are, or how they're used. They don't know who has ownership, or how to opt in or out. They don't know how to find out if they opted out of something five years ago, and whether that decision needs to be revisited.

"We must starting building privacy in by design, and make sure it's thought of first, not last."

However, she too echoed Caldicott's point that sharing health information is crucial to patient care, and just because care needs to be given to governance, that doesn't mean that health bodies should give up, or attempt to scale back on information sharing.

"We have to be careful that there isn't so much [for health workers] to consider, and there are so many risks, that we end up in a place where they just won't do it. In our experience it can be far more detrimental to the patient not to share, than to share. Often there's a risk management decision to take, that may mean that you're breaching data protection principles, but if you don't, what would the risk be to the patient as an individual? It could be a case of if you don't share that information, someone is doing to die. So it's a risk management decision, just like any other business decision."

Monaghan's point is that privacy and data protection principles are just white noise when lives are at stake.

In Caldicott's view, consent should be seen as a "hierarchy". Patients usually give an extremely high level of consent where the information sharing is directly related to their healthcare – not many people fear for their personal data when in severe anaphylactic shock. But a far lesser degree of consent is usually given if that data is being used for commercial concerns.

"If it is about their care, patients see information sharing as being in their interests. We also need to look at whether the patient needs to be identified for the purpose that whoever wants the information to be shared is describing. If the data is completely anonymized then used for research, that's fine. But patients give less consent if the sharing is for the profits of commercial organizations, so there's a hierarchy of consent. If the data isn't anonymized, what's the justification for the organization to have it?"

Again, care.data falls down under the rigors of this analysis. There was no thought given to the notion of hierarchy of consent. Consent was assumed, and uniformly applied to all forms of information sharing.

When the care.data programme was paused in February 2014, NHS England to its credit – although in all honesty it had little choice - embarked on a project to get more feedback on what had gone wrong, and how to put it right.

Eve Roodhouse, programme director for care.data at the HSCIC explains what her organization has been doing in that time, and how it would attempt to improve the programme in its next phase.

"In February 2014 NHS England agreed to listen to and work with professionals and patients to get their feedback and reconsider how to implement care. data. To help us understand the views and concerns of professionals, patients, and the public last year we met with almost 3,000 people across over 145 local and regional meetings and events."

Those people included patients and other members of the public, and also GPs and others from the NHS and various other medical groups, including the BMA. NHS England has put some of the concerns it heard into a document on its website. They include worries about who will have access to patient information and how it will be used, the risks of the disclosure of medical records, lack of clarity over the benefits of care.data, and confusion as to how it differs from other NHS information collection.

Basically the scale of confusion and concerns encompasses almost every aspect of care.data, which is perhaps unsurprising given everything discussed in this chapter so far.

The HSCIC developed an 'action plan' from these concerns, and quickly set up what it called 'pathfinders', and what most other people would call a 'trial'. It began working with a small number of GP practices, and a handful of Clinical Commissioning Groups (in all that amounts to 265 GP surgeries and around two million patients) in order to work out how to run the programme properly. Needless to say much pain and some expenditure could have been avoided had this been done initially, but it is at least encouraging that the right noises are being made, and the right actions finally happening. Even better, the entire trial is being scrutinized by an independent panel chaired by the National Data Guardian herself, Dame Fiona Caldicott.

Roodhouse said that the pathfinder stage will be considered a success if Caldicott is able to give it her seal of approval.

"If the national data guardian feels she can tell the secretary of state that the proposals and safeguards in place are satisfactory, that's a measure of success," stated Roodhouse.

MEDICAL PRIVACY IN THE FACEBOOK AGE

In chapter five we discussed social media, and especially how Facebook drives consumers' attitudes to privacy, much as the firm attempts to claim the reverse. Dr Sundiatu Dixon-Fyle, senior expert, healthcare practice, from consultancy McKinsey, questions how much patients today really care about privacy.

"There has been a huge focus on data privacy concerns," she said, speaking at the same event as Caldicott and Roodhouse. "But is this really such an issue for patients who are already sharing private things about themselves on Facebook?"

This provoked an outraged response from Med Confidential's Sam Smith.

"People choose what they put on Facebook and what they do with it, whereas care.data was done to them by the system," said Smith.

He went on to describe his vision of how care.data could be improved.

"What if the NHS was to look at the public interest rather than looking to give data to their mates in the commercial sector? It would work if you could give people a list [of what might happen to their data], and let them choose what to opt out of. That list would have to include allowing people to opt out of data being shared with commercial organizations," he said.

Finally on care.data, at the time of writing the programme is still paused, with conflicting reports emerging from various bodies within the NHS as to when patients in the pathfinder phase will be written to. It is widely expected to re-commence some time late in 2015.

DOES OBAMACARE ABOUT PRIVACY?

Whilst the US has largely managed to avoid the privacy catastrophe that is care.data, it does have its own issues. The Patient Protection and Affordable Care Act (PPACA), commonly known as the Affordable Care Act (ACA) or more simply 'ObamaCare', was made law by President Obama in March 2010. Whilst it has been successful in helping millions of American citizens obtain medical insurance, it has been criticized for many things, including its effects on privacy. One of the most concerning issues is that visitors to the Health-Care.gov website, where US citizens can go to arrange their health cover, can be tracked by commercial companies.

According to news organization the Associated Press (AP), these companies can uncover details like the visitor's age, income, and ZIP code on top of certain medical data including whether the person smokes or is pregnant. And as we have discussed several times in this book, in the age of big data, once you have just a handful of data points, it's not too hard to find out the rest and clearly identify an individual.

The problem with the site is down to its embedded connections to various external, commercial firms, something which is not unusual for a government website on the face of it, except that there are apparently many more connections on HealthCare.gov than most other US federal sites.

A spokesperson for Medicare told various media outlets in January 2015 that external vendors "are prohibited from using information from these tools on HealthCare.gov for their companies' purposes." He explained that the US government uses them to measure the performance of HealthCare.gov so citizens can receive "a simpler, more streamlined and intuitive experience."

And although HealthCare.gov's privacy policy claims that "no personally identifiable information is collected" on its site, the data points uncovered by AP's investigation suggest that that statement is untrue.

Just a few days after these concerns around HealthCare.gov came to light, and following pressure from both lawmakers and privacy advocates, the Obama administration took the decision to scale back the release of consumers' personal data to private companies.

This failed to satisfy everyone however, with Senator Chuck Grassley of Iowa for one demanding more information.

"The [Obama] administration is reversing itself only days after claiming consumers were protected and only after the Associated Press disclosed the problem and two US senators weighed in," he wrote on his website. "It's still unclear how consumers' information is being used. Even with this reversal, I still expect a complete response from the administration about how this information was used and by whom. People using HealthCare.gov should have the confidence that their information is secure and not being used for sales pitches by outside firms. The administration should be able to provide assurances with accuracy and credibility."

One theme which has persisted throughout this chapter is that the barrier for what constitutes identifiable information is lower today than it ever has been. We have found over and again that very little data is needed in order to reliably identify an individual, often by cross-referencing information with other data sets. We have discussed anonymization and pseudonymization and found both to be lacking when it comes to protecting individual privacy.

And the reason for that, largely, is big data, which along with the internet of things is the topic of the next chapter.

References

https://medconfidential.org/blog/

https://medconfidential.org/how-to-opt-out/

http://www.independent.co.uk/news/uk/politics/government-told-to-make-it-easier-to-opt-out-of-caredata-database-10019135.html]

http://bigstory.ap.org/article/c08e8f9667c54c86b36976ab8a338128/apnewsbreak-govt-reverses-health-care-privacy-problem

https://www.gov.uk/government/organisations/health-and-social-care-information-centre

http://www.legislation.gov.uk/ukpga/2012/7/contents

http://www.care-data.info/

http://www.computing.co.uk/ctg/interview/2387142/personal-data-should-become-private-property-not-googles-or-gchqs-says-david-davis-mp

http://data.parliament.uk/writtenevidence/committeeevidence.svc/evidencedocument/health-committee/handling-of-nhs-patient-data/written/17671.pdf

http://www.dailymail.co.uk/health/article-2654581/One-five-cancer-patients-delay-visiting-GP-three-months-noticing-symptoms.html

http://www.dailymail.co.uk/health/article-2686216/Young-women-Google-illnesses-GP-especially-think-embarrassing.html

http://www.hscic.gov.uk/hes

http://www.hscic.gov.uk/media/12443/data-linkage-service-charges-2013-2014-updated/pdf/dles_service_charges__2013_14_V10_050913.pdf

http://bma.org.uk/working-for-change/negotiating-for-the-profession/bma-general-practitioners-committee/lmc-conference/gpc-chair-speech

https://www.gov.uk/government/publications/iigop-report-on-caredata

http://www.england.nhs.uk/wp-content/uploads/2015/01/care-data-presentation.pdf

http://www.grassley.senate.gov/news/news-releases/grassley-government%E2%80%99s-reversal-healthcaregov-privacy-problem

CHAPTER 9

The Internet of Things and the (not so) Smart Grid

In 1891, Nicola Tesla, the brilliant and eccentric scientist and inventor of the Tesla coil, the radio transmitter and fluorescent lamps, amongst other things, presented a lecture at the American Institute of Electrical Engineers in New York City where he proposed a technology more appropriate to a comic book than a sober lecture hall. Tesla's idea in a nutshell was for a global network of strange metal towers broadcasting both electricity and information into the atmosphere. As a proof of concept, and also certainly as an effort to disprove the doubters, he gave his address whilst holding a glowing gas discharge tube in each hand, powered by electrified sheets of metal standing at each end of the stage – though crucially not physically connected to the tubes.

It took Tesla over a decade to convince enough people of the idea to enable the construction of the Wardenclyffe Tower, a 187-foot steel behemoth straight out of a 1950s B-Movie (a genre it predated by half a century), with a 55 ton steel dome – or cupola - at its summit. See Figure 9.1.

Next to the tower stood the complex's main building (designed by renowned architect Stanford White), which was populated with various electromechanical devices, generators, electrical transformers, X-Ray devices, Tesla coils, a plethora of bulbs, tubes, wires and even, apparently, a remote controlled boat.

Below both buildings was a shaft, sunk 120 feet straight down into the Earth with 16 iron pipes spanning 300 feet out from it under the ground. Tesla described these pipes as anchors, and their design as "to have a grip on the earth so the whole of this globe can quiver."

The tower's purpose was to discharge an immense voltage into the atmosphere in order to use the Earth itself, or more specifically, the ionosphere, as an electrical conductor.

Although the technology was never put to use, and Tesla's dream of a global network of these towers making power and communications technology available for all was never realized, reports suggest that trials of both Wardenclyffe

CONTENTS

FIGURE 9.1 The Wardenclyffe Tower.

(which apparently drew so much current that it caused the local city generator to fail) and smaller prototypes proved that it did actually work.

AND THE POINT OF ALL THIS?

Wardenclyffe was supposed to compete with Thomas Edison's electricity network, which began providing power to paying customers in 1882. In its early years many people were extremely dubious about the merits of an electricity utility as most preferred to trust their own generators. Power was just too precious a resource to trust to someone else.

The point of all this is that it mirrors the situation today with cloud computing. In the same way that buying electricity became cheaper and more reliable than generating it yourself, maintaining mass storage capability, or hosting a large amount of processing power is no longer something individuals or most firms need to concern themselves with. There are plenty of companies offering cloud computing services over the internet, and entire armadas of computers, servers, platforms and software can be launched within moments of the corporate credit card's use.

As Christopher Millard, Professor of Privacy and Information Law and head of the Cloud Legal Project in the Centre for Commercial Law Studies, Queen Mary University of London, explains, the internet of things ('things' in this context could be sensors, smartphones, printers, wearable devices, tablets, cars, home appliances, or anything with a chip and an internet connection) coming together with cloud computing is about to cause a lot of grief for legislators, and potentially consumers.

"We're on the cusp of the cloud meeting the internet of things," says Millard. "We're trying to understand how to make sense of the internet of things and cloud using existing technological and legal concepts," he added, explaining that the law as it stands is unfit to deal with such new ideas.

"There will soon be many times more 'things' connected to the internet than people," he continues. "There are all these devices out there now, which could be your fridge, washing machine, or even something you eat. This could be a game changer as to whether our online lives can ever be private."

He says that the cloud "unsettles" legislators and regulators, who try to apply traditional legal principles to it. Whilst this will change in time, it's nothing new. The law has always been several paces behind technology, and is one reason why both the US and UK legal systems have courts and a judiciary tasked to interpret rules and apply them intelligently. The UK legal system in particular has a tenet of resolving the idiomatic antithesis between the spirit (or intention), rather than the letter (or precise wording) of the law, by generally preferring the former. The US, by contrast, is slightly more divided on this issue, especially when it comes to the Constitution, with 'Living Constitution' scholars advocating an interpretive strategy, and 'Originalist' scholars backing a more rules-based approach. The point is that the law can often afford to lag technology to at least a small degree as long as its underlying principles are sound, and as long as the regulators and judiciary actually understand the latest developments enough to bend anachronistic rules around them.

However, Millard evidently feels rather less comfortable with the existing situation, especially when it comes to data.

"The law is a bit of a mess. Regulators used to know where data was, but when it comes to data, the law is completely obsolete. It uses the same principles today as it used in the 1970s. The core principles are still sound, but a bureaucratic nightmare has evolved around them."

He continues to discuss the many factors at play when considering the concept of privacy in the cloud.

"Can you control the way in which your data might be collected, seen and used? And do you use the controls you already have? My anecdotal observation is that most people don't take even the most trivial and basic care of their privacy. The most popular passwords for instance are 'admin' and 'password'. [Vendors] shouldn't be selling kit that is by design open to anyone who wants to try to look into it," he argues.

Millard proposed two-factor authentication as one solution. He concedes that most people view it as a "bit of a pain", but suggests that it hugely improves security.

"The law doesn't specify which technology you should use, but we may get to a point where it's just not enough for people to have random, weak passwords, so we need to force people to use some other form of authentication."

Beyond the question of how people authenticate themselves on cloud services, there's the trust issue. Should we trust cloud providers with our precious data?

The only logical answer is that each cloud provider must be assessed on a case by case basis, it would make no sense to automatically distrust them all because the whole idea of the cloud is in some way untrustworthy, just as it would be irrational to decide that every cloud provider is a safe bet. Firms and individuals consuming cloud services (which increasingly means all firms and most individuals) can draw some comfort from the fact that any cloud vendor who develops a bad reputation for security and privacy will quickly go out of business.

Then there's the fact that your data is by no means safe just because you've carefully kept it out of the cloud, as the UK's tax authority HM Revenue and Customs found in November 2007 when discs containing the personal details of 7.25 million families claiming child benefit disappeared from a courier's motorbike. A junior employee at the organization breached government security rules by sending the sensitive information across the country by unrecorded post. The fact that the data had been kept out of the cloud was scant consolation to banks, building societies and the general public, as they all feared breaches in the wake of the leaked information – and some even predicted a banking crisis as a direct result.

BACK TO THE INTERNET OF THINGS

But cloud security is a rabbit hole from which we may never emerge if we delve any deeper into that particular discussion. One of the first references most people make when confronted with the term 'internet of things' is the concept of the internet-enabled fridge.

Alison Powell, Assistant Professor in Media and Communications at the London School of Economics, is not a fan.

"The internet fridge has been a myth for at least 15 years, the notion that it's a good idea for a fridge to have contact with the internet. What might it want to do? Order new eggs? Report on missing milk? Say the jam has mold? What kinds of things might the internet-enabled fridge do that the person possessing it couldn't do in a more efficient and more cognitively worthwhile way? The greater social benefit of the internet-enabled fridge remains one of the great mysteries."

But of course the internet of things is much more than an arguably pointlessly connected fridge. It's sensor networks, smart meters (which we'll come back to later in this chapter) and an ever expanding variety of devices.

"In this world of connected objects," Powell continues, "we imagine they're in contact with one another through the magic of the cloud. Data goes into the cloud then comes back to connect objects together. The notion is that it's a seamless set of connections.

"But we miss details. The first is that there is no cloud. When we're talking about the internet of things, what are we actually talking about? We're talking about data acquisition, aggregation, analytics and actions taken on that data, and on the analytics that relate the data together, it goes from personal to systemic. In the set of relationships that unfold along this stack, there are imbalances of power."

What she means is that it's the data generated and transmitted across this network which should interest us, rather than the network itself. Many if not all of the nodes on the internet of things are constantly generating data, often about individuals, or groups of people. Sometimes that's with that person's knowledge and consent, but not always.

Powell gives the example of a fitness tracker, a simple wristband which monitors its user's movement. It passively collects data, such as your location, the number of steps you have taken, together with the information you provide when you register the device, which often includes, name, date of birth, height, weight and contact details. The fact that someone has purchased it and attached it to their arm implies knowledge that they are participating in a relationship, but do they understand the full extent of that relationship? Powell calls the fridge a "benign example" because we know what a fridge is and we can place it in context, but other examples, including our wristband, are slightly more nebulous. Have its users fully understood what the wristband's manufacturers and many partners will do with that data? Do they recognize that their data will exist outside of their control for years, perhaps even decades?

Some insurers have suggested that they may charge lower premiums for health insurance customers who agree to wear a fitness band, but there is nothing stopping them raising fees for those whom they feel are not exercising enough.

"The data from fitness trackers is aggregated and analyzed both by us and by the firm that provided it," says Powell. "The data is valuable to us as we can ask if we've walked up enough stairs today. Am I getting fitter? It's a story we're telling ourselves about ourselves. Now we tell that story through data.

"At same time, those analytics are available to the firm that sells fitness trackers, and anyone else they're selling aggregated fitness tracker data to. That data has a life in the wider ecosystem. It's no longer the story we're telling, it's our data double. It's out in the world having a life, creating relationships about a single person and groups of people who undertake similar actions. The results of the analysis of those data doubles are open to lots of different entities," she says.

This issue is compounded on a massive scale in the concept of 'smart cities', where networks of sensors monitor and control everything from traffic flow and parking spaces to electricity usage and refuse collection. It's a supposedly aspirational concept, and many major cities are busily peppering themselves with sensors to pave their way to smartness, but this intelligence comes at a cost to privacy.

It also gives rise potentially to new business models, Powell says, as firms set up sensors to monitor human traffic around a city, perhaps even passing through turnstiles, and then sell this data on transport authorities.

"It results in interesting economic possibilities, but it all depends on the individual losing control over personal data," she adds.

The internet of things on this scale, both macro (in terms of pervading an entire city) and micro (in terms of tracking every tiny movement of an individual), raises interesting questions of how we consider privacy. How much of our lives now are not online? When there are objects out there passively recording every trivial detail of our day, without our consent, which is then analyzed, brokered and sold on in ways of which we're not even aware, where does that leave the concept of privacy? Is it already an anachronism?

"Do we need to say goodbye to privacy in the way that we have traditionally thought about it?" asks Powell.

"Maybe we need to say hello to the idea of personal responsibility, individually and as a society. We may not be able to see how our data interacts with other data and services, which increases the potential for there to be an imbalance of power. People who can perform more analytics gain more power. Or there could be an imbalance where the government errs on the side of having more data about individuals than it needs."

For Powell, and many others, this is a dangerous path, and an entirely new way of understanding how data should be treated is needed.

"We tend to overlook quality of liberty," she begins. "When we collect data about ourselves for ourselves, it's part of a story we can tell about ourselves. Liberty is about our ability to shape that story and control to whom we tell it to and how. When we lose that control we need new ways to control liberty. We can't have a moat or a wall around our data, so maybe we need new ethical framework, a way to increase the social responsibility people feel around their ability to tell their own stories and to change their minds."

Powell's final point is an interesting one, as once there is a body of data out in the wild about an individual, it becomes a perpetual description of that person. The individual in question may change their mind, and decide over time that actually they feel differently about something. It could be something trivial like suddenly preferring the color green over blue, or not liking baked beans any more, or it could be rather less trivial like their political affiliation. You might change as a person, but your data double won't necessarily toe the line.

"Perhaps we need an ethics of data that permits these abilities to address the inequities that can result from the emerging economies of the internet of things," summarizes Powell.

This ethical approach should ideally naturally devolve from effective data protection legislation. However, lawmakers in the EU can't even agree on data protection law for technology which has been around for the last couple of decades, let alone anything only emerging now.

So how should this ethical framework look? For a start it should include the concept of being responsible with our own data, it's hard to make a convincing case for one's privacy having been invaded when you've, metaphorically speaking, wandered around town with your name, address and bank account details written in bold letters on your T-shirt. So the use of good, strong passwords and perhaps even two-factor authentication on important online accounts would be a great place to start.

For the ethics, we return to the first chapter, and Gartner's Frank Buytendijk's three points:

1. Think through what you're doing with data (whether it's your own or someone else's), and ask yourself what could possibly go wrong?
2. Would you treat your own personal data in this way? Does it feel right?
3. Monitor for unintended consequences and be prepared to act to set them right.

The first rule applies to everyone, and the latter two more to firms dealing with our data. They are clearly subjective, and what feels right for one person could send another running screaming for the hills, but they at least provide a basic framework for society to being to find some sort of accord for what might be an acceptable way to treat data.

DATA TRAWLING

One of the biggest problems with the internet of things is that it hoovers up massive amounts of potentially personal data secretly, and indiscriminately. Ian Brown, Professor of Information Security and Privacy at the Oxford Internet Institute argues that this is a dangerous setup.

"It's often trivial technologically just to collect everything," says Brown. "But you shouldn't collect everything just because you can. Users need to be given control, and you need to limit who has access to that data. You also need good security around the data, otherwise your access controls aren't actually much help."

Among the best methods of protecting data both in storage and in transit is encryption. Pairing that technology with the principle of data minimization (in other words, only harvesting, storing and transmitting as much data as is actually needed for a specific purpose) ensures that if a system is hacked, or suffers some form of breach, much less data will be compromised.

But few if any systems within and around the concepts of the internet of things and big data adhere to these principles. They are designed to suck up and disseminate as much data as possible, and security is generally weak or almost entirely absent.

Then there's the lifetime of that data. Currently most consent options, where they're given at all, are binary. You're either in or you're out. But what if you only want to agree to share some data today, not in perpetuity?

"You might be willing to share your location right now with a service," continues Brown. "But you might not want anyone not in your immediate family to know everywhere you've been in the last week."

But when it comes to the internet of things, the bigger consent issue is that most of the time you have no idea what's happening to your data. It's hard to choose whether to opt in or out of something if you've no idea that it exists. "In the internet of things, how do all these sensors tell you what they're doing with all this data?" Brown asks, rhetorically.

A good example is the 'spy bins', litter bins in London's financial center (known as 'the City') sporting embedded chips which track WiFi signals from smartphones in order to monitor passers by. They caused a media storm in August 2013 when the press caught on to their activities, with the public unhappy at the thought of being tracked without the opportunity to opt out. The idea was that smartphone owners could be monitored regularly going into a branch of McDonald's for example, then could be served a targeted ad from Burger King.

"It can also be used by retailers to track your movements around a shop [which is happening today]," says Brown. "And over time organizations can build up a detailed picture of where you go and what you've been doing. You only need to sign into their website once and they can link all these records together."

It's worth noting that it is possible to tweak a phone's settings to stop it sending out these trackable 'pings', or unique identifiers (MAC addresses, for the technically minded), but it's something that most users will never do, partly because they are unaware of any need.

Despite his distaste at the many privacy invasions perpetrated by spy bins and the like, Brown acknowledges the economics of the internet; that data is the new currency and if you expect free services then you should brace yourself for junk mail and targeted ads (and a host of other minor and not so minor assaults). Whilst he accepts this as the modern web's transactional system, he proposes a fundamental change to the way the data is controlled.

"Could we do targeted advertising to people's phones in a privacy sensitive way?" he asks. "I don't want the internet to go away and revenue streams to all these companies to be cut off, so could we develop a system where your phone, a system under your control, builds your profile and keeps it there? It can then work with ad exchanges and publishers to show you targeted advertising, so you get the benefits without building up detailed profiles which exist in the wild."

This comes back to Powell's idea of personal responsibility for data, and would go a long way towards resolving the thorny issue of consent, where consumers find it hard to opt in or out of things like spy bins if they have no idea it's happening. If they're able to define on their phones which details they're prepared to give away for certain services, and either set other information as permissible for ad hoc requests like spy bins, or completely lock down anything not directly related to a service they've asked for, then the value exchange is still there, only now it only happens when both parties are fully aware of it.

Sadly this system doesn't currently exist, and the examples of the privacy invasions of the internet of things keep coming.

In fact we don't need to go far for our next example, it also happened in London, a city which couldn't do a much better job of striving to abuse your privacy if it tried.

The issue in this case is its congestion charging scheme, which appears to be designed with the specific intention to violate drivers' privacy. A network of static cameras built around the city's center monitors and tracks vehicles' registration plates. Whilst this does enable the transport authority to know who has entered the restricted zone during charging hours, it's also a sure way to know who has gone where, and when. It could have been designed much more simply, and have been far more respectful of citizens' privacy. For example, drivers could be given top up cards which sit on their dashboards, or are attached to windscreens. These then talk to transponders based at the zone's perimeter which can remove the relevant funds, all without identifying the car or its driver.

Even some of those firms most invested in the internet of things, and who stand to make big profits from the concept in future, believe the existing system is incompatible with the notion of privacy. Wim Elfrink, who heads up networking firm Cisco's smart cities team told the Guardian newspaper in 2014 that citizens must be allowed to opt in or out of schemes such as these, and that their data must be handled securely.

"Having security policies, having privacy policies is a given. I think you have to first give the citizens the right to opt-in or opt-out. Then all these policies, longer term, security and privacy are going to be the biggest imperatives. If we don't solve this, people will opt-out more."

THE DANGERS OF BEING SMART

So our privacy is now under threat from dustbins, street cameras, and our very cities. And whilst the internet fridge may still be a myth, the internet of things is already penetrating our homes in several guises, including the smart meter.

The idea of smart meters is that they will enable the more efficient and ultimately cheaper consumption of energy, a goal few would argue against. They monitor a household's energy or water consumption for instance, enabling the utility to more accurately bill their customers, and also providing them with a much clearer picture of who is consuming what and when. That in turn helps them to plan their own production cycles and configure their services in ways which are better suited to the public's needs. The data captured by smart meters can also help consumers to change their habits for the better – putting on dishwashers at night when electricity is cheaper, for instance.

However, as with many other aspects of the internet of things, some smart meter systems – notably those in use around Europe, have not been designed with privacy in mind. Many smart meters in use by various electricity utilities in the UK for instance are programmed to send energy consumption readings back to the provider every fifteen minutes. As Brown explains, this is more dangerous than it perhaps sounds.

"The EU wants eighty per cent of European households to have smart meters by the end of this decade, but they really could have been designed in a more privacy friendly way. The data captured by the smart meter should stay under the household's control, and send only the minimum necessary information back to the utility, rather than what it does now. Studies show that you can surmise all sorts of things about household activities from the frequency of current readings. You can see what time they get up, what kids of appliances they use, when they use them, and what they watch on television," says Brown.

Mike Mitcham, head of Stop Smart Meters UK, a campaign group which aims to warn the public about the dangers of smart meters, told the audience at the Alternative View 5 conference in 2014 that it's not obligatory to have a smart meter, but that utilities are forcing the issue because of the value to themselves, not the value it brings to their customers.

"Smart meters are not mandatory, you have the right to refuse them," began Mitcham. "It's a globally synchronized initiative. There are already more than a million installed in the UK with 52 million more to come, and there are many more across the world in the US, Australia and in other regions. The utilities are calling people up and telling them that smart meters need installing, and then ripping out perfectly good older meters.

"Worldwide the smart meter market is expected to reach half a trillion dollars by 2050, so this is big, big business. [The meters] constantly monitor and measure how you're behaving at home and what you're doing with your energy and water use, and they communicate that back to the nearest cell tower, almost in real time through a government gateway known as the DCC, and finally it gets passed on to your utility provider. To do this smart meters contain two microwave transmitters, one that communicates with cell towers using pulse mobile phone signals, the other is designed to communicate with a new generation of smart appliances via pulse Wi-Fi signals. So when your old TVs and washing machines die, they'll likely be replaced by something that's smart, which means it has an RFID chip in it which is able to communicate with the smart meter and anyone else who has access to that data about how you're using it."

This is not wholly without consumer benefit, as households can then see their energy use in detail via an in-home display unit. However, this is nothing that a twenty dollar energy monitor from Amazon couldn't also do, without transmitting that data wirelessly to a utility provider, and without giving that provider the means to remotely disconnect you.

Mitcham claims that smart meters also carry health risks.

"Smart meters give out an intense pulse of microwave radiation every two seconds. In a single 24 hour period, smart meters can expose you to up to 190,000 pulses of microwave radiation, 365 days per year. A single smart meter can expose you to between 160 to 800 times more radiation than a mobile phone."

Back to the privacy issues, it's not only utilities which receive data from smart meters, but also potentially law enforcement agencies. They can get access to data that enables them to track citizens' activities at home, including details such as what and when they eat, when they sleep, whether that sleep's broken, their showering habits, what appliances they use and when, and whether they prefer the TV or the treadmill, amongst other things.

Mitcham added that smart meters can also show whether someone has mental health problems, or has ever left the children home alone. But does any of that matter if you have nothing to hide? We'll return to that question later in this chapter.

STRIDING OVER THE CREEPY LINE

Of more obvious concern is a recent patent application from Verizon for a smart TV detection zone which will be able to determine who's sitting in front of the TV, what they're doing, what kind of facial expression they have, what kind of mood they're in, and whether they're arguing.

"It's sold on the premise that if you're having an argument with your partner, the smart TV detection zone will know, and will be able to serve up a targeted ad for marriage counselling," says Mitcham.

In chapter two, Gartner's Buytendijk introduced the concept "crossing the creepy line". His point was that if you exploit your users' data in the context of the relationship you have with them, then that's often fine. So if your airline makes you a hotel offer at the destination you're travelling to with them, few people will object. But your television spying on you and offering implied judgment on your marriage or relationship? Either the research and development heads at Verizon have astonishingly high creepy thresholds, or ethics just isn't high on their key performance indicators.

Samsung's privacy policy is explicit about the intentions of its Smart TV sets. It explains that the TV will listen to people in the room in an attempt to spot voice commands, but adds: "If your spoken words include personal or other sensitive information, that information will be among the data captured and transmitted to a third party."

Parker Higgins, an activist for the Electronic Frontier Foundation, compared this policy to an extract from George Orwell's novel 1984, describing the protagonist's 'telescreen':

'Any sound that Winston made, above the level of a whisper, would be picked up by it, moreover, so long as he remained within the field of vision which the metal plaque commanded, he could be seen as well as heard. There was of course no way of knowing whether you were being watched at any given moment. How often, or on what system the Thought Police plugged in on any individual was guesswork.'

Lance Cottrell, chief scientist at cybersecurity firm Ntrepid, described the monitoring by Smart TVs as just part of the larger internet of things trend.

"Sensors are going into everything, and will continue to do so. It is important for everyone to take the time to disable the sensors they don't really want or need. Increasingly people need to think about what things they really want to keep private, because it is almost impossible to protect everything without going completely off the grid.

"Monitoring by smart TVs is part of a larger trend towards tracking all kinds of activities and behaviors. Location tracking, financial tracking, and web tracking also provide very invasive levels of information about us."

Also on the theme of companies going well beyond their mandate is data analytics firm Onzo, which lists 'Load Disaggregator' amongst its available services. This product "identifies appliance level consumption from granular energy use data, without the need for appliance or plug level metering."

Onzo can apparently also enable a utility to attempt to predict illness amongst its customers

"Your smart meter will be able to predict falls," says Mitcham. "So if you start using your appliances differently, you might be suffering from an illness, it's a marker for a urinary tract infection, for instance. And illnesses can be precursors to falls. If the British Gas smart metering team thinks you're due for a fall they can send intervention. But that of course goes well beyond the mandate for an energy company."

Needless to say spy agencies are rubbing their hands with glee at the prospect of all this remote monitoring. In the past they'd have had to sneak into a building and hide a bug in a lampshade to find out what was going on in a particular room, but the internet of things has presumably resulted in a string of redundancies amongst stealthy technicians at GCHQ and the NSA.

Speaking at a summit for In-Q-Tel, the CIA's venture capital firm (which allows it to invest in technologies it sees as potentially useful for its operations in the future), CIA director of the time David Petraeus said of the internet of things: "'Transformational' is an overused word, but I do believe it properly applies to these technologies, particularly to their effect on clandestine tradecraft.

"Items of interest will be located, identified, monitored, and remotely controlled through technologies such as radio-frequency identification, sensor networks, tiny embedded servers, and energy harvesters — all connected to the next-generation internet using abundant, low-cost, and high-power computing, the latter now going to cloud computing, in many areas greater and greater supercomputing, and, ultimately, heading to quantum computing."

He took a brief pause from salivating over the prospect of all this free data to concede that the internet of things prompts a rethink of "our notions of identity and secrecy." If the director of the CIA is acknowledging that a technology is eroding the very concept of privacy, then it's high time, or possibly even too late, to start worrying.

Mitcham claims that the NSA's new $1.5bn data center in Utah (completed in late 2014) is designed to sift through all the new data cascading out of the internet of things like an untapped oil geyser (only vastly more valuable and infinitely more dangerous). The US government states that the installation is designed to support the 'Comprehensive National Cybersecurity Initiative', although how it does that is classified. According to an interview with Edward Snowden the facility was originally known as the 'Massive Data Repository' within the NSA, but was renamed to the 'Mission Data Repository' because the former was apparently considered to be too creepy. Quite how the NSA defines "too creepy", given its activities detailed in chapter two, remains a mystery for now.

BUT WHY SHOULD I CARE? I'M NOT DOING ANYTHING WRONG...

"But hey you've got nothing to hide right, you're not doing anything wrong?" asks Mitcham. To illustrate his point, he uses the hard hitting example of Anne Frank, a Jewish writer and victim of the holocaust.

"She had nothing to hide either," says Mitcham. "She was a sweet, innocent 13 year old girl when she started writing her diaries. In the mornings and evenings, Anne Frank's family had access to water, a gas stove and some electricity to power a light bulb. The Frank family would not have lasted a day with the smart grid. If someone says to you that they have nothing to hide, history tells us that that might not always be the case whether you're doing something wrong or not."

And there are security fears over the smart grid too. By installing a smart meter into your home, utility firms are effectively uploading the details of your energy and water usage onto the internet. When connecting their computers to the web, most people do so behind the protection of a firewall and anti-virus software, because the internet is basically the wild west. If your computer is compromised, your data is at risk. But with a web-connected smart meter, it's your energy supply that's at risk. And smart meters are being rolled out globally at a time when cyber warfare is massively on the increase.

Stuxnet, the computer worm probably designed by the US and Israel, which attacks industrial control systems and successfully disrupted Iran's nuclear programme, is still out there in the wild, in the sense that it's available for anyone with some technical nous to adopt and use. The smart grid will bring around 440 million new entry points into the energy grid. This wouldn't be a major issue if smart meters were designed to be secure, but unfortunately they're not. Or if they are, then that design has failed.

There have been numerous media reports of smart meters being hacked time and again with ease.

"Smart meters could be hacked to under-report consumption and this should act as a warning," Alejandro Rivas-Vásquez, principal adviser in KPMG's Cyber Security department told The Register. "If the technology could be hacked for fraud, hackers with more nefarious intent may use these flaws for other purposes."

Mitcham argues that if a smart meter can be breached that easily, then your power supply can be disconnected that easily.

"I know there are people out there doing this, because there are dedicated search engines like ShowdownHQ which helps hackers seek out insecure devices online and hack them. The number two most searched for item when I checked recently was industrial control systems."

Speaking to EnergyNow.com in 2012 former CIA Director James Woolsey said the US government's oversight of grid security is inadequate and attacks on the grid are "entirely possible".

"No one is in charge of security for the grid, whether it's cyber or transformers or whatever," claimed Woolsey. "You can search forever through the federal code to try to find who that person might be. And a so-called 'Smart Grid' that is as vulnerable as what we've got is not smart at all, it's a really, really stupid grid."

So why is anyone bothering with smart meters? The concept is in part sold to consumers on the basis that it will save them money. But if the smart meter program comes in on budget, and history tells us that major national infrastructure projects don't, then it will cost the UK £12 billion. That equates to roughly £400 per home.

Mitcham calculated that if a home has two smart meters, it will save something in the region of £23 per year.

"So if you believe your energy company will give you that saving back, then it will take 16 years for you to see it, and I'm not convinced the energy companies will show you that saving. Pilot tests across the world have shown that 91 per cent of people with smart meters don't save money. That's great news if you're an institutional shareholder in big energy."

Could it be that the smart meter rollout is happening not for the benefit of consumers, but for big business? Mitcham argues that one of the main beneficiaries is IBM.

"Whilst the EU is cheerleading the internet of things, they're doing so on behalf of the real driving force behind it which is IBM in my opinion. IBM is pushing the smart concept in every major industrial sector, and that is a little more than worrying to me given IBM's track record in spear-heading invasive population tracking technology."

Mitcham refers to 'Hollerith' (see Figure 9.2) when he talks about IBM's 'track record'.

FIGURE 9.2 World War II era Hollerith poster.

In the 1880s Herman Hollerith, an employee of the US census Bureau, came up with the idea of creating punch cards containing searchable data such as gender, nationality, and occupation for the population. The system worked, and in 1911, via a series of sales and acquisitions, found its way into the corporate structure of IBM (then called the Computing-Tabulating-Recording Company (CTR)).

One of the system's big customers was the German government, who in 1933 announced its intention to conduct a national census, in part in order to identify Jews, Gypsies and other ethnic groups the Nazis deemed undesirable. In this way, it is thought to have assisted the Nazis in their pursuit of the holocaust.

In his presentation Mitcham compared the Hollerith poster with a still taken from a recent advert commissioned by the EU supporting the internet of things, which showed a person beneath a shining street lamp (see Figure 9.3). The two images may be superficially slightly similar, but this is highly likely to be a coincidence given that evoking such controversial and inflammatory imagery gains little and risks losing a lot. Mitcham however sounds less convinced, though his point about the extent to which the internet of things will track us remains valid.

"[The Hollerith imagery] seems to have been resurrected in the internet of things advert in modern times. I'm at a loss as to why this imagery is being evoked for population tracking in 2014. Is a coincidence, a sick joke, or something else? Hollerith was used by the Nazis to profile and identify [what they saw as] undesirables. The smart grid and the internet of things is going to profile all of us, all of the time."

The big tech firms, like IBM and Cisco, and some consulting and financial firms are now sponsoring internet of things awareness programs in schools.

FIGURE 9.3 EU Internet of Things advert.

"Corporations are moving into schools and trying to tee up this industry for the future," explains Mitcham. And in March 2015 IBM announced that it plans to pour $3 billion into its internet of things business unit over the next four years. The Hollerith imagery is almost certainly coincidental, and some of the risks discussed in this chapter may not appear in the real world, but the fact remains that the internet of things is coming, and privacy and security will both suffer as a result.

But should we care? The Anne Frank example is an extreme one, so can we feel safe in the absence of a fascist dictatorship? Our governments may be far from ideal, but they at least aren't currently attempting to racially segregate us or worse.

To answer this question we need to look at some other broad trends in data usage. Energy and utility firms are queueing up to see how we use our appliances and consume water and power. The medical industry, through schemes like care.data in the UK and sites like healthcare.gov in the US, is enjoying ever greater insight into our health and lifestyles. And in the UK, the tax authority HMRC has announced its intention to sell our tax data to private firms. None of these initiatives, or invasions if we want to use a less kind term, is designed to save citizens money, they are designed to enable companies to make money at citizens' expense.

"Your bank might like this data too," says Mitcham. "They now feel they have the right to ask if you eat steak before they give you a loan. I can foresee a future where before you're given a mortgage, you have to give up your last three years of smart meter data, or before an insurer agrees to covering you. If you're not prepared to do that you'll either not be covered, or you'll have to pay a premium."

Currently we can opt out of the smart meter rollout, though utility firms have proven themselves to obfuscate this right in the past. We can't opt out of street cameras and sensors or devices which track our WiFi signals, but we can refuse to buy Smart TVs, or at least switch off their voice command features.

With enough pressure and momentum, concepts like Powell's personal responsibility for data, and plans like Brown's idea for smartphones to allow users to define exactly which of their data is open for consumption could assuage many of the issues outlined in this chapter, whilst still permitting the internet economy to function. There are also better ways of designing things like congestion charge zones. The internet of things isn't a bad idea of itself, it just needs to be designed with security and privacy at its heart.

References

http://www.damninteresting.com/teslas-tower-of-power/

http://www.theguardian.com/news/2014/apr/04/if-smart-cities-dont-think-about-privacy-citizens-will-refuse-to-accept-change-says-cisco-chief

http://stopsmartmeters.org.uk/the-smart-meter-agenda/

https://aftermathnews.wordpress.com/2013/01/03/verizon-detection-zone-cameras-microphones-watch-tv-viewers-and-listen-to-their-conversations/

http://www.nsci-va.org/WhitePapers/2011-10-19-SmartGrid%20Security-Stephens.pdf

https://fas.org/sgp/crs/misc/R42338.pdf

https://www.youtube.com/watch?v=nDBup8KLEtk

CHAPTER 10

Biometrics and The Future

Imagine your personal data as a chest full of treasure; gems, jewellery gold coins and whatever else floats your boat. Now imagine that you keep this treasure in a well-fortified castle, high up on a hill surrounded by thick walls. So far so good. Now imagine the door. Tall and sturdy, made of solid oak strengthened by thick iron supports. The lock, however, is a flimsy little thing made of plastic which breaks when you give the door a decent shove. That's about how effective passwords are at protecting your data.

In several chapters in this book we've discussed the inadequacies of the password as a means of authentication, and of protecting sensitive information. One of the main reasons for this fact is that humans are just so very bad at coming up with hard to guess words. Security applications vendor Splashdata compiles a list each year of the most common passwords in use, and the result is fairly depressing reading for anyone with an interest in security (and indeed anyone who values imagination). Here are the top five from this particular hall of shame. If you see a password you use yourself for anything you actually care about in this list, then you'd be well advised to change it immediately!

1. 123456
2. password
3. 12345
4. 12345678
5. qwerty

If this list was your sole piece of insight into the human race, you'd assume the species comprises a bunch of unimaginative, witless morons who probably deserve to have their data stolen.

And it's not just consumers who are guilty of truly world-class uninspired password selection either. In June 2014 an ATM belonging to the Bank of Montreal was successfully hacked by two ninth Grade boys. That's two fourteen-year olds outwitting the combined minds of a major bank's security staff.

Matthew Hewlett and Caleb Turon discovered an old ATM operator's manual online that showed how to get into the cash machine's admin mode. During their school lunch hour one day, they went to an ATM belonging to the Bank of Montreal to try it out.

"We thought it would be fun to try it, but we were not expecting it to work," Hewlett told local newspaper the Winnipeg Sun at the time. "When it did, it asked for a password."

Expecting little, Hewlett and Turon tried a random guess at the six-digit password, using what they knew to be a common choice. Although the newspaper doesn't report which password they tried, from what we know, it was likely to have been '123456', since the more popular option 'password' has eight letters and is therefore too long. It worked, and they were in. The boys then immediately went into the bank itself to let staff know that their ATM security was less sophisticated than what many people employ on their laptops.

But the bank's staff didn't believe them, telling the boys that what they had done "wasn't really possible." So Hewlett and Turon went back out the ATM, changed its surcharge setting and amended its welcome screen to read 'Go away. This ATM has been hacked.'

This bought them an interview with the branch manager, and a note for their school explaining that they were late back from lunch because they had been assisting the bank with its security.

At this point, most people will be simultaneously pleased that the vulnerability was discovered by two enterprising and ethical teens, rather than a hacker out to make a quick profit, and also hopeful that their own bank doesn't require two fourteen-year olds to tell it how to secure itself properly.

One method of measuring password strength is by using the concept of 'information entropy'. This scale is measured in 'bits', and doubles for each bit you add to it. So a password with six bits of strength would need two to the power of six (that's 64, for those of you without easy access to a calculator) guesses before every possible combination of characters was exhausted – cracking a password by attempting all possible sequences is known as a 'brute force' attack.

So for each additional character you add to your password, the principles of information entropy dictate that its strength doubles. However, probability dictates that on average a brute force attacker will only need to try half of the possible combinations of characters in order to find the correct one. And in fact your password is likely to require even fewer guesses, since humans are so bad at generating truly random passwords. Even if you manage to avoid any of the options from the hall of shame, a study by Microsoft in

2007 which analyzed over three million eight-character passwords revealed that the letter 'e' was used over 1.5 million times, whilst 'f' was used only 250,000 times. If the passwords had been truly random, each letter would have been selected about 900,000 times. The study found that people were far more likely to use the number '1' than other numbers, and the letters 'a', 'e', 'o', and 'r'.

And an examination of the results of a phishing attack on users of early social network MySpace in 2006, which revealed 34,000 passwords, showed that only 8.3 per cent of people bothered to come up with mixed case passwords, or to use numbers of symbols.

And as if all of that doesn't make it easy enough for hackers, anyone with access to your Facebook page and other social media probably knows your date and place of birth, where you live, your hobbies and the corresponding information relating to your immediate family too. Those details, coupled with a small measure of insight into human psychology will usually offer up your password in short order. And if not, there's always the brute force option, or you can just google 'password hacks' and find something in the region of 13.9 million results including thousands of how-to guides.

YOUR BODY AS YOUR PASSWORD

So we can agree then that passwords aren't great, so what are the alternatives? One which has been gaining popularity in recent years is biometric technology, where you literally are the password – or more specifically part of you. It could be a retinal scanner at an airport, or fingerprint recognition on your smartphone, in either case it's considerably more secure than '123456'.

However, whilst the development undoubtedly has much to offer in terms of security, like all new technologies it is not without its controversies and risks.

The police in the US have been using biometric data for many years, in the form of ID cards and DNA fingerprinting for instance. On top of those techniques, since 2011 they've had the Mobile Offender Recognition and Information System (MORIS), a device which can plug into an iPhone, and is able to verify fingerprints and even irises. Meanwhile in 2014 the FBI announced that its 'Next Generation Identification System' had reached "full operational capability" in late 2014. This system contains data on fingerprints, palm prints, iris scans, voice data and photographs of faces.

And researchers at Carnegie Mellon University are in the final stages of developing a new camera that's able to make rapid, high resolution iris scans of every individual within a crowd at a distance of ten meters.

Similar things have been happening in the UK. The British police have begun using facial recognition software to quickly scan through their databases of criminals and suspects. But not everyone in these databases is a criminal, some are people who have been brought in to a police station for questioning, but never actually charged with a crime.

Alan Miller MP, chair of the UK Parliament's science and technology committee, warned the government of the risks.

"As we struggle to remember ever more passwords and pin numbers in everyday life, the potential benefits of using biometric technologies to verify identity are obvious. However, biometrics also introduces risks and raises important ethical and legal questions relating to privacy and autonomy.

"We are not against the police using biometric technologies like facial recognition software to combat crime and terrorism. But we were alarmed to discover that the police have begun uploading custody photographs of people to the Police National Database and using facial recognition software without any regulatory oversight—some of the people had not even been charged."

The Information Commissioner's Office, the UK's privacy regulator, was asked to adjudicate, but ruled that no current legislation covers the use of photographs in this way. In effect, it's a legal black hole and therefore the police's activities are entirely within the law.

The UK even has a 'Biometrics Commissioner', who is charged with reviewing police retention and use of DNA samples, DNA profiles and fingerprints. The government website which describes his activities says the Biometrics Commissioner is independent, which one assumes means he doesn't answer to the government. However, it also admits that he works "with the Home Office", the central government department which administers affairs relating to the UK, so quite how independent he is we will only discover when he is called upon to rule in a matter relating to government handling of biometric data.

The fact that he has no remit over police use of photographs didn't escape the notice of the Parliamentary science and technology committee, who recommended in December 2014 that the statutory responsibilities of the Biometrics Commissioner be extended to cover the police use of "facial images".

Miller expressed his disappointment that the UK government has still failed to provide any leadership or guidance around biometrics, despite pledging to do so over two years ago.

"Management of both the risks and benefits of biometrics should have been at the core of the Government's joint forensics and biometrics strategy. In 2013, my Committee was told by the Government to expect the publication of a strategy by the end of the year. We were therefore dismayed to find that, in 2015, there is still no Government strategy, no consensus on what it should include, and no expectation that it will be published in this Parliament."

SO WHAT ARE THE RISKS?

This book has dealt extensively with government surveillance. It's pervasive, invasive, and it's not going away any time soon. But couple this obsession with surveillance together with biometrics, and the potential for privacy violations increases exponentially.

For example, the city of New York operates a network of around 3,000 cameras called the 'Domain Awareness System', essentially a CCTV network much the same as that used in London and many other cities. If a crime is committed and the police know roughly where and when it happened, they can scan through the relevant recording histories to find it.

But what if systems such as this were equipped with facial recognition technology? Anyone sufficiently motivated would be able very simply to track you throughout your daily routine.

"A person who lives and works in lower Manhattan would be under constant surveillance," Jennifer Lynch, an attorney at the Electronic Frontier Foundation has been widely quoted as saying.

And this threat is fast becoming a reality. The Department of Homeland Security is working on a five billion dollar project to develop what it calls the Biometric Optical Surveillance System (which becomes no less disturbing when you refer to it by its acronym: BOSS). This system aims to be able to recognize people (and it is able to do so because organizations like the NSA have been harvesting people's photographs for years and building vast databases) with 90 per cent certainty at a range of 100 meters, and it has been predicted to be operational by 2018.

Things become more worrying still once your DNA profile gets digitized. For one thing various commercial bodies including insurers will want to get hold of the data to scan your profile for risks and revenue-generating opportunities ('Hi there, we've noticed that you have a genetic predisposition towards colon trouble, why not try our new herbal range of teas, proven to ease such complaints in over 80 per cent of cases' is a fake, but yet disturbingly believable example of what could happen). Worse still, what if some government agency one day purports to have found a genetic sequence indicating a propensity towards crime?

Alternatively, what happens when a malicious party appropriates your genetic code? You can change your password, or the locks on your front door, but your DNA sequence?

THE FUTURE OF BIOMETRICS

Miller's committee released a report which identified three future trends in the ways biometrics will be used. First was the expansion of what it termed "unsupervised" biometric systems, like fingerprint authentication on your smartphone; then the proliferation of biometric technologies which could be used to identify individuals without their consent or knowledge; and finally the linking of biometric data with other types of big data as part of the massive individual profiling efforts discussed at length in earlier chapters.

MOBILE BIOMETRICS

The first trend – mobile biometrics – is arguably where the area is currently seeing the most explosive growth. Submitting evidence to the committee, Dr Richard Guest, from the University of Kent, rated consumer-level biometrics, like the fingerprint scanner on Apple's iPhone 6 "something of a gimmick value". But actually it's rather more than that. Sticking with the iPhone 6 (though other models, such as the Samsung Galaxy S6 also include biometric authentication), it enables financial transactions via its 'Apple Pay' system, which is authenticated via its biometric scanner. Similarly, Barclays Bank has announced that it will be rolling out a biometric reader in 2015 to replace the current PIN system for its corporate clients, to allow them to access their accounts online.

Biometric technology on mobile devices is still a relatively new concept, with only the latest smartphone models from the major manufacturers being fitted with biometric readers, and the practical applications at the time of writing are few. However when Apple first released the iPhone in June 2007 there were just a handful of apps available to users (admittedly largely because Apple was initially reluctant to allow third parties to develop software for the platform). Seven years later, by June 2014, there were over 1.2 million apps, and that figure is growing daily. The "unsupervised" possibilities of biometric technology on mobile devices is likely to be quickly exploited in ways its inventors could barely have imagined.

It has also, as of April 2015, already been hacked. Fortunately for users of the Samsung Galaxy S5 it was hacked by security researchers rather than a group with more nefarious aims (some would argue that some security researchers, with their habit of selling any flaws they discover to the highest bidder, whether that's law enforcement, a hacking group or a shady government department, are nefarious enough by themselves). What they discovered was that a flaw in Android, the phone's operating system, allows hackers to take copies of fingerprints used to unlock the device. They concluded that other Android-based phones could be similarly vulnerable.

This is especially alarming as fingerprints are set to become increasingly popular over the next few years as a way of authenticating financial transactions in particular, with the Apple Pay system, and a similar offering from Paypal.

This isn't even the first time that a phone's fingerprint scanner has been beaten by hackers, although it is the first way that has been found so far to steal biometric data from a mobile device. In a rather more prosaic hack, a German group the 'Chaos Computer Club' in 2013 used a photo of a person's fingerprint on a glass surface to fabricate a fake finger that was successfully used to unlock a phone.

Some could be forgiven at this point for thinking that perhaps passwords aren't so bad after all, but what this is really an argument for is two-factor authentication. Once hackers have to build a prosthetic finger AND guess your password, they're going to have to really want to get at your data before they go to those lengths.

CLANDESTINE IDENTIFICATION OF INDIVIDUALS

Biometric technology like facial recognition systems are able to identify individuals without their knowledge. In November 2013 supermarket giant Tesco announced that it would be installing screens positioned by payment tills which scan its customers faces, then display targeted advertising to them. Their cameras are able to work out customers' age and gender, and the algorithm behind it all also takes into account time and date, and also monitors customer purchases.

Simon Sugar, chief executive of Amscreen, the firm behind the technology, said: "It is time for a step-change in advertising – brands deserve to know not just an estimation of how many eyeballs are viewing their adverts, but who they are too."

His use of language is interesting; brands "deserve" to know who's viewing adverts. Quite why they're entitled to this information isn't explained

"Yes it's like something out of [2002 film] Minority Report, but this could change the face of British retail and our plans are to expand the screens into as many supermarkets as possible," Sugar added.

Privacy campaign group Big Brother Watch described the potential for abuse as "chilling".

"Should we really be increasing the amount of surveillance we're under so some companies can sell more advertising?" it asked on its blog. "Secondly, the technology isn't going to stay the same and be used in the same way," it continued.

This is yet another step in the evolution of supermarkets' desire to know everything about their customers. But how can they work out anything useful from a quick scan of our faces? Surely there must be a master database showing what we look like and who we are so these till scanners have something to find a match with – where does that information come from? The answer is, we give it away ourselves in our social media accounts. It's trivial technologically to scrape a database together from Facebook, Twitter and LinkedIn, take people's mugshots, names, and whatever else they make easily accessible (usually almost everything), then use facial recognition software to search for a match to the data streaming back from the in-shop scanner.

"Given the number of CCTV cameras across Britain [and many other parts of the world] that could be adapted to use this technology, the potential to track people in real-time is huge," argues Big Brother Watch.

Whilst there was a brief media outcry after Tesco made its announcement, and whilst Facebook removed its own facial recognition data (used to automatically identify its users on photographs uploaded to the network) under pressure from regulators in 2012, most consumers remain relatively unconcerned.

The pattern that's repeated itself in the last couple of decades is one of privacy being eroded in increments. What seemed outrageous a few years ago – like Facebook posts defaulting to publically visible where they had before been private – is now just expected.

"The fact shops feel they can scan you without your permission is a shocking indictment of how privacy is under attack in an unprecedented way," continued Big Brother Watch. "Those who argue you have nothing to fear if you have nothing to hide may well think twice about the shops they visit, whether they seek sensitive medical and legal advice or what streets they walk down.

"People accept a degree of surveillance for law enforcement purposes, but these systems are solely motivated to watch us to collect marketing data. People would never accept the police keeping a real-time log of which shops we go in, but this technology could do just that. It is only a few steps short of a surveillance state by the shop door," it concluded.

This covert identification of individuals, as mentioned earlier, is also used by police forces. A pilot project known as the 'Neoface system' being run by Leicestershire Constabulary uses a database of 92,000 facial images, which largely come from CCTV and police cameras. Commenting on the project in its evidence to the Parliamentary committee, the ICO explained that police biometric identification goes well beyond facial recognition. "The surreptitious collection of information about individuals that they would not necessarily expect" could also come from "a fingerprint or genetic material left behind", and not just from "facial recognition in live or recorded images," it stated.

LINKING BIOMETRIC DATA

An earlier report from the science and technology committee entitled 'Responsible Use of Data' covers the UK government's work with the Economic and Social Research Council's Administrative Data Research Network to "facilitate access to, and linkage of, de-identified administrative data routinely collected by government departments and other public sector organizations."

The UK government is especially keen on "joining the dots", as civil service blog from late 2014 calls it, linking disparate datasets together and coming up with consensus on common identifiers, so if you want to tell people that your data relates to the Empire State Building, you can do it in a commonly understood way that easily links to other data on the same subject.

"Our vision is that anyone should be able to discover and link together related sources over the web," writes the cabinet office, effectively the UK government's corporate HQ, in a blog. "For example, DCLG [Department for Communities and Local Government] wants to develop smarter ways of joining-up disconnected data on housing, schools, parks, and retail facilities – empowering people to make more informed choices about where they want to live. We are doing this by publishing our data as Linked Data. These sources could be open data, linked over the public web, or could equally be private information shared in a more secure and protected environment," it states.

All of which sounds perfectly noble and reasonable. But Professor Louise Amoore from Durham University, giving evidence to the committee, gave her view that the likely future trajectory was moving towards "the integration of biometric data" into a "much larger and rapidly growing array of digital big data" in ways that were "capable of producing profiles or behavioral maps of individuals and groups". Amoore's views were echoed by the British Standards Institution which predicted that the identification of individuals would "be possible using a wider range of non-traditional biometric data sets and… by combining data sets using 'big data' approaches".

This is possible because there are currently no meaningful regulations in place to limit the collection and sharing of certain biometric data, including facial recognition.

Amoore went so far as to suggest that analytics could even use the linkages between biometric and other easily accessible types of data to understand and predict a person's behaviour.

"[There are] analytics engines that can mine biometric data that is available on the internet, and link that to other forms of data," stated Amoore. "That moves us more in the direction of indicating not just who someone is but suggesting that one might be able to infer someone's intent from some of the biometric data."

Dr Richard Guest from the University of Kent stated that the 'Super-Identity Project' (a trans-Atlantic project funded by the Engineering and Physical Sciences Research Council examining the concepts of identity in both the physical and cyber world) had proved that biometric data could be linked with "cyber activity and personality assessment" data in such a way that made it possible to obtain "unknown elements of identity from known elements".

In other words you start with a photo of someone's face, and quickly end up with their name, address, television viewing habits and favourite brand of cereal (and much, much more).

THE SOLUTION

So that's all very well but what can be done about it? We've explored the issues of big data in earlier chapters, but given that reams of our personal data has already been harvested, catalogued, packaged up and sold on, it's very unlikely at this point that we're going to convince data brokers and marketers to stop using it or delete it entirely. And given that all of this is already out there, how can we govern how it interacts with biometric data which is now increasingly flooding into servers all over the world from our smartphones, street cameras and even shopping tills?

Big Brother Watch suggests that biometric data should fall under the same guidelines as the UK National DNA database (a system set up in 1995 which carries the genetic profiles of over six million people, with samples recovered from crime scenes and taken from suspects). Broadly, these guidelines dictate that DNA profiles of anyone convicted of an offence can be stored permanently, but those taken where no conviction follows can only be stored for up to six months.

Until recently, innocents' DNA profiles could be legally stored for six years, but the Protection of Freedoms Act 2012, which came into force in the UK on 31st October 2013, dialed that back significantly. Since then, the National DNA Database Strategy Board stated in its annual report for 2014 that almost 8 million DNA samples had been destroyed in its efforts to comply with the new legislation.

Big Brother Watch compares the rules for the DNA database with the current system around biometric data. Currently biometric data stored by the government for 'national security determinations' can be kept for two years, but with the potential for indefinite renewal (which renders the initial two year time limit utterly meaningless).

"This is grossly excessive and judging from past cases of how anti-terrorism legislation has been applied it is far from certain that it will be limited to cases of credible threat to national security," the group states on its blog.

Its other proposal is rather more general, and would help to safeguard all personal information.

SAFEGUARDING PRIVACY IN THE AGE OF BIOMETRICS AND BIG DATA, AND OTHER IMPOSSIBLE TASKS

Big Brother Watch recommended that the UK introduce custodial sentences for serious breaches of the Data Protection Act 1998. This would even be quite simple to achieve; under Section 77 of the Criminal Justice and Immigration Act 2008 a Secretary of State can implement a custodial sentence of up to two years for a serious breach of the Data Protection Act.

"No new primary legislation would be required and it would send a clear message that the government takes the security of personal information seriously."

The current law is defined by Section 55 of the Data Protection Act, which states that it is generally unlawful for a person to "knowingly or recklessly without the consent of the data controller obtain or disclose personal data or the information contained in personal data, or procure the disclosure to another person of the information contained in personal data" without the consent of those who control the data.

But rather than jail time, the current penalty for committing an offence under Section 55 is a maximum £5,000 fine if the case is heard in a Magistrates Court and an unlimited fine for cases tried in a Crown Court.

The introduction of custodial sentences for this type of offence has reared its head many times in the UK. The last proposal came from Lord Marks of the UK's House of Lords in late 2014.

"To put it bluntly, the threat of fines is frequently insufficient as a punishment," Lord Marks said during the Lords debate. "There is a risk that payment of fines may be regarded and treated as no more than a necessary expense by unscrupulous publishers who act with intent to circumvent the Data Protection Act."

However, the proposal failed. In fact, it was never even put to a vote in order to progress through to the House of Commons. Rather oddly, Lord Marks withdrew the proposal when other members of the House of Lords criticized his timing.

CONCLUSIONS

So what have we learnt so far? The main key takeaway which summarizes in just a few words what this book is attempting to say, is that the very concept of privacy is under threat from recent (and some not so recent) developments in technology. Several of the world's largest and richest governments have been proven to have been snooping on their citizens, and indeed anyone unfortunate enough to have their data pass through various breached servers, cables and entire networks. What Edward Snowden's leaked trove of documents showed us was the dizzying scale of the espionage, and the almost total absence of governance and oversight around it. Where is the judicial review of security agency requests to examine data belonging to groups and individuals? Where are the rigorous governing bodies holding these agencies to account for breaching their own rules? Where are the high profile casualties – the senior heads rolling for their lack of respect for the privacy of their citizens? They are all lacking.

And the most frustrating part (at least for this commentator)? The fact that the news breaking out and becoming common knowledge has changed almost nothing. It's still all going on, right under our noses.

But that is far from the full picture. Private firms are playing very much the same game, snooping, harvesting and sucking up as much data about us as they possibly can. Often this is with the intention of turning an indirect profit. Supermarkets want to know more about us than we know ourselves so they can convince us to spend more money in their stores by targeting us with very specific advertising. Diaper offers before we've even told our families that we might be expecting a new arrival, to cite one famous example. Media outfits want to profile us to within an inch of our lives so they can show their own advertisers the types of people visiting their pages, because sponsors will pay more for a certain number of the 'right' viewers, than a larger number of anonymous unknowns. And then there are other firms turning our data into a direct profit. Data brokers like Acxiom, who gather and store detailed profiles on almost every adult in the UK and US alone, then sell that data on in a business model worth hundreds of millions of dollars (and growing), absolutely none of which goes back to the people whose privacy has suffered in the collection of the data in the first place.

Most of us are also guilty of giving highly personal data away freely, with little or no care for the risks or consequences. Most people are aware that Google, and operators of other search engines, are not charitable organizations, and that since their services like web search are largely free, somewhere along the line there must be a catch. But that's usually as far as the thinking goes, and so they are deemed to consent to the subsequent information pilfering. However, when directly shown that everything they type into a search engine, every website they visit and how long they spend there, and everything they write or even receive in an email is stored and analysed and used for profit, most people express shock and even outrage.

Personal data is given up with if anything even greater abandon to firms like Facebook, Twitter and other social media outfits. And this is far from low value information, but intimate details of our lives: where we live, work and shop, our daily routines, where, when and how we travel, what we buy, and even, in the form of photography, what we and our children look like.

Even more intimate information is gathered up and stored by our hospitals and other care providers, but not exclusively to increase the quality of our healthcare. Both the US and UK are guilty of serious breaches of patient trust, with a profiteering approach to patient data that has quite rightly been met with scorn and disbelief on both sides of the Atlantic.

The narrative follows a familiar theme in the world of mobile, where free apps like Angry Birds are downloaded by hundreds of millions of people, the vast majority of whom will not read the terms and conditions, and therefore be completely unaware that their mobile devices are scanned, their contacts and sometimes even personal messages read and sold on to advertisers.

And even our cities themselves are spying on us, with an unimaginable number of sensors, cameras and other devices pinging our phones, and monitoring and tracking us as we go about our lives. The simple act of visiting your local store to buy a pint of milk could result in dozens of new additions to your data doubles, residing in cyber space and ever-evolving without your knowledge or consent. Here's a brief list of some of the privacy violations this act could instigate:

1. Logged on CCTV on the street. Image scanned and matched with photograph scraped from social media.
2. Phone logged by smart sensor embedded in lamp post.
3. Travel card scanned accessing public transport.
4. Phone logged again by sensors in shop. MAC address matched with customer profile from previous visits. Route around shop monitored.
5. Purchase logged and added to customer history. Profile updated.
6. Face scanned at till. Identity matched with photo from database.
7. Profile updates and transaction information packaged and sold on to advertisers.

None of these actions improve our lives or enrich us to any great degree. It's also worth noting that the above list is what might happen without the person in question deliberately interacting with a connected device in any way. Perform a web search to check on the store's opening hours, or update your social network on the way and the list grows significantly.

SO WE SHOULD ALL GO LIVE IN A CAVE?

So what can we actually do to improve things? The good news for Europeans is that the new data protection Regulation and Directive, which should hopefully creak into force some time in 2018 if the lawmakers manage to remember their purpose, will go some way towards helping the situation. Although final negotiations are ongoing at the time of writing, the new rules will force firms to treat data security more seriously, in part by increasing the financial penalties that regulators are able to impose upon them. However, this increase is tempered by the fact that those same regulators may find it harder to enforce data protection legislation given that their governance responsibilities (basically checking up on potentially dodgy firms) could see a huge increase in workload without a corresponding increase in their budgets.

So we can't rely on the law to resolve the situation. And the industry is unlikely effectively to police itself. Although Acxiom has made a positive gesture by making some of the information it holds on US citizens accessible to them, in truth it's such a small subset of the data it holds as to be meaningless, and it's hard to escape from the cynical view that it's more an attempt to deter regulators from imposing tighter controls than it is a genuine revolution in commercial responsibility.

Where does that leave us? The answer is, it leaves us in part needing to fend for ourselves. But maybe that's not such a bad solution. We have shown alarming disregard for our online privacy and security, and no amount of legislation nor even goodwill from corporations is going to protect us when we can barely lift a finger to protect ourselves. There needs to be a cultural shift towards personal responsibility for data, only then will we see some progress in the battle to preserve privacy in the big data age. And that means people stop using things like 'password' and '12345' for their passwords, and instead start using technologies such as two-factor authentication for access to anything remotely important, which includes personal email, not just internet banking.

And this notion of responsibility extends to social media use too. Social networks need to evolve to provide clear indications of their default privacy settings, including notices about the potential dangers of uploading geo-tagged photos, and telling everyone in the world that you're off on holiday for a fortnight and your house is going to be unoccupied. This isn't a plea for governments to become nannies, but rather a call to help consumer understanding of what's really happening with their data. If people choose to share their every intimate detail with the wide world, then that should be permitted, but it should be done with a full understanding of the consequences. And that rule applies to everything described in this book. Consumers need to fully understand what they're getting in to, only then can they provide an informed consent.

But these changes won't be sufficient in isolation, governments and legislators aren't off the hook. If individuals are solely responsible to protect themselves, then privacy will become something only for the privileged few, those who know better, and know how the system works.

Pressure groups like Liberty and Privacy International have shown that it is possible to incite change, with their February 2015 victory in the case to prove that some of GCHQ's mass surveillance activities were unlawful. With privacy-first services like Ello being formed, some at least are now viewing it as a selling point, and that will help privacy to start being built in to systems by default. These are small, but important steps.

But there is more that commercial and public bodies should be doing. Whilst we can never expect profiteering corporations to put individual privacy first, there are some basic rules which should be followed:

- Privacy must be built in to new systems and tools, not added as an afterthought. That means clearly identified options with reasonable explanations (no more Hamlet-length terms and conditions), and the possibility to opt out of all or parts of a service based on a thorough understanding of what will happen to private data at each step. Consumers should also have the means to check what has happened to their data later, together with a simple means to hold that body accountable should they subsequently learn that promises have not been kept.
- Organizations must be legally obligated to collect only the minimum data necessary for each specific task. That data must be held for the minimum duration necessary for that task, and the transfer of that data between different systems must also be kept to a minimum. Furthermore, access to that data should be restricted to as few parties as possible.
- There needs to be a widespread understanding that individual can very often be identified from anonymized and pseudonymized data. This means that it should be treated as identifiable data, with the same safeguards. Aggregated data is the only truly anonymous type of data we have available today.
- A system of ethics should be accepted and agreed as the baseline expectation for the ways in which private data will be treated. This includes thinking through what will happen in future to data, and what could possibly go wrong. "Monitor for unintended consequences and be prepared to act to set them right," as Gartner's Buytendijk said.
- Finally, as Paul Sieghart concluded at the end of 'Privacy and Computers', we must accept that "No system of safeguards will ever be perfect."

And that seems a fitting place to end. No system is ever going to be perfect. Data breaches and leaks will continue. Privacy intrusions will persist. But if we can change the accepted societal norms back to where they arguably used to be, where minimal data sharing is the default position and anything else comes with a big red flag attached to it explaining the situation, then we'll be in a better, safer position in future.

References

http://www.publications.parliament.uk/pa/cm201415/cmselect/cmsctech/734/73405.htm#note22

http://www.bbc.co.uk/news/technology-32429477

http://research.microsoft.com/pubs/74164/www2007.pdf

http://archive.wired.com/politics/security/commentary/securitymatters/2006/12/72300?currentPage=all

http://www.bigbrotherwatch.org.uk/2013/11/shop-door-surveillance-start/

http://www.publications.parliament.uk/pa/cm201415/cmselect/cmsctech/245/24502.htm

https://quarterly.blog.gov.uk/2014/10/15/joining-the-dots/

http://www.southampton.ac.uk/superidentity/index.page

https://www.gov.uk/government/uploads/system/uploads/attachment_data/file/387581/NationalDNAdatabase201314.pdf

http://www.fbi.gov/news/pressrel/press-releases/fbi-announces-full-operational-capability-of-the-next-generation-identification-system

http://geneticprivacynetwork.org/tag/biometric-data/

http://www.nytimes.com/2013/08/21/us/facial-scanning-is-making-gains-in-surveillance.html?_r=0

https://en.necessaryandproportionate.org/

http://www.ispreview.co.uk/index.php/2015/02/uk-tribunal-rules-gchq-nsa-mass-internet-surveillance-sharing-unlawful.html

Index

Printed in the United States
By Bookmasters